Barbados in Bloom

Photography - Derek St. Romaine

Design - Eightzeronine Design Associates Inc.

Digital Colour Imaging - Dynamic Colour Imaging

Photo Captions - John L. Webster, PhD

Published by Wordsmith International

Distributed by Miller Publishing Company
Edgehill, St. Thomas, Barbados, West Indies.
Tel: (246) 421 6700 Fax: (246) 421 6707
E-mail: miller@caribsurf.com

© 2004 Wordsmith International

All rights reserved. No part of this publication may be reproduced
or transmitted in any form or by any means, electronic or mechanical,
including photocopy, recording or any information storage and
retrieval system, without permission in writing from the publisher.

Printed in Singapore

ISBN 976 - 8081 - 12 - 0

Contents

5 - Foreword
by Peter Seabrook

7 - Barbados — A Horticultural Society
by Victor Roach, President of the Barbados Horticultural Society

Home Gardens in Barbados
a selection of 15 home gardens

12 - Francia

20 - Grassy Hills

28 - Frantasia

36 - Gibbs Hill House

46 - Calypso Cottage

54 - Olive Wood

64 - Laxybones

72 - Bellerive

80 - Mango Bay

88 - Dar es Salaam

94 - Bachelor Hall

102 - Tanglewood

110 - Cane Heaven

120 - Glendale

130 - Eusteen's Garden

Botanical Gardens in Barbados

136 - Andromeda Gardens

144 - Welchman Hall Gully

154 - Flower Forest

164 - Orchid World

174 - Orchids in Barbados

186 - Palms in Barbados

198 - Index of Scientific and Common Names of Plants

200 - Acknowledgements

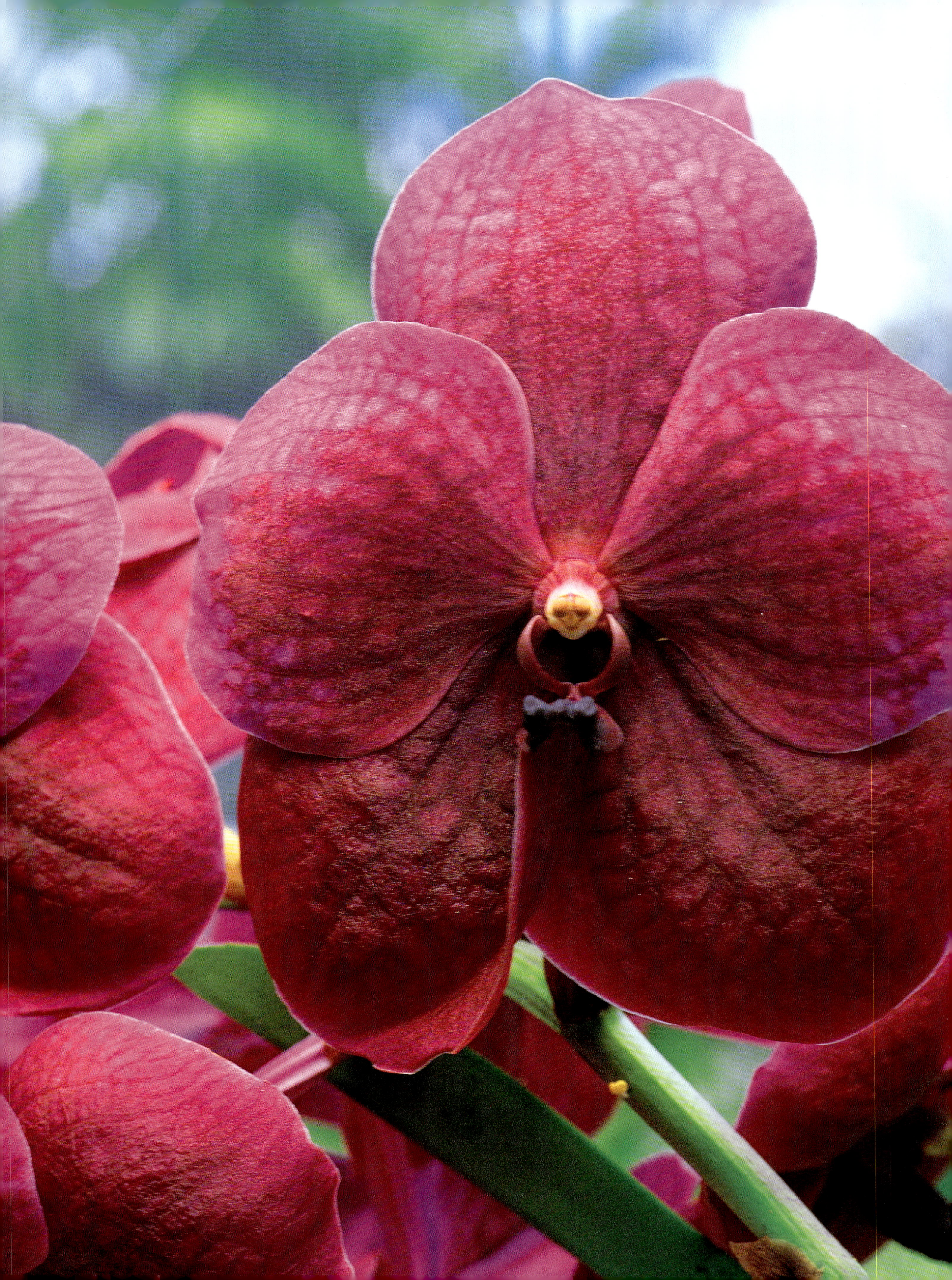

Foreword

The big smiles from Jean Robinson and her team of helpers at the Chelsea Flower Show in the late 1980's first introduced me to the charm, stunning colour, luxuriant growth and sheer delight of gardens and gardening 'Barbados-style'.

Trips to Barbados with television cameras - both BBC and then WGBH Boston and its Victory Garden Team - soon followed. I will never forget our first visit to Audrey Thomas - what gardening skill and what a garden! It was, and is, a chocolate box picture in the finest English Cottage Garden mode, executed with tropical plants. Their brilliant colours and rapid growth demand a true green-fingered touch and constant attention to achieve such beauty.

This book and the remarkably fine pictures capture all of this and more. Here you can revel in marvellous private and public gardens, with everything from historic to modern, and beloved community to chattel house gardens.

Great buttresses at the base of tropical trees, twining stems, aerial roots and the steamy tropical forest atmosphere have all been brilliantly captured by Derek St Romaine, whose photographic mastery is exceptional. He opens our eyes to flower detail in orchid bloom close-up as well as to wide-angle landscapes.

Those bright blue skies, silhouetted swaying palm trees, rich green forest floors and seas are all here. Just a hint of spicy nutmeg fragrance brings them all to mind, these pages allowing so many happy memories to be rekindled.

My thanks and congratulations to everyone who has contributed to this very fine record of Barbados in Bloom.

Peter Seabrook, AH (RHS), VMH.

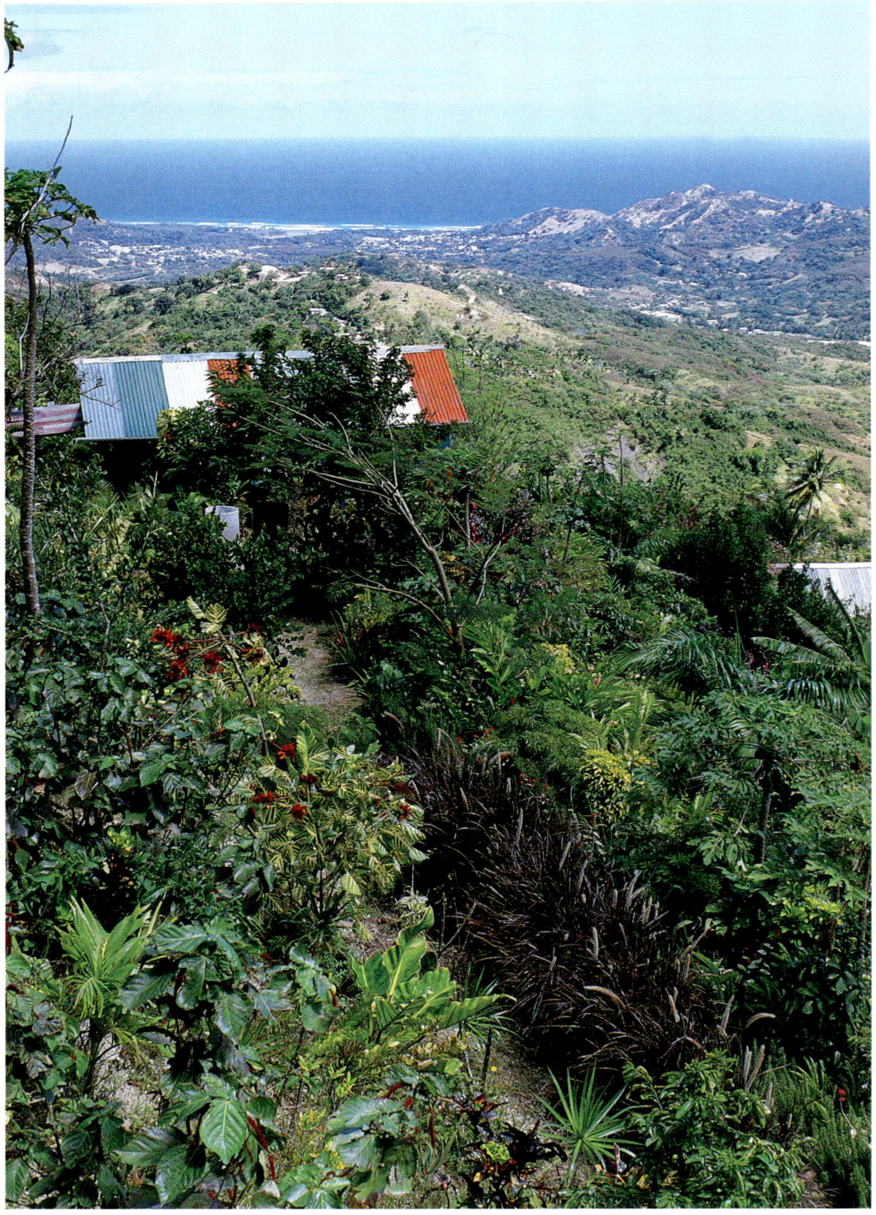
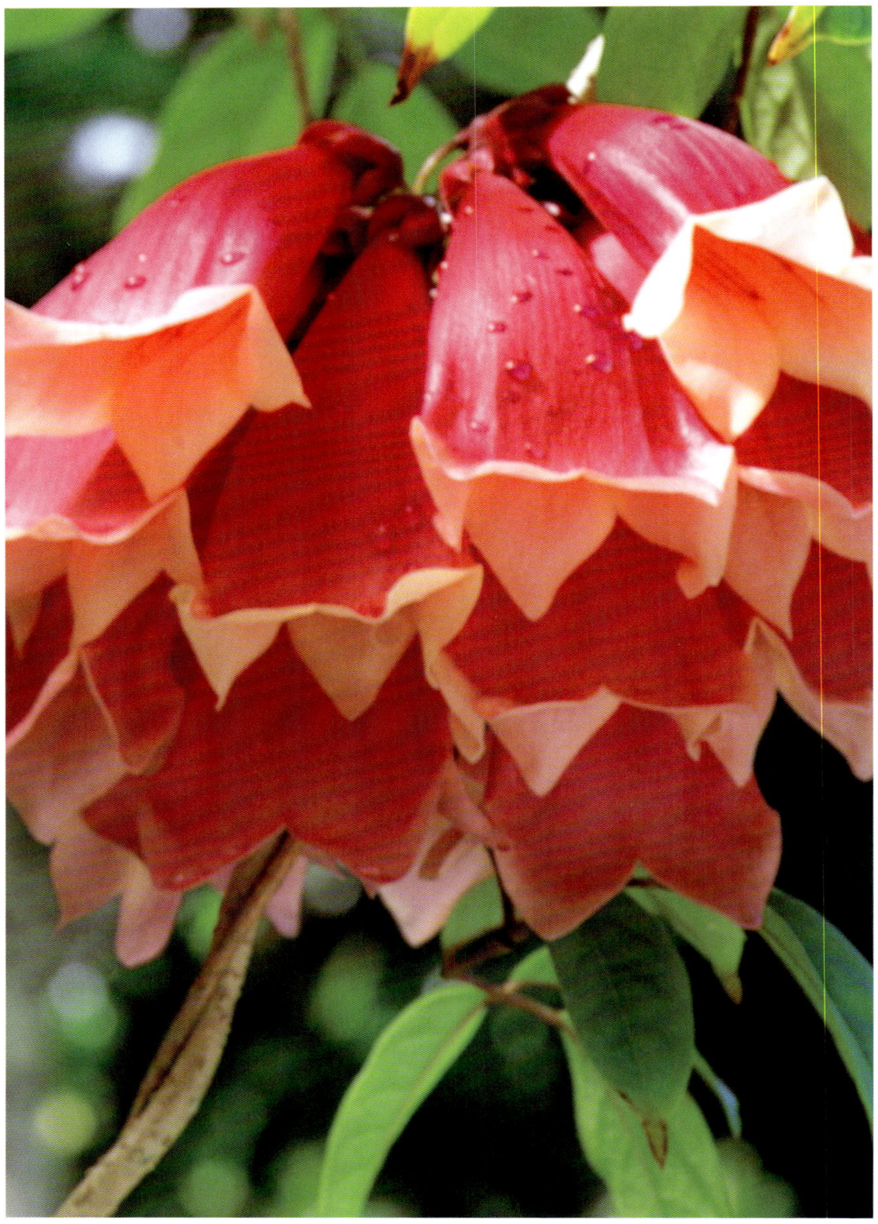
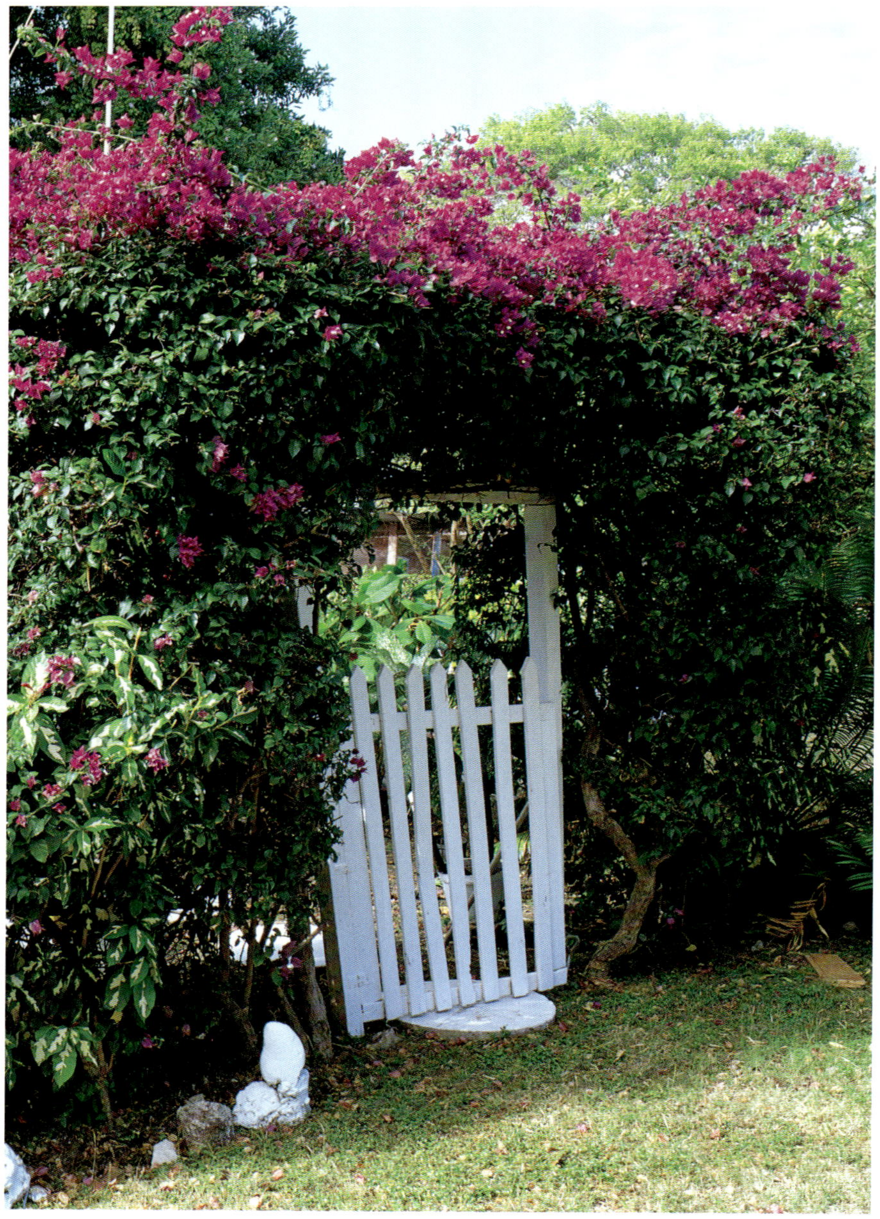
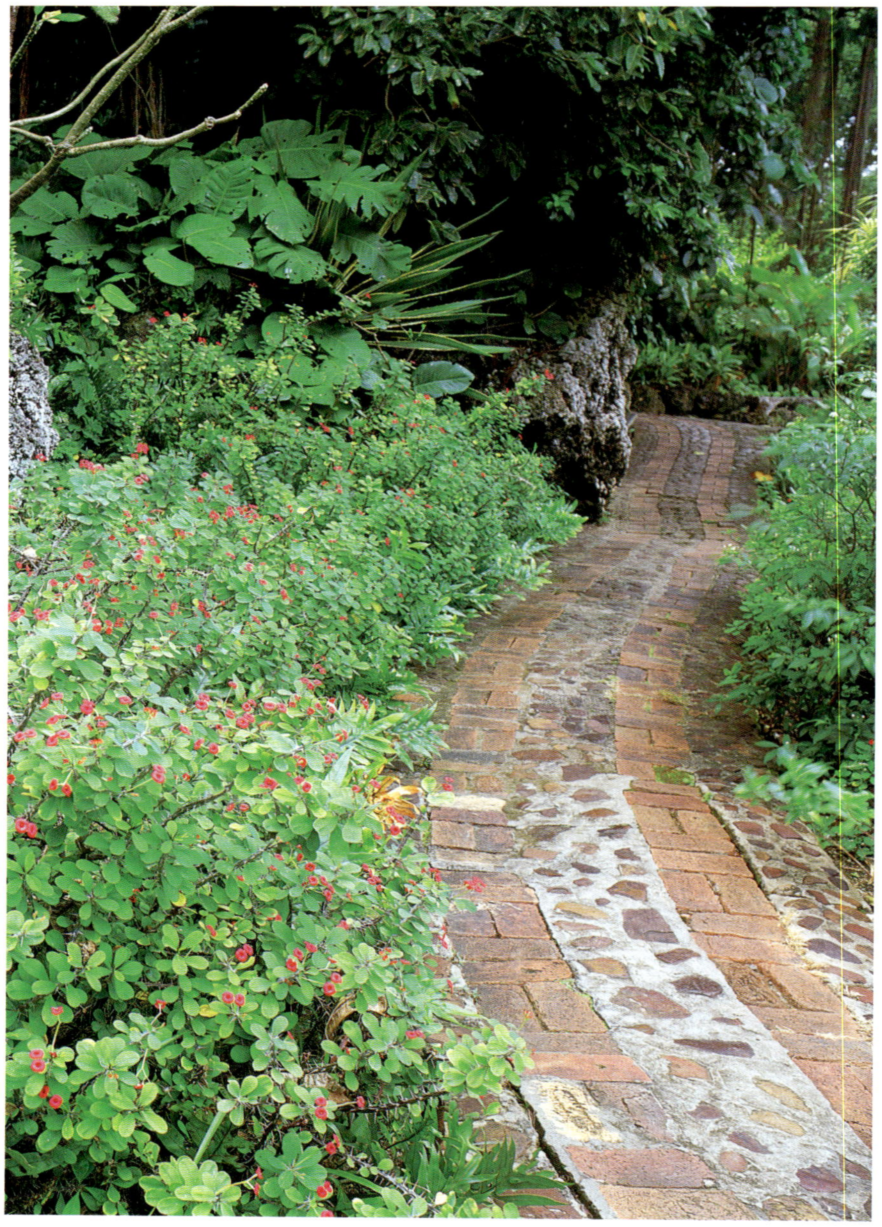

Barbados – A Horticultural Society

Barbados enjoys a pleasant, tropical climate with a mean annual temperature of 26.7 degrees celsius, seldom rising above 31 degrees celsius and rarely falling below 20 degrees celsius. The climate is seasonal with a marked dry season from February through June, at which time in low-lying areas of the island there may be little or no rainfall. Despite the island's small size, there is quite a range in rainfall with coastal regions receiving about 50 inches (1270 mm) annually and the highest central regions some 80 inches (2000 mm). Limited water resources, combined with the shallow soils of what is geologically a young island, can present quite a challenge to farmers and gardeners.

The English settlers who arrived in Barbados in 1627 found an island that was densely forested and uninhabited, but within a relatively short time the forest cover was almost entirely removed to allow the land to be intensely cultivated. Today, the native and naturalized flora comprise about 700 species of flowering plants compared to some 2000 species for the entire Lesser Antilles. Only two flowering plant species are unique or endemic to Barbados, one a gully shrub and the other a woodland vine. This floristic paucity is not surprising as Barbados is relatively flat and ecologically less diverse than its neighbouring volcanic islands. It is also comparatively young and the prevailing winds are in the wrong direction for wind dispersal from the older islands of the Caribbean. Nowadays the island's cultivated flora probably amounts to several thousand species, as from the earliest days of settlement there has been a steady steam of deliberate plant introduction.

Historical records indicate that just as exotic plants were introduced to Barbados, so too did seeds and cuttings from the island find their way to the hot houses of England and Europe. The early 19th century was a particularly intensive period of plant exchange for the island as the then Governor, Lord Seaforth, was a great plantsman and was even dubbed the 'Botanical Governor'. He was responsible for introducing many new garden species to Barbados from the St. Vincent Botanical Gardens and beyond. In turn, these plants were spread to other parts of the British realm. In our current era, the late Iris Bannochie, founder of Andromeda Botanical Gardens, deserves special mention as an indefatigable plant collector who introduced myriads of new plant varieties to the island's gardens.

In terms of institutions, the Barbados Horticultural Society has played a pivotal role in the island's horticultural development. Established by an act of incorporation in April 1928, it is one of the oldest such societies in the Caribbean. Since its inception, interest in horticulture has grown tremendously in Barbados, touching every level in our community.

This development is in keeping with one of the main objectives of the Society, which is to promote understanding of, and to encourage interest and participation in, all aspects of horticulture among citizens and other residents of Barbados and its visitors, to the end that the island's ambience may steadily improve and the people be afforded increasing aesthetic enjoyment and creative satisfaction from horticulture.

This ideal speaks for itself as we look around at the

Opposite from top left: Hilaby Community Garden with its incredible view over the Scotland District of the East coast of Barbados. The pathway is bordered on the right side with Purple Fountain Grass, *Pennisetum setaceum* cv: 'Purpureum', and on the left with Coral Trees, *Erythrina variegata* • **Top right** – Flowers of New Guinea Creeper, or New Guinea Trumpet Vine, *Tecomanthe venusta*, a woody climber from New Guinea. It is a member of the *Bignoniaceae* and produces its flowers directly on the old wood • **Bottom Right** - Crown of Thorns, *Euphorbia milli*, border a paved path at Andromeda Gardens. The paving on the edges is created from bricks brought as ballast in the holds of sailing ships of centuries past as the ships sailed from England to collect the sugar produced on the island and take it back to England. The bricks were used in the construction of chimneys at the sugar factories and many carry their manufacturers name or city. The centre of the path is paved with 'iron stone' concretions collected in the Scotland District area surrounding Andromeda • **Bottom left** – Purple Bougainvillea, *Bougainvillea spectabilis*, forms a delightful arch over a rustic gate

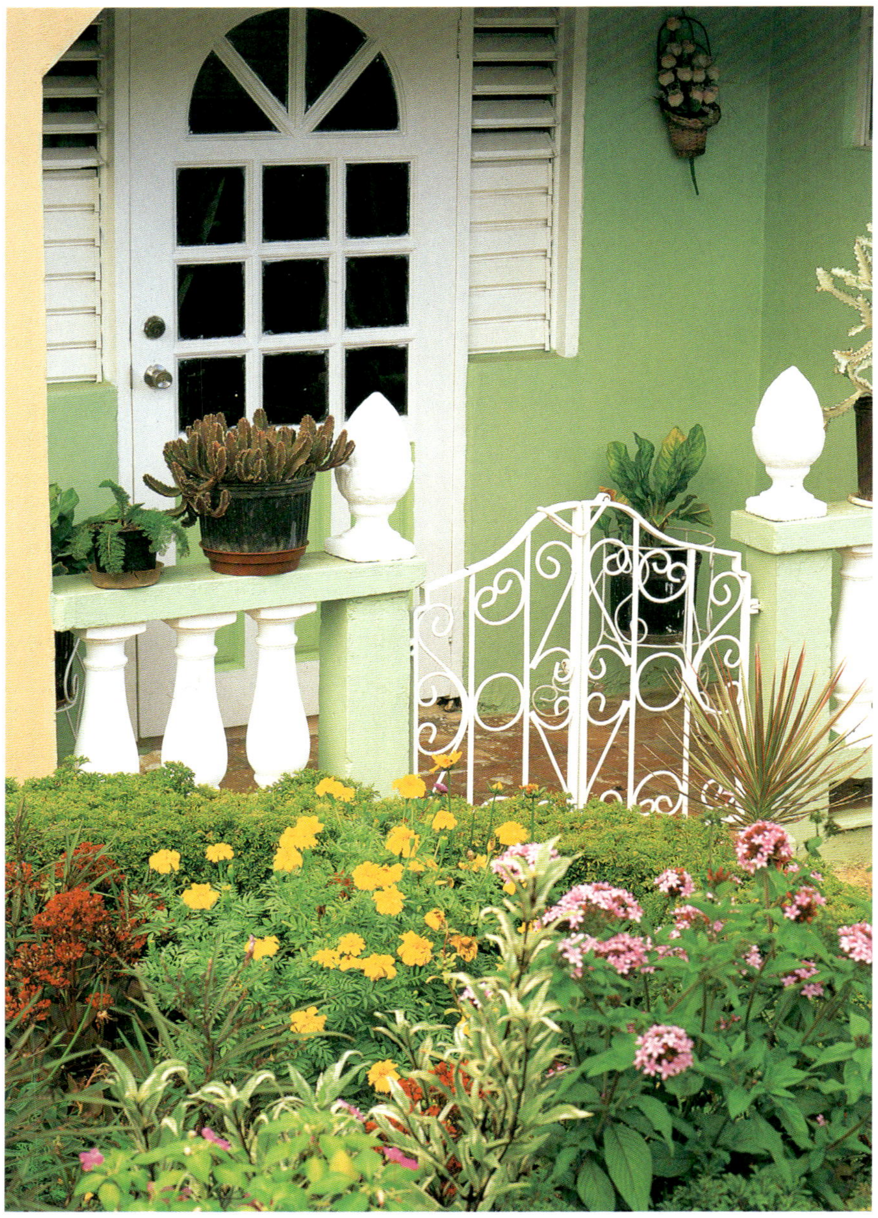
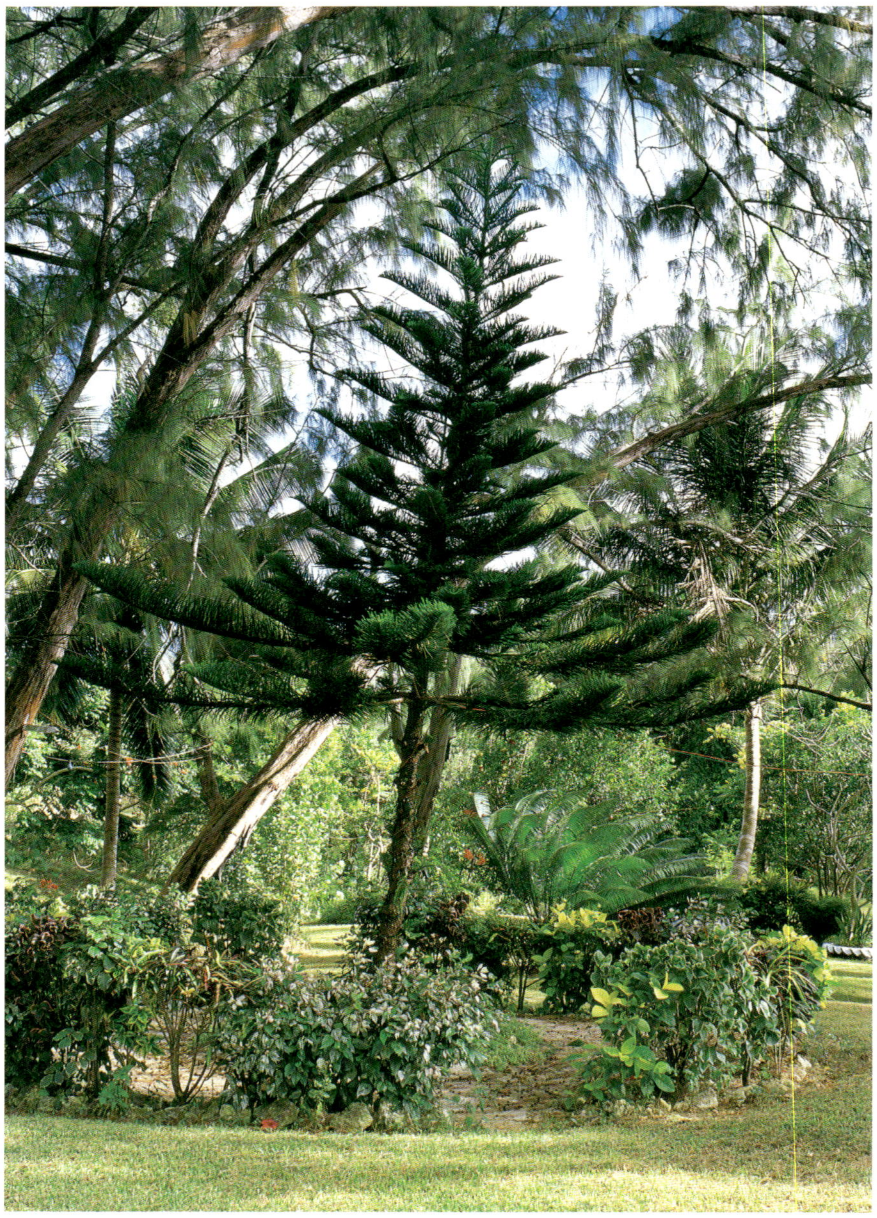
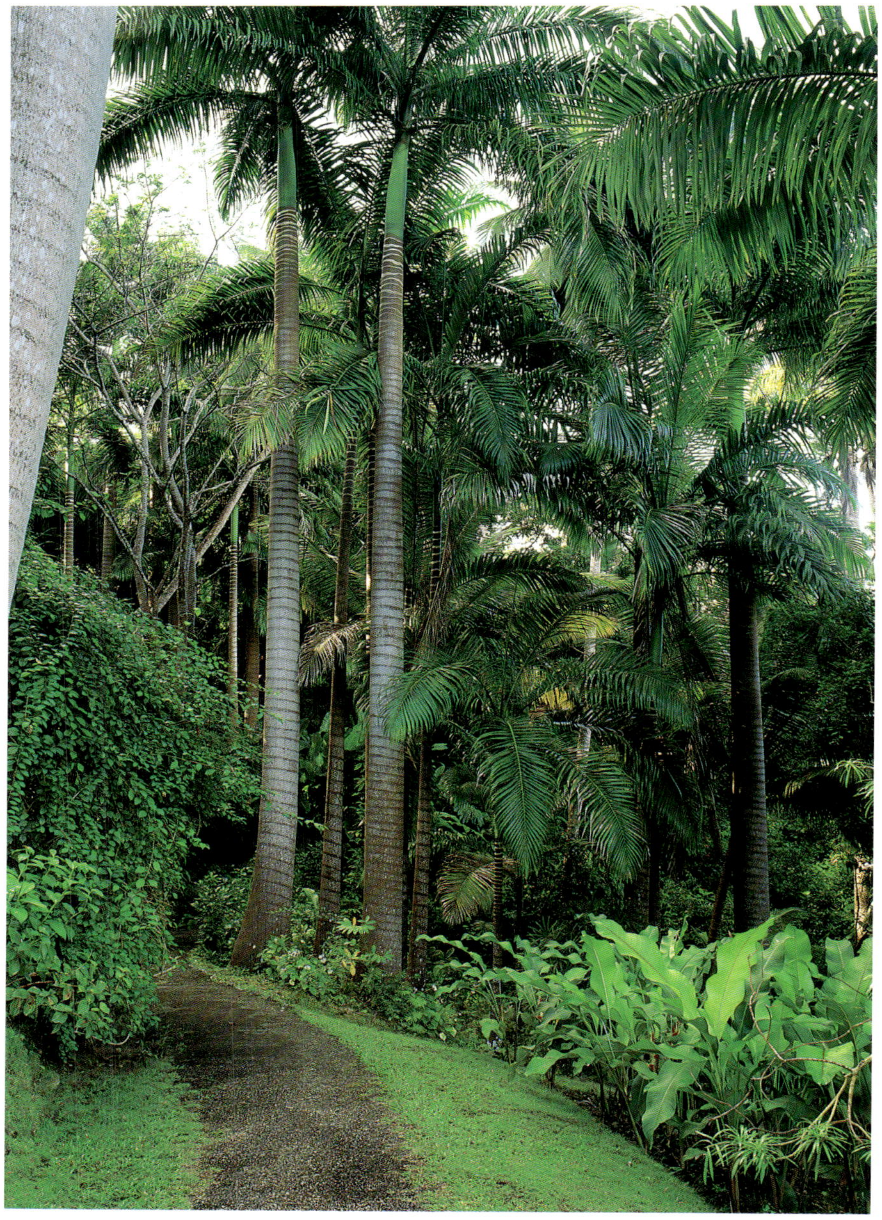
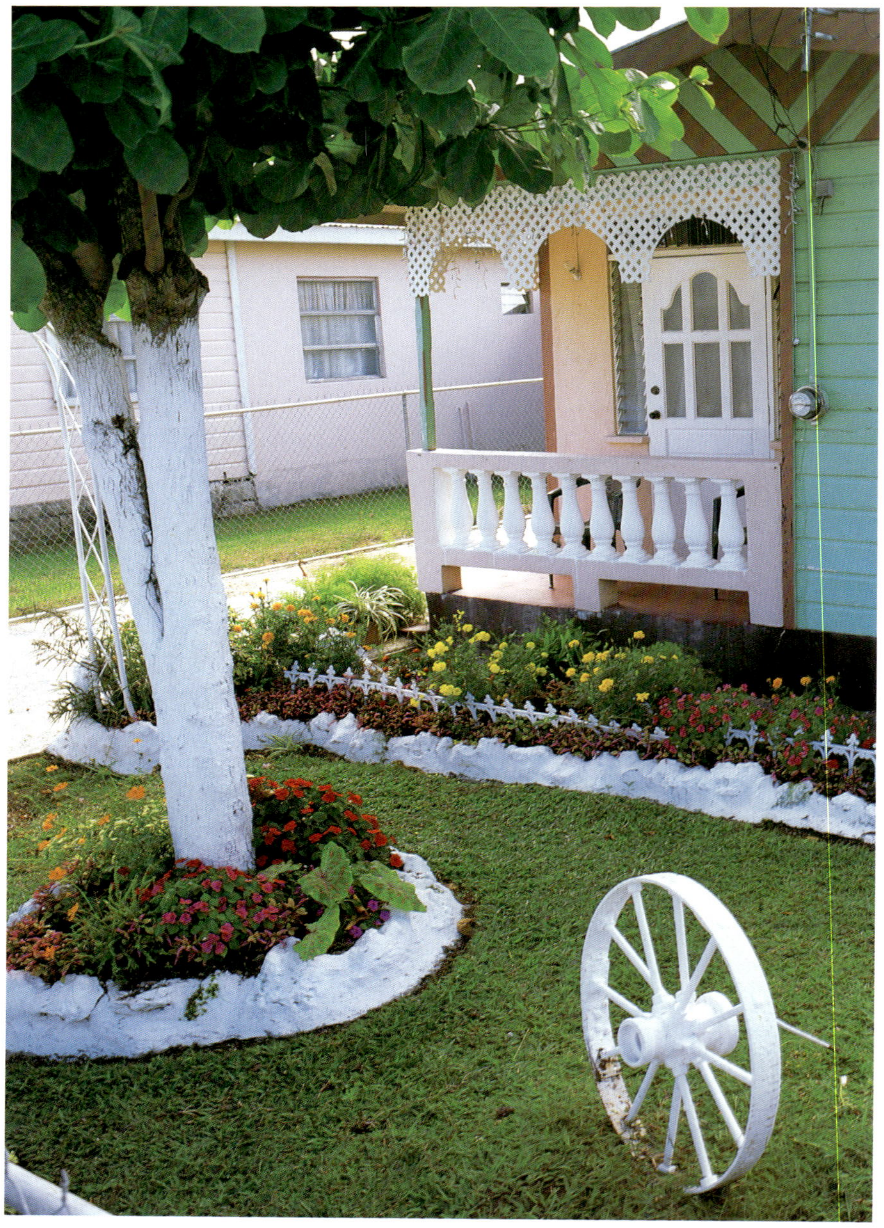

various parks, homes, gardens and landscapes that add to the beauty of present day Barbados. The society has also developed an "Open Garden Programme" in recent years, which provides a welcome opportunity for locals and visitors to visit many of the lush and beautiful gardens found at private homes.

At the community level, most villages in Barbados have their own special 'liming spot' and in recent times more and more residents have taken it upon themselves to clean up these areas, plant gardens and add their own forms of artistic decorations, ranging from painted tree stumps to decorated tyres and home-made sculptures. Barbadians are by nature both creative and proud, so as one village built its own community garden it was inevitable that a neighbouring village would soon follow suit, keen to have their own version that was just as good if not better.

The Government of Barbados, in the form of the Community Independence Celebrations Secretariat of the Prime Minister's Office, has further fuelled this trend of community spirit and environmental improvement by facilitating the national Mini-Parks Competition. The basic objectives of this programme are to maintain pride in the physical environment of Barbados and to promote community-mindedness through direct involvement in the maintenance of the natural landscape. The Mini-Parks Competition, with judging criteria based upon the use of suitable plants for the area, recycling techniques and the development of community spirit, has done a great deal to promote environmental friendliness and a greater appreciation of the value of beautiful gardens.

At the international level, the Barbados Horticultural Society has won a magnificent eleven gold and six silver-gilt medals at the Chelsea Flower Show in London, considered by many to be the most prestigious flower show in the world. This means that in the seventeen consecutive years that the Society has been participating, Barbados has won a medal on each occasion. This is a tremendous achievement by any standards and much credit needs to be given to all the many volunteers who have worked so hard over the years to earn such great distinction for Barbados in the horticultural world. The ongoing success of the Barbados Horticultural Society at the Chelsea Flower Show has greatly stimulated interest in horticulture in Barbados, including the advent of an ever-growing number of oversees visitors coming to the island specifically to view and experience our gardens.

The publishing of this beautiful, world-class book, Barbados in Bloom, now promises to provide a further fascinating glimpse into some of our most magnificent private and botanical gardens, as well as a captivating visual record of many of our outstanding plants. In addition, and very importantly, Barbados in Bloom proudly recognises and highlights the excellent work being carried out in Barbados by a wide range of dedicated and highly talented garden enthusiasts, gardeners, landscape architects, landscapers, plant nurseries and environmentalists, both professionals and amateurs alike.

Victor Roach
President
Barbados Horticultural Society.

Opposite clockwise from top left - Simple private garden including Marigolds, *Tagates lucida*, Pentas, *Pentas lanceolata*, and *Dracaena marginata* cv: tricolour • **Top right** – The Pride of Wilson Hill Community Garden. Large Mile Trees, or Casuarina trees, *Casuarina equisetifolia*, provide shade to the park and a Norfolk Pine, *Araucaria hetrophylla*, creates a focal point • **Bottom right** - Community gardeners recycle discarded items and work them into their designs as objects d'art. Here a discarded metal wheel from a piece of agricultural equipment has become a sculpture amongst the flowers of Marigolds, *Tagates lucida*, Busy Lizzies, *Impatiens walleriana*, and Tea Plant, *Alternanthera tenella*. • **Bottom left** – A grove of West Indian Royal Palms, *Roystonea oleracea* becomes a focal point on a path at the Flower Forest. The path is bordered by *Gmelina hystrix* on the left and a clump of *Heliconia wagneriana* on the right •

HOME GARDENS IN BARBADOS

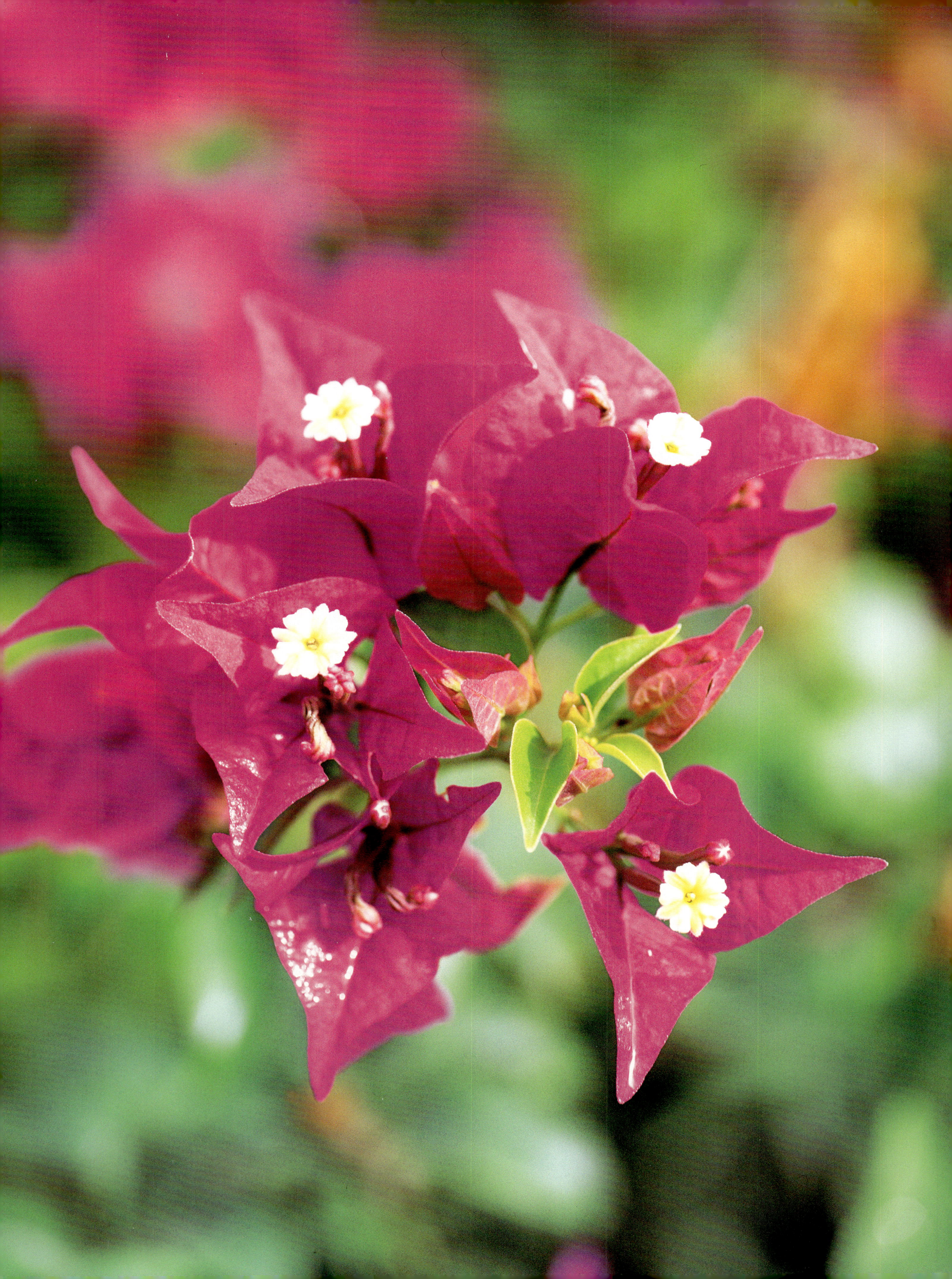

Francia

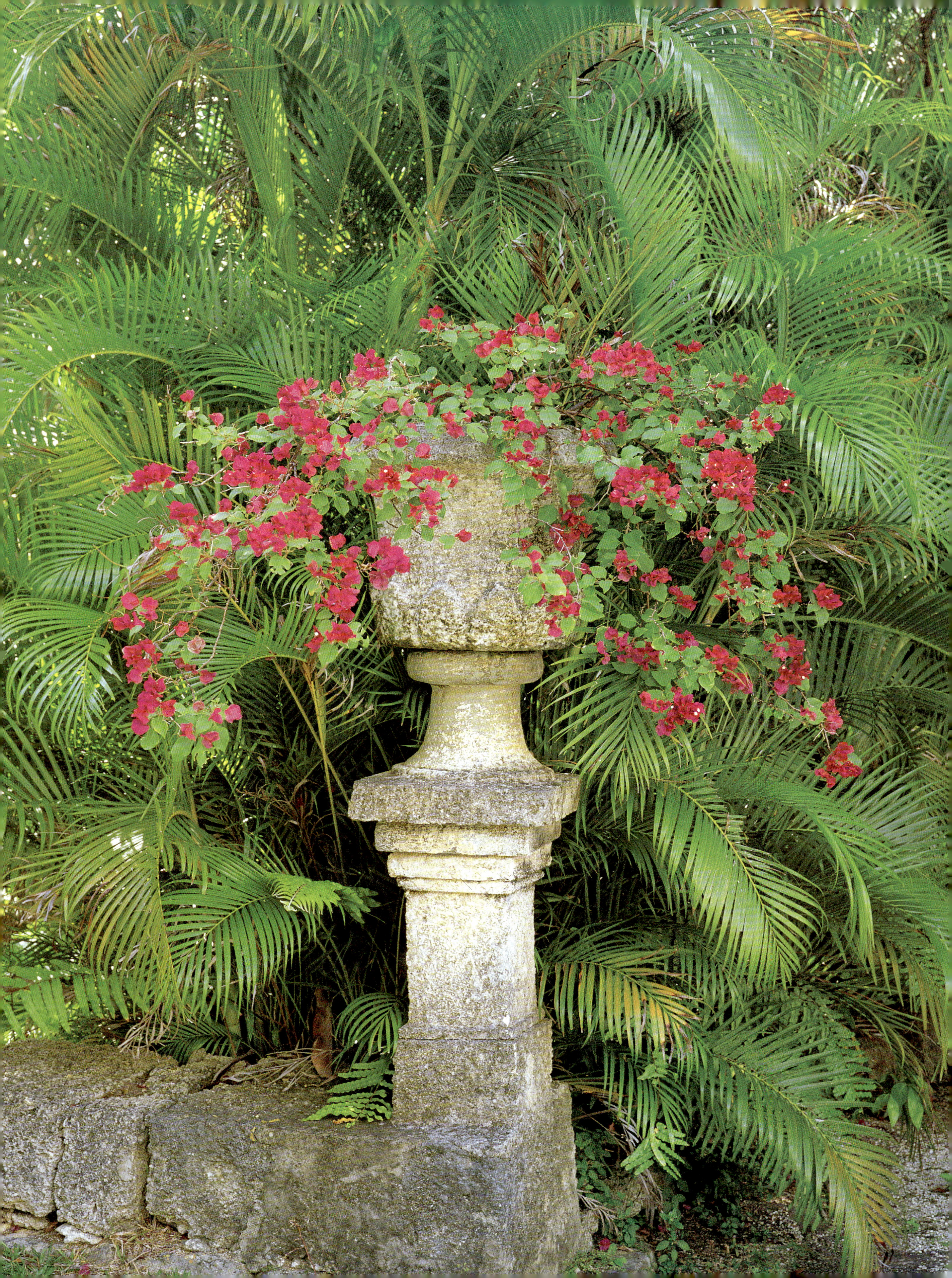

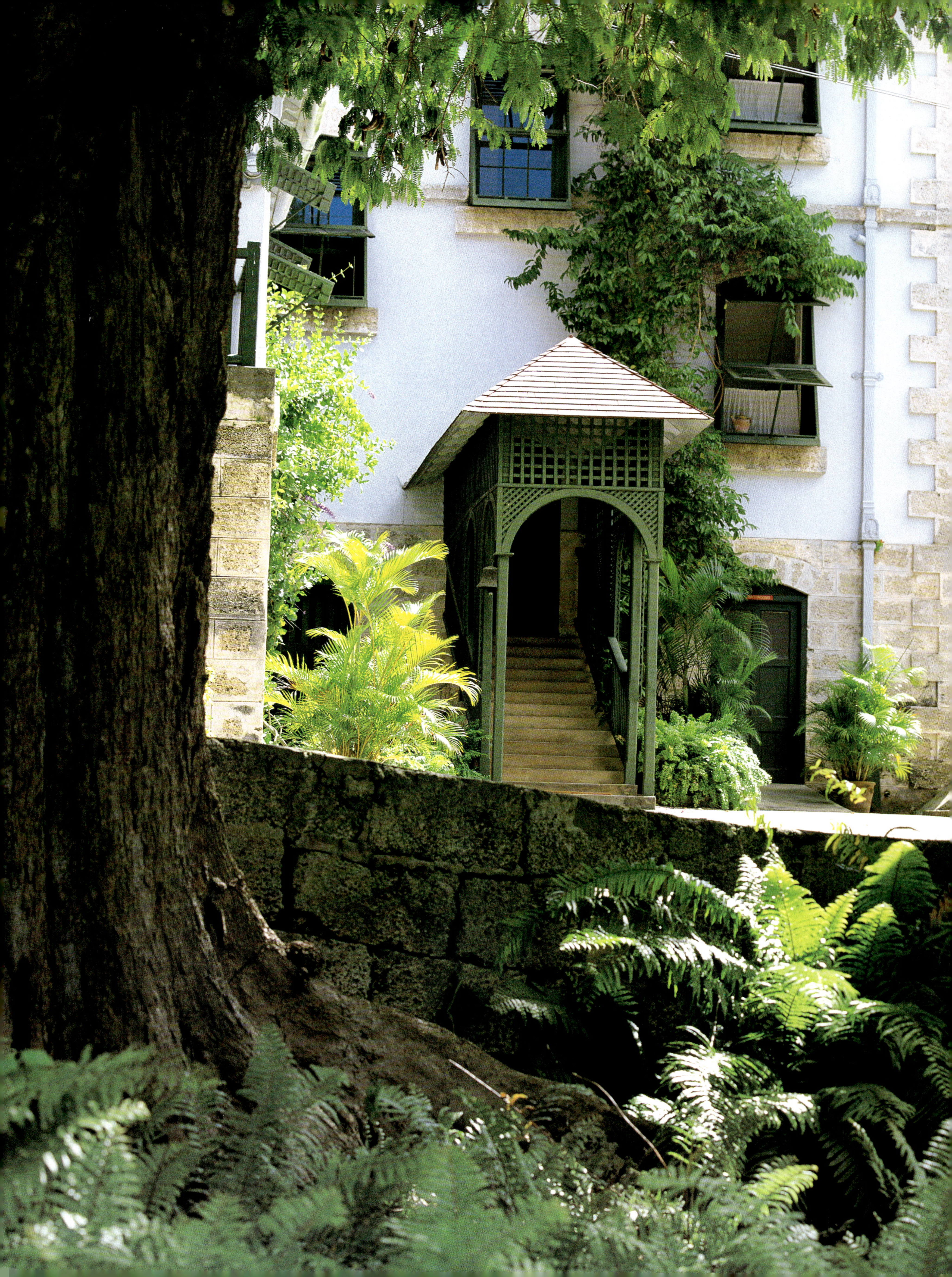

Opening page: Bougainvillea, *Bougainvillea spectabilis*, on a coral stone pedestal against a backdrop of Golden Palms, *Dypsis lutescens*. Bougainvilla are large woody climbers from South America. The vibrantly coloured 'flowers' are actually paper-like bracts that surround the small white tubular flowers. The Golden Palm is a multi-stemmed or clustering palm whose trunks can attain a height of 25 feet. *Lutescens* is Latin for "growing yellow" and refers to the colour development of the petioles, which may vary from green to yellow through to bright orange, dependent on the amount of sunlight the plant receives. The Golden Palm originated in Madagascar and is also known by the common names, Areca Palm and the Yellow Butterfly Palm. It is unquestionably the most used of all palms in landscaping in Barbados; it is easy to grow and hardy, it makes a superb screen and it is a wonderfully elegant plant.
• **Opposite**: Part of the plantation yard is shaded with a large Tamarind Tree, *Tamarindus indica*. Above the doorway, a Rangoon Creeper or Quisqualis, *Quisqualis indica*, climbs the wall next to the house's original cast iron drainpipe. Clumps of Golden Palms, *Dypsis lutescens*, frame the entrance way. • **Above**: A view of the house from the top terrace of the garden, with variegated Bougainvillea cultivar to the right and two species of Acalypha, *Acalypha wilkesiana* and *Acalypha godseffiana*, to the left.

Above: Coral stone balustrades are a feature of the gardens at Francia. The large tree is a Lucky Seed Tree, *Thevetia peruviana*, that produces bright yellow flowers. However, all parts of the Lucky Seed Tree are poisonous, especially the seeds, as a result of the presence of cardiac glycosides or cardiac toxins which act directly on the heart. A very poisonous milky juice is also exuded by the plant. • **Opposite**: A coral stone lily pond, full of character and charm

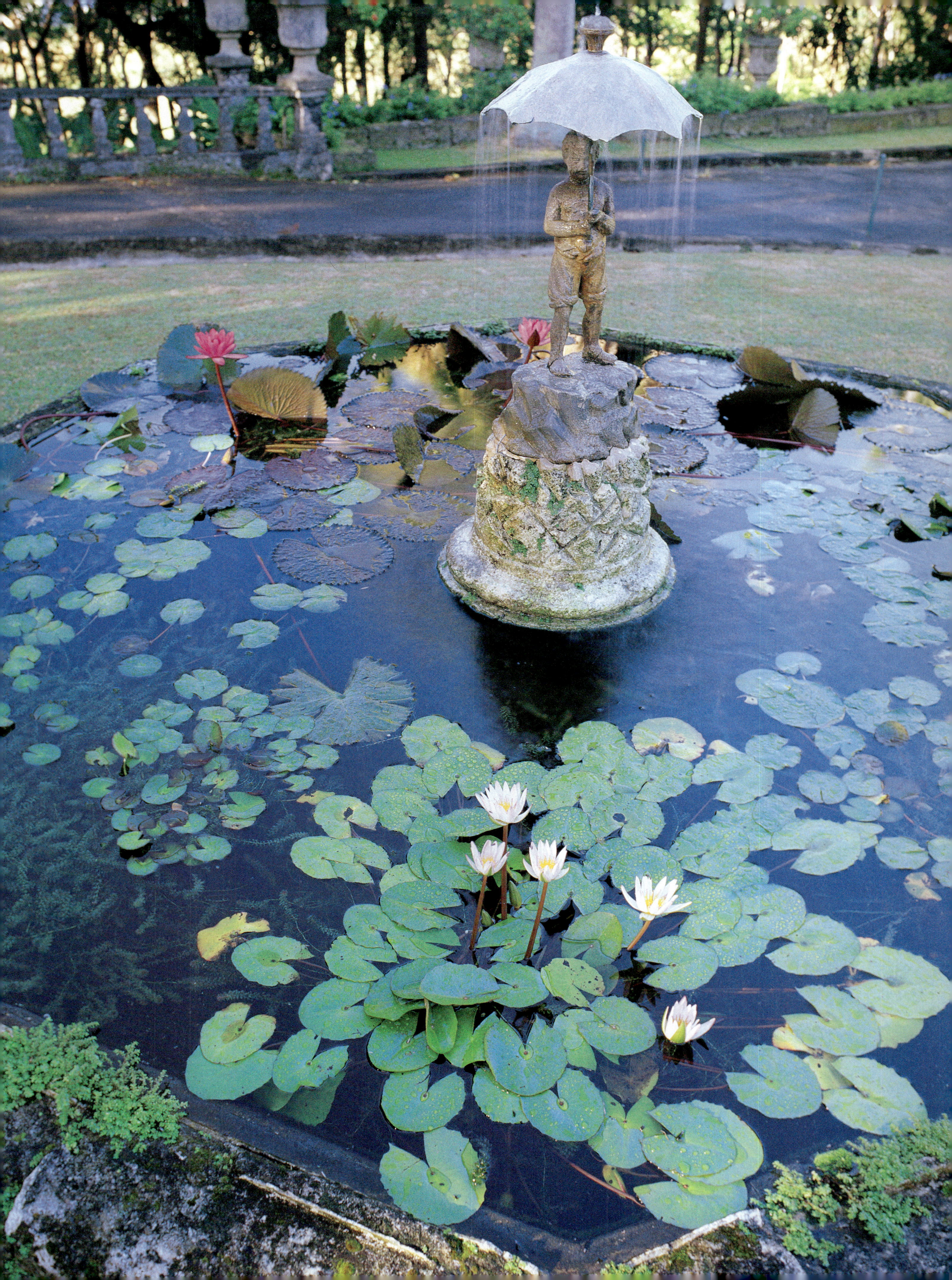

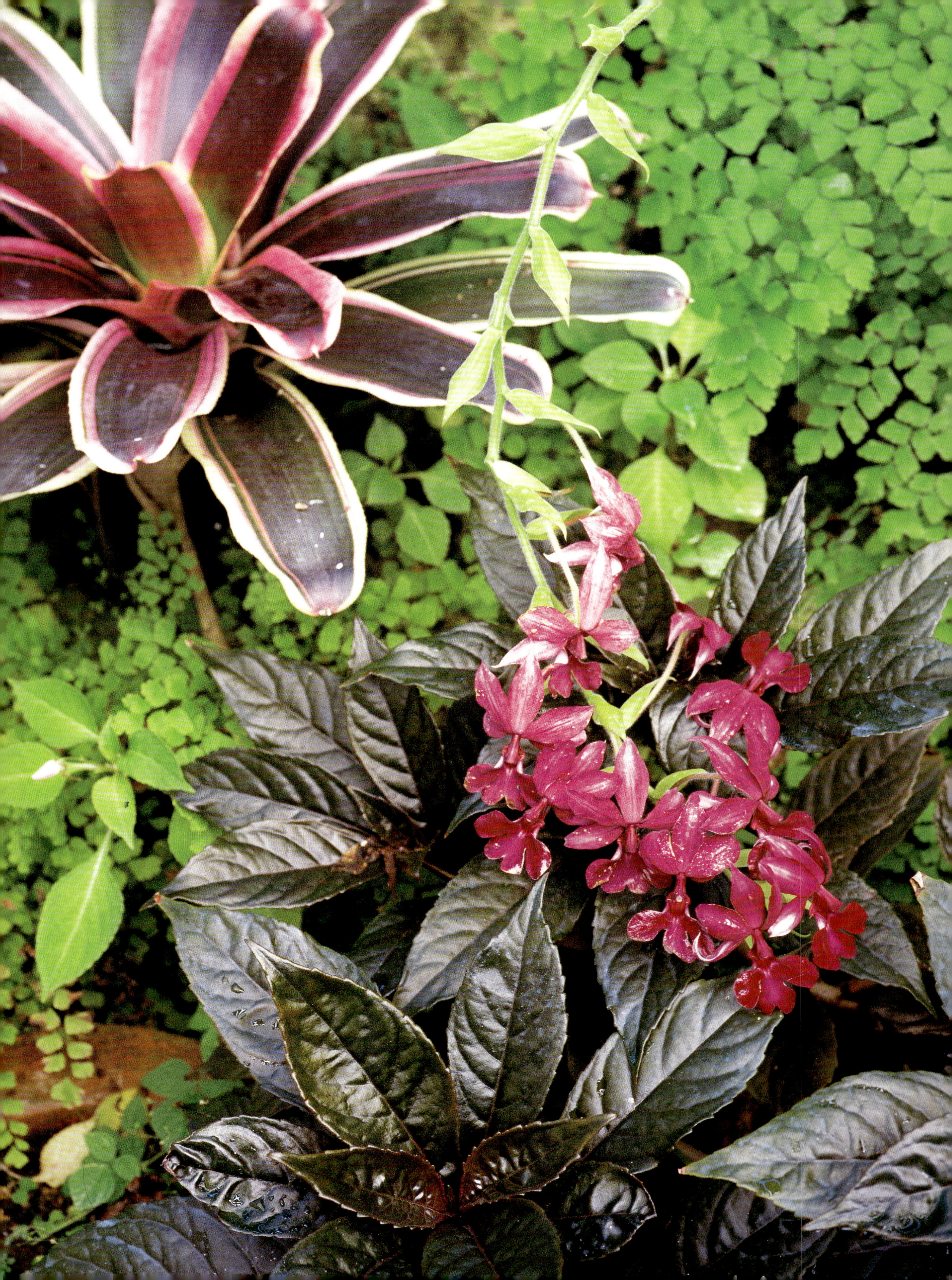

Opposite: A Bromeliad, *Neoregelia carolinae* cv: 'Volkaert's Pride', can be seen in the top left, with Maiden Hair Fern, *Adiantum sp*, in the background. In the centre of the photograph can be seen the flower of an Orchid, of the genus *Calanthe* • **Top**: Plumbago, *Plumbago auriculata*, borders the bottom of the steps, while *Acalypha godseffiana* adorns the stone pots. Plumbago, although a woody, climbing shrub, is used extensively for borders and hedges as it responds well to clipping and pruning. The flowers, which are borne in terminal clusters of about 6" in diameter, are available in various shades of blue, from light blue to a strikingly dark, cobalt blue. There is also a white variety (*P. auriculata* var. 'alba'). Plumbago is a native of South Africa • **Above**: Wild flowers and ferns grow on and around the coral stone walls of an old pump that was formerly used to supply water for the animals and general domestic use. Behind the green door can still be found a full set of drip stones, which were once used to collect and filter drinking water.

GRASSY HILLS

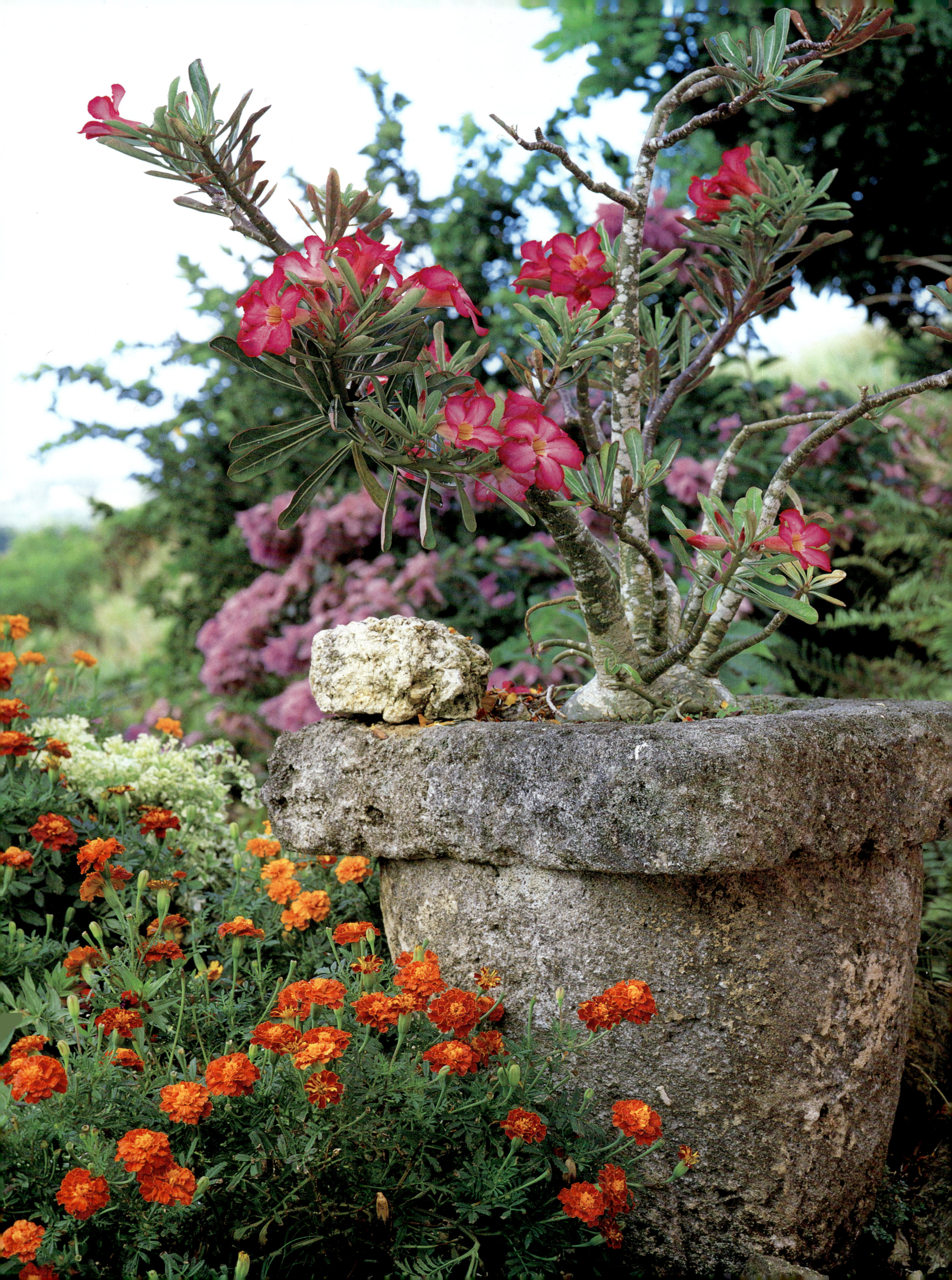

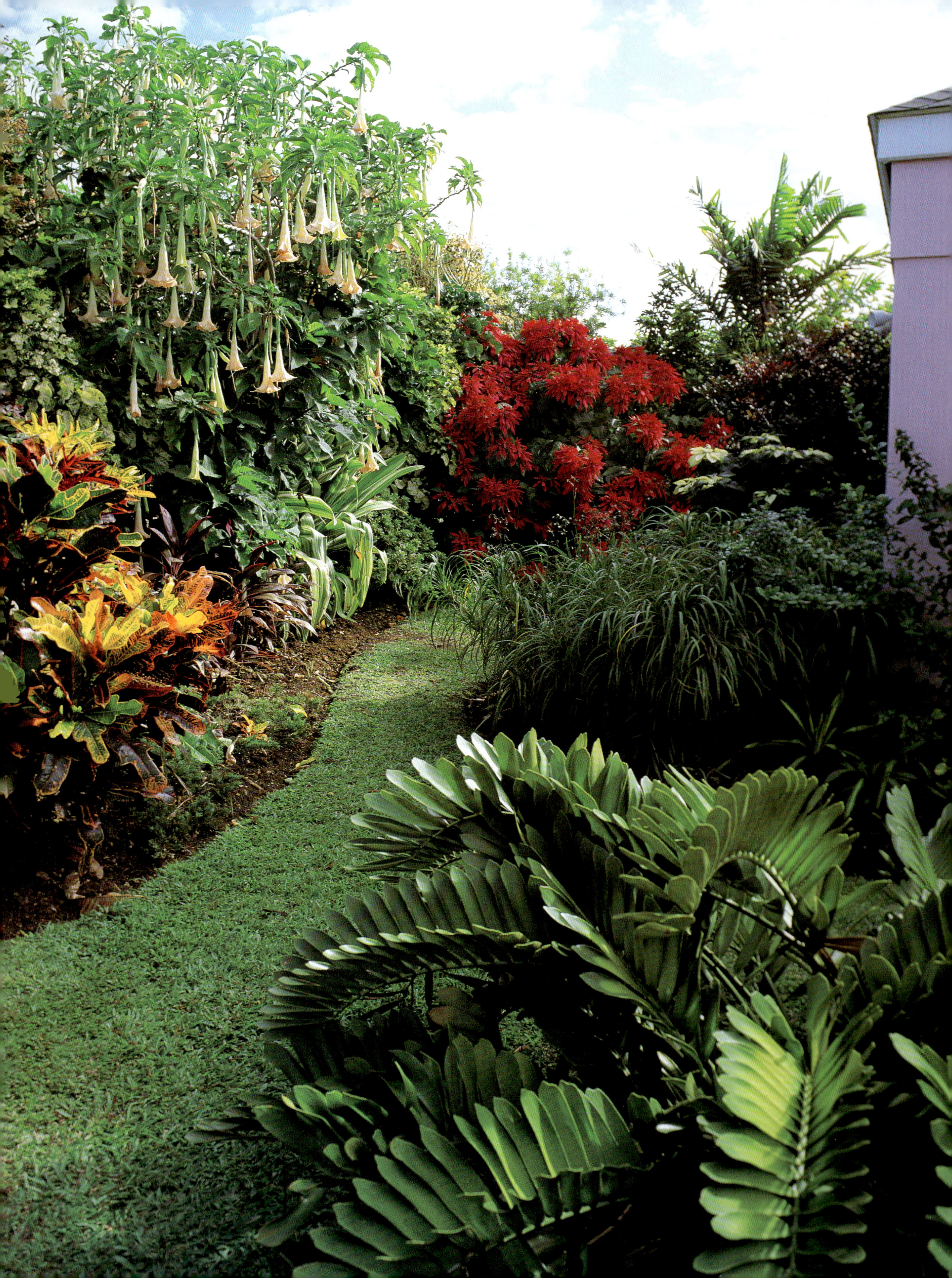

Opening page: A Desert Rose, *Adenium obesum*, planted in an old Barbadian coral dripstone, formerly used to cool and filter drinking water. Marigolds, *Tagates lucida*, can be seen in the foreground. Desert Roses, native to sub-Saharan Africa and Arabia, are members of the *Apocynaceae* (Dogbane family) which includes mostly tropical species such as *Allamanda, Beaumontia, Carissa, Mandevillea, Nerium, Plumeria*, and *Tabernaemontana*. They contain several cardiac glycosides and, in Eastern Africa, are used as a fish and arrow poison. The Adeniums are considered to be very toxic to livestock. Whereas Adeniums flower throughout the year, they are most showy during the drier months of the year, typically, late December through June in Barbados. Annual pruning encourages branching and subsequently heavier flowering. Hundreds of new cultivars are introduced annually by growers in Thailand. •
Opposite: From left to right: Crotons, *Codiaeum variegatum*, with a spectacular display of Angel's Trumpet, *Brugmansia versicolor*, hanging above them, and an equally stunning display of Poinsettia, *Euphorbia pulcherrima*. A variegated Crinum or Spider Lily, *Crinum asiaticum* cv. Variegata, peeps out from below the Angel's Trumpets. Crinum Lilies, members of the *Amaryllidaceae* and natives of Tropical Asia, are huge lilies, reaching heights of up to 6 feet and about the same in width. Mature bulbs may weigh as much as 20 pounds! Many of them, such as this variegated cultivar, are grown for their attractive foliage but gardeners will also be rewarded periodically with beautiful clusters of flowers. Poinsettia, native of Tropical Central America and Mexico, are considered a flowering plant of the Christmas season. The species name in Latin means "most beautiful", and how appropriately chosen a name, as is so strikingly displayed in this photograph. The "flowers" of Poinsettia are actually large brightly coloured bracts with the tiny, almost insignificant flowers located in the centre. Flowering in Poinsettia is initiated by decreasing day length – longer hours of darkness – hence their flowering during, and after, the Christmas period. Consequently, Poinsettia plants need to be located away from night time light sources to ensure maximum flowering; Lower right – Cardboard Palm, *Zamia furfuracea*. The Cardboard Palm is not a palm but a member of the Cycad family. It is considered a "living fossil" as the Cycads have survived on earth since the age of the dinosaurs. The Cardboard Palm, a native of Mexico, is effective as an accent or specimen plant and is very suitable for beachside plantings because of its salt resistance. It also makes an excellent container plant. The Cycads reproduce by producing cones, male and female cones being produced on separate plants. These cones, when produced, add significantly to the uniqueness and visual appeal of this plant • **Above**: Flowers of Angel's Trumpet, *Brugmansia versicolor*. The Brugmansias are members of the *Solanaceae* (Nightshade family) which includes well known crop plants such as eggplant, potatoes, tobacco, and tomatoes. All parts of the plant are toxic to man. The flowers are very fragrant during evening hours.

Above: From left to right: Variegated Wild Pineapple, *Ananas bracteatus* cv: 'Variegata,', *Bougainvillea glabra*, Corkwood Tree, *Sesbania grandiflora*, Bismark Palm, *Bismarkia nonbilis*, Lower right – Plum Pudding Poinsettia, *Euphorbia pulcherrima* cv: 'Plum pudding', so called as it is adorned with plum-purple coloured bracts. • **Opposite:** Flowers of the Blue Butterfly Bush. *Clerodendrum ugandense*.

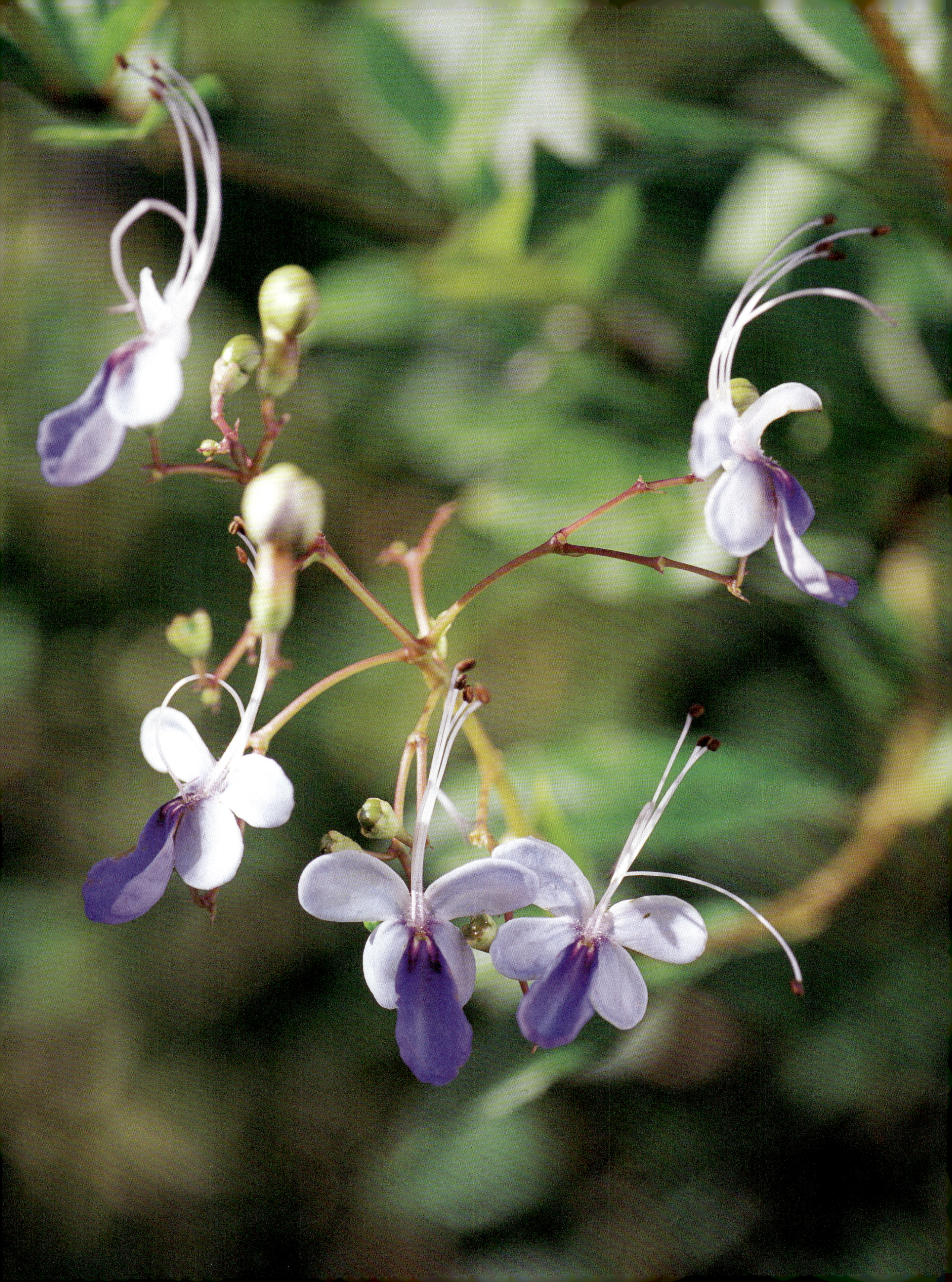

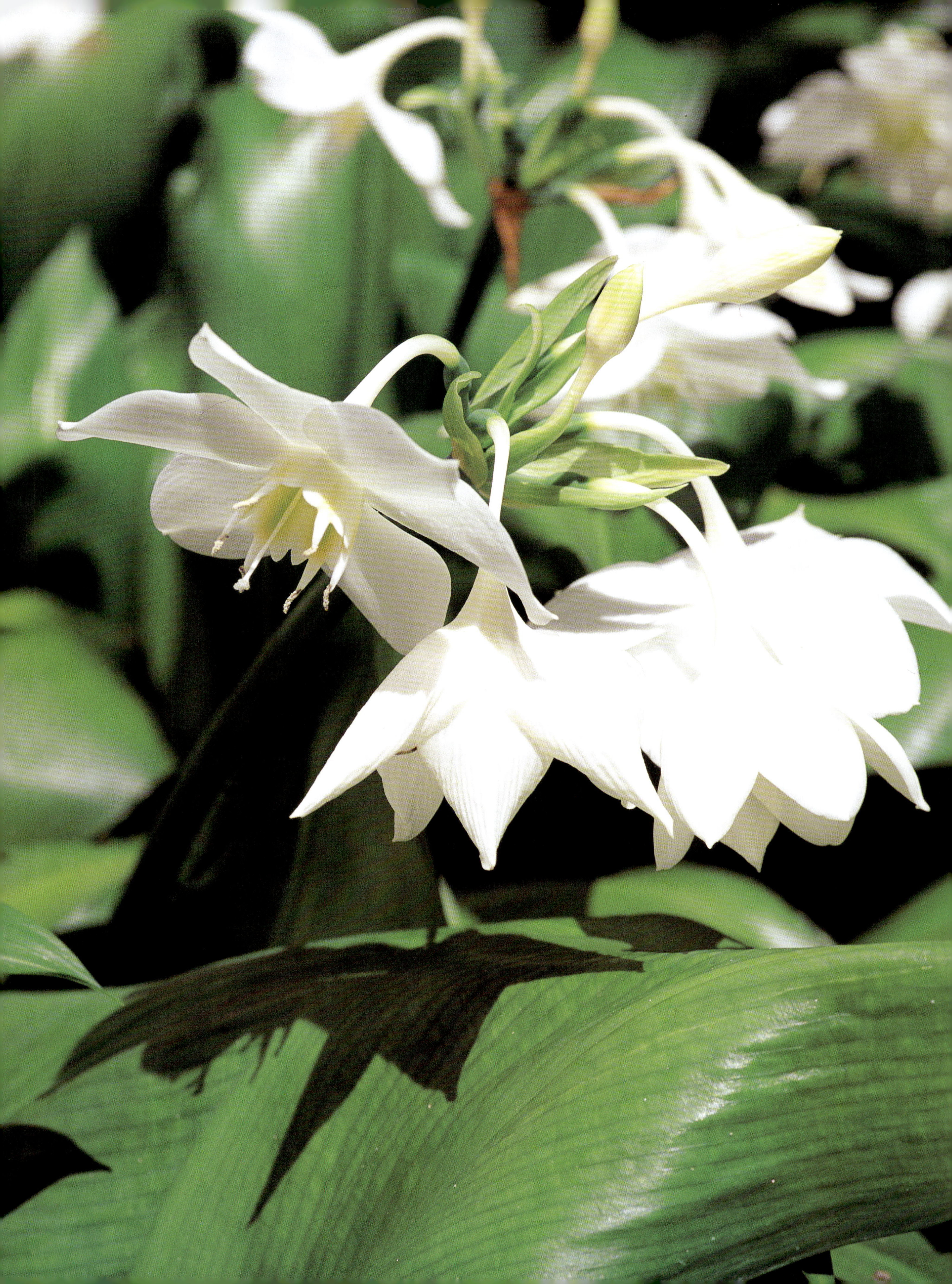

Opposite: Amazon or Eucharist Lily, *Eucharis amazonica*, is a native of the Andes of Columbia and Peru, not the Amazon as the name would lead you to believe. • **Above, clockwise from top left**: The Spirit of the Garden • Mother-of-thousands, *Kalanchoe daigremontiana*. This plant, a member of the *Crassulaceae*, exhibits the interesting and unusual phenomenon of producing its offspring as tiny replicas of itself along the edge of its leaves. • Close up of the trunk of a Bottle Palm, *Hyophorbe lagenicaulis*, showing a pair of emerging inflorescences. The Bottle Palm is a small to medium sized palm originating in the Mascarene Islands, reaching a typical height of 10-15 feet when mature. It usually has only 5-6 leaves but is much prized for the swollen, bottle-shaped, form of its trunk which develops as the plant approaches maturity. • Snow Bush, *Breynia disticha*, forms a contrasting backdrop to a stand of hybrid Crotons, *Codiaeum variegatum*. Snow Bush, a native of Melanesia and a member of the *Euphorbiaceae*, is cultivated for its striking variegated foliage which is typically mottled with white, red, purple and pink. It is usually grown as hedges and the white mottling lends the appearance that snow has fallen on it, hence its name.

FRANTASIA

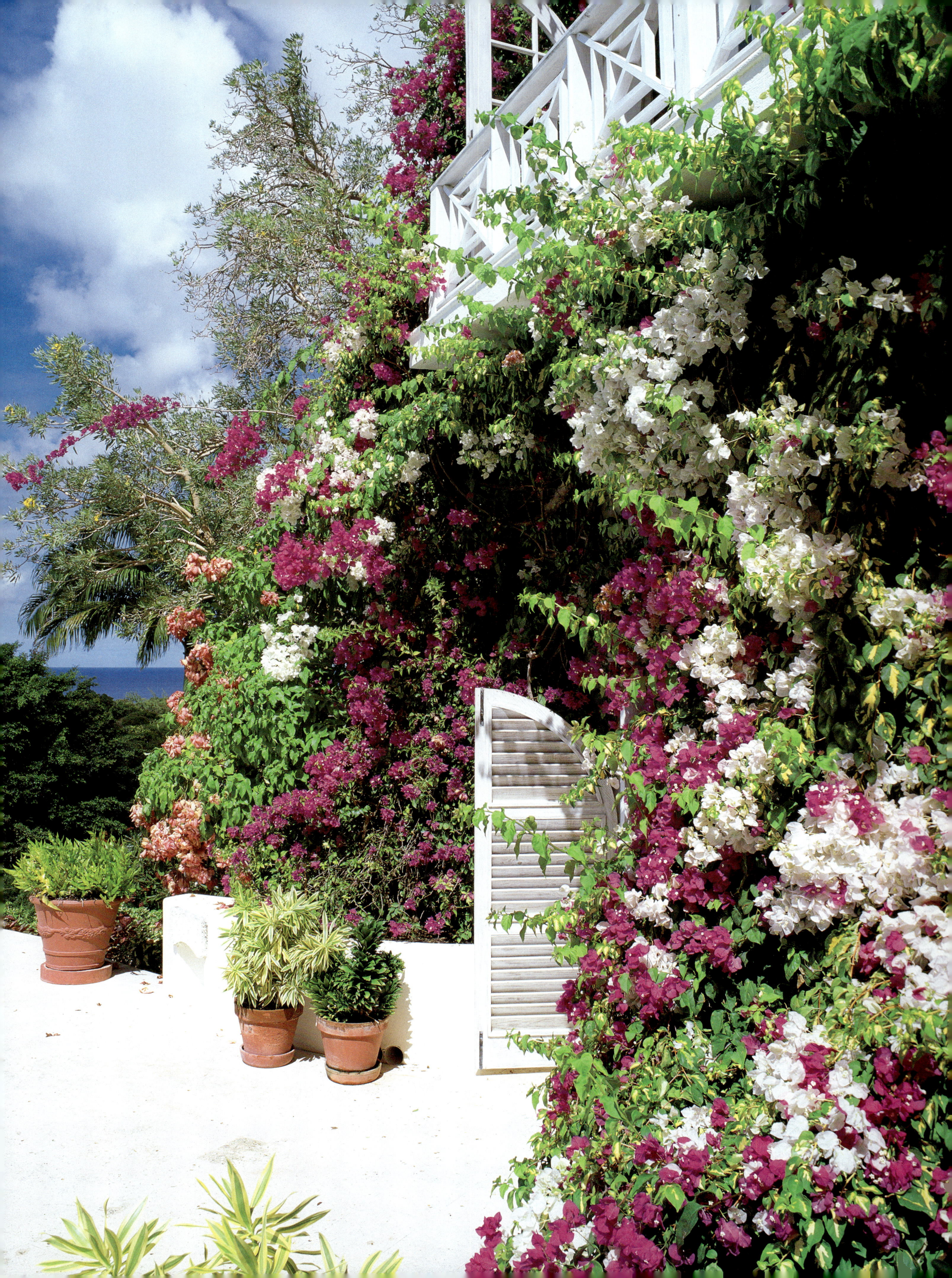

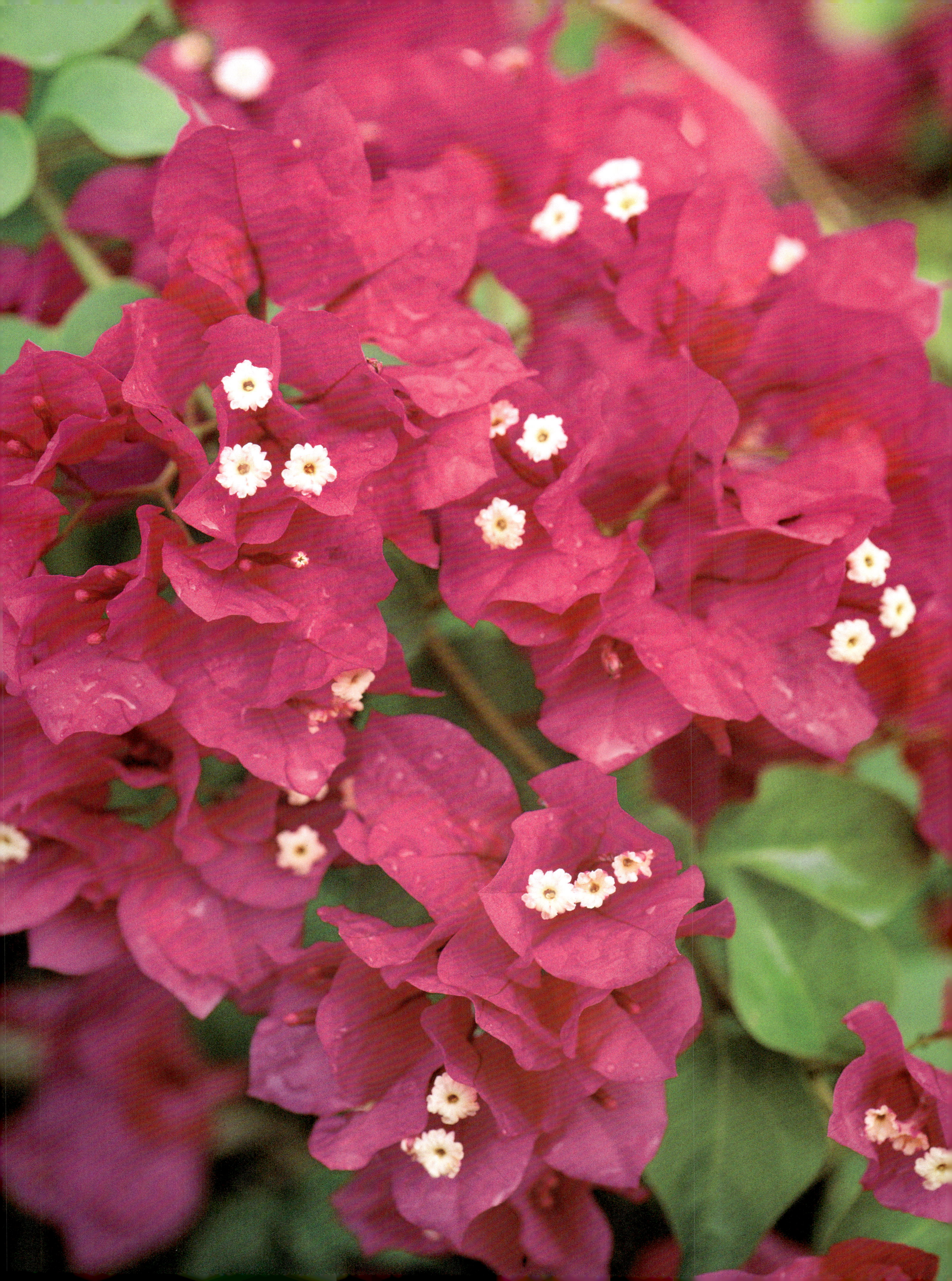

Opening page: Bougainvillea species, *Bougainvillea glabra* and *Bougainvillea spectabilis* • **Opposite:** *Bougainvillea* up close • **Above**: West Indian Royal Palms, *Roystonea oleracea*, with Purple Fountain Grass, *Pennisetum setaceum* cv: 'Purpureum', and Bougainvillea in the foreground

Above: Bougainvillea growing on the walls has effectively softened the lines of the building, while adding a splash of colour and integrating the building into the landscape. Bougainvilleas are naturally large woody climbers so this is their normal mode of growth • **Opposite**: Sage, *Lantana camara*. In Barbados this beautiful plant is considered a common roadside weed.

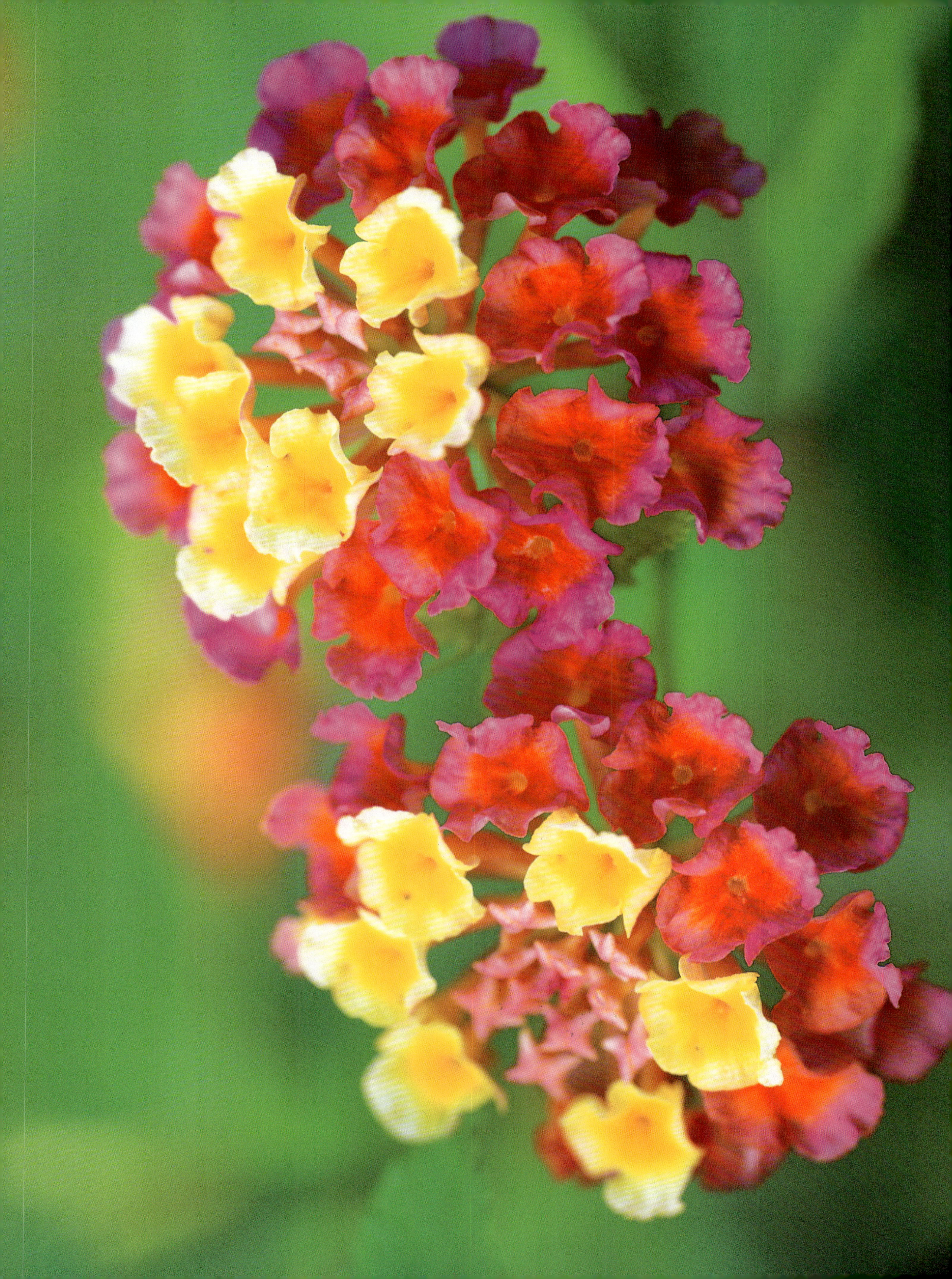

Above, clockwise from top left: Ixora, *Ixora casei* • Hybrid *Hibiscus* • Hybrid *Hibiscus* • Mussaenda, *Mussaenda erythrophylla* cv:'Rosea'. The plant's 'flower' colour comes from bracts and not the small, often yellow, white or orange, flowers at the center of each bract. This is the same colour-producing system found in Bougainvillea. **Opposite**: Peace and tranquillity — A gazebo located in the midst of assorted tropicals including from left to right: *Acalypha godseffiana*, Firecracker or Coral plant, *Russelia equisetiformis*, Giant Elephant Ear, *Alocasia macrorrhiza*, *Dracaena marginata*, Bougainvillea, and an Umbrella Plant, *Cyperus alternifolius*. Various palms abound in the background including a Queen Palm, *Syagrus romanzoffiana*, whose leaves overhang from the left

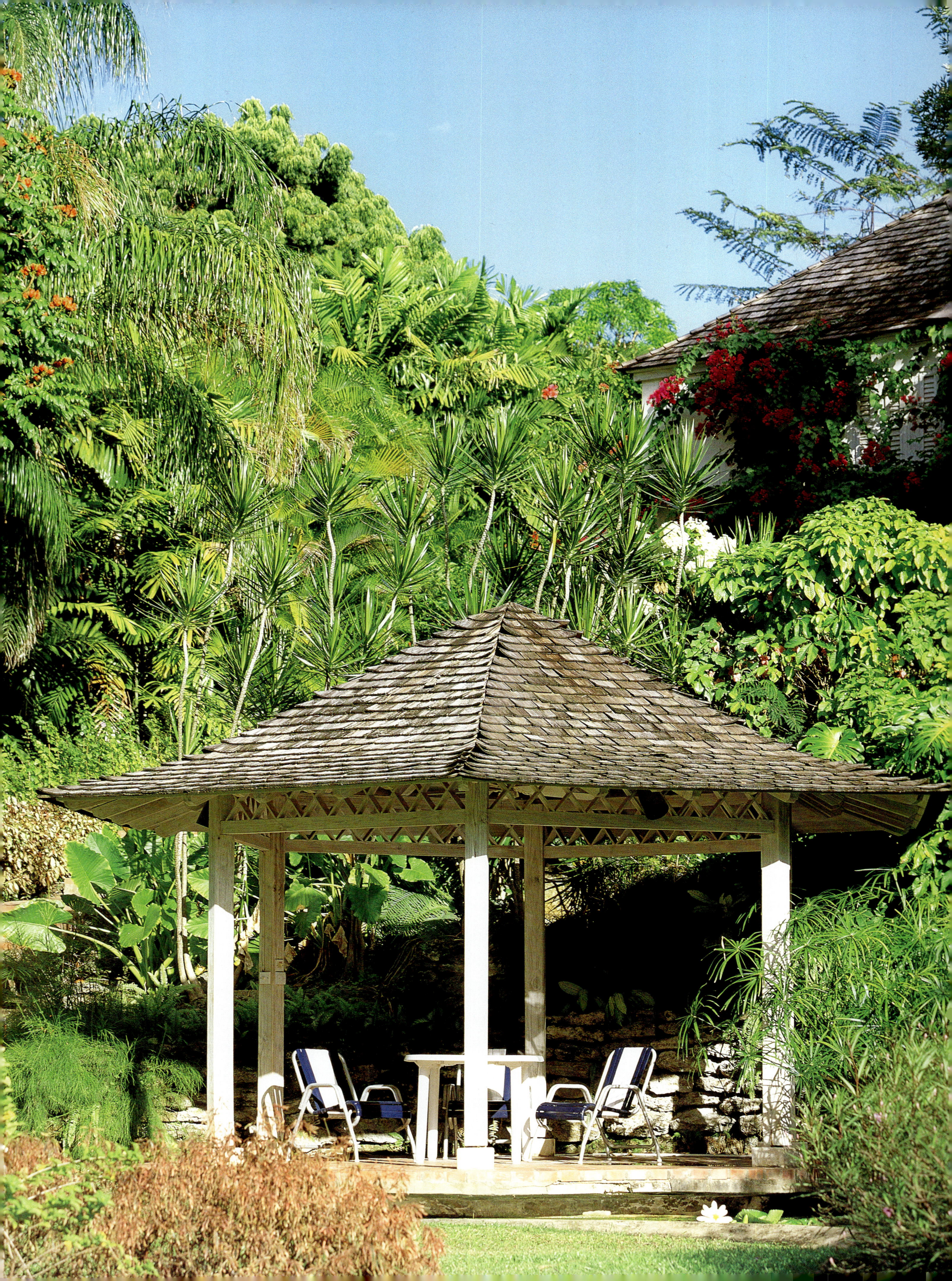

Gibbs Hill House

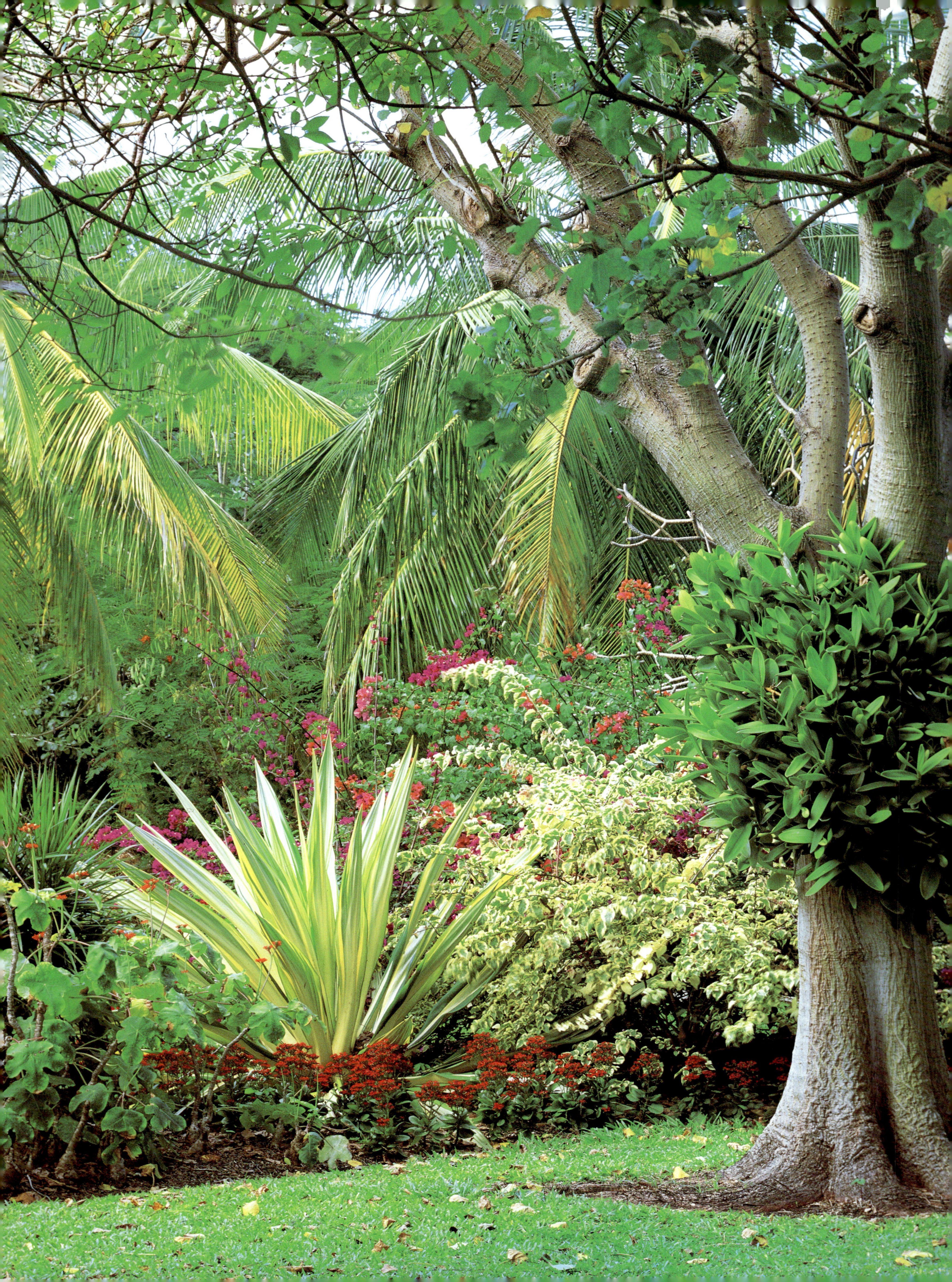

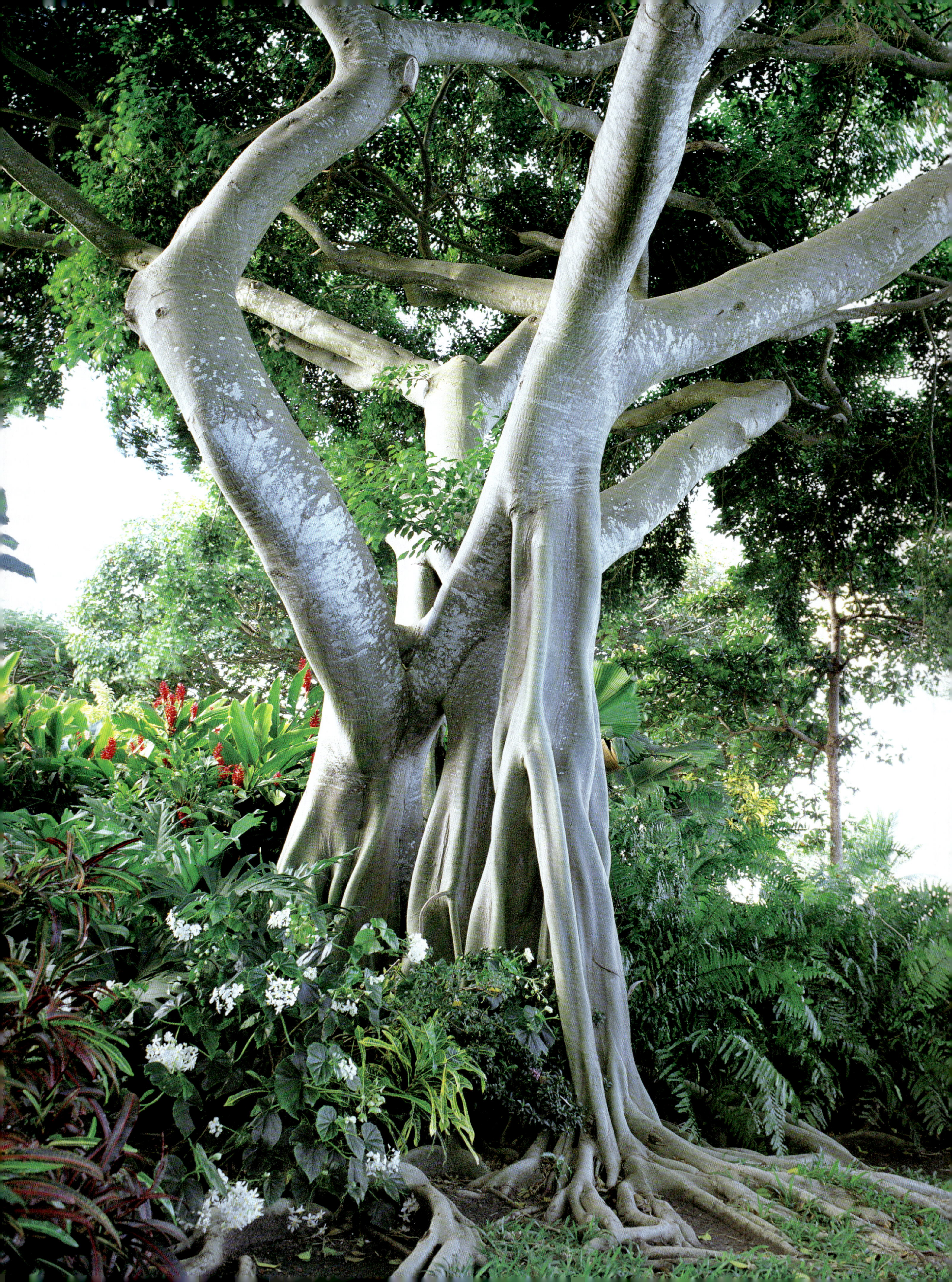

Opening page: Bottom centre —Mauritius Hemp, *Furcraea foetida* cv., 'Medio Picta', makes quite an architectural statement with its tall, slender variegated leaves; Kalanchoe, *Kalanchoe blossfeldiana*, displaying masses of red flowers, and a variegated *Bougainvillea* to the right. The background is dominated by the leaves of Coconut Palms, *Cocos nucifera*, and additional Bougainvilleas in full flower; Bottom left —Buddha Belly or Gouty Foot plant, *Jatropha podagrica*, a succulent and native of Guatemala, develops an interesting swollen trunk. • **Opposite**: *Ficus* with a skirt of aerial roots, made radiant with the silver glow of the natural light • **Above**: Snow-on-the-Mountain, *Euphorbia leucocephala*, from Central America and a member of the *Euphorbiaceae*, exhibits an incredible display of creamy white bracts throughout the Christmas period. Like the Poinsettia to which it is related, Snow-on-the-Mountain requires periods of increasing night hours, typically in excess of twelve hours of continuous dark, in order to initiate flowering. Plants should always therefore be located away from sources of night time lighting. It is not uncommon to see a Snow-on-the-Mountain that has been planted near to a street light, one half white and the other half, the side towards the street light, still green as the constant lighting has prevented the initiation of the flowering cycle in that side of the plant. In Barbados, Snow-on-the-Mountain and Poinsettia are often planted together to create a stunning contrast in colours at Christmas time.

Top: The striking inflorescence of the Umbrella or Octopus Tree, *Schefflera actinophylla*, a native of Australia, resembles the tentacles of an octopus, giving rise to one of its two common names. This highly ornamental tree is grown especially for its large palmately arranged leaves, which resemble the spokes of an umbrella, hence the other name, Umbrella Tree. • **Above**: Frangipani, *Plumeria rubra*. The Frangipani have previously dropped all their leaves and after a period of dormancy, are just beginning to flower, with minimal leaf production. During this period of dormancy the full sculptural character of the leafless, multi-branched Frangipani tree can be fully appreciated. • **Opposite**: Clusters of coconuts hang invitingly from a Coconut Palm, *Cocos nucifera*. In the top right background may be seen a recently opened inflorescence, the start of the next crop of coconuts. The water from a freshly cut cococut is extremely refreshing and enjoyed by all.

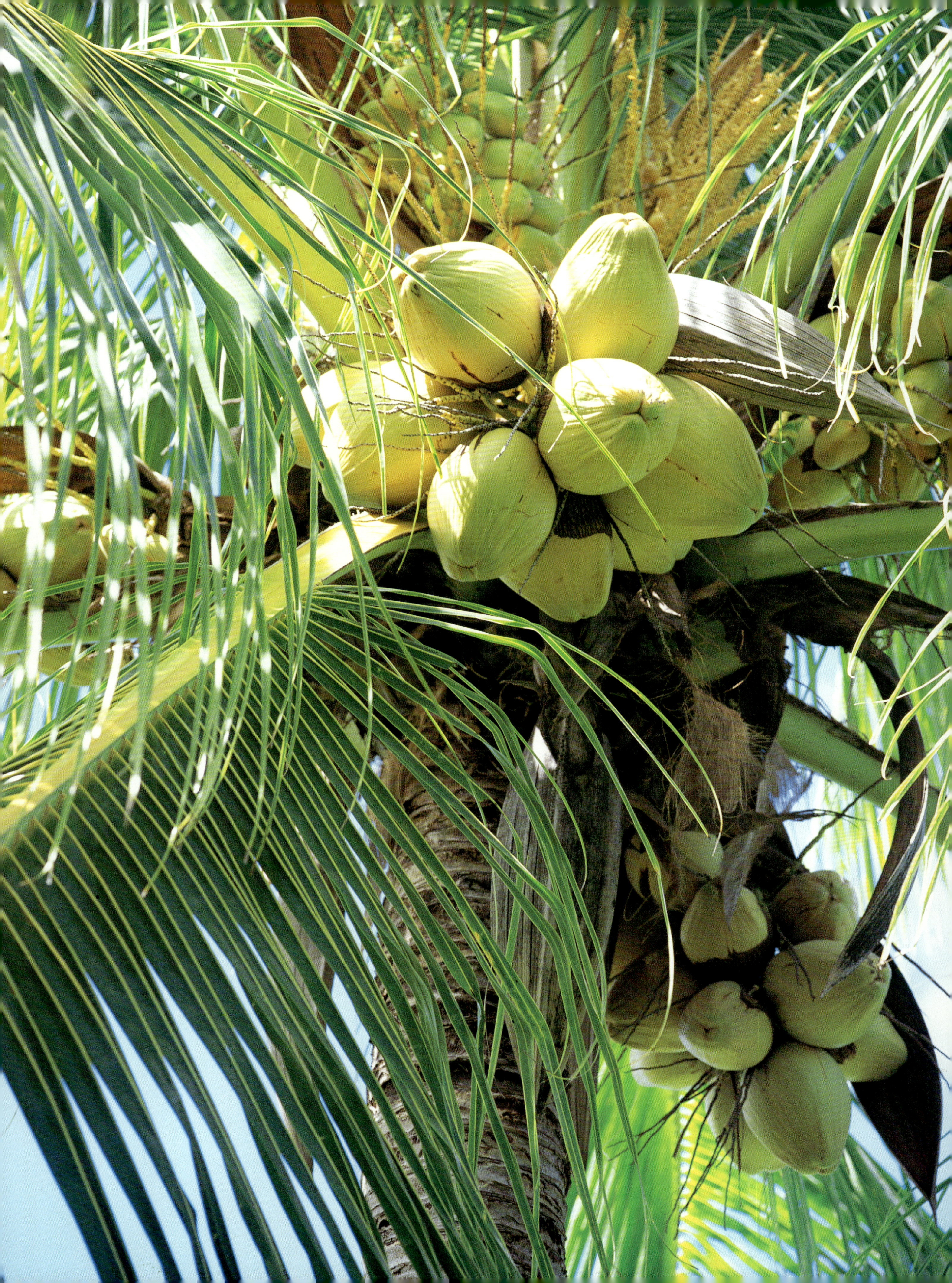

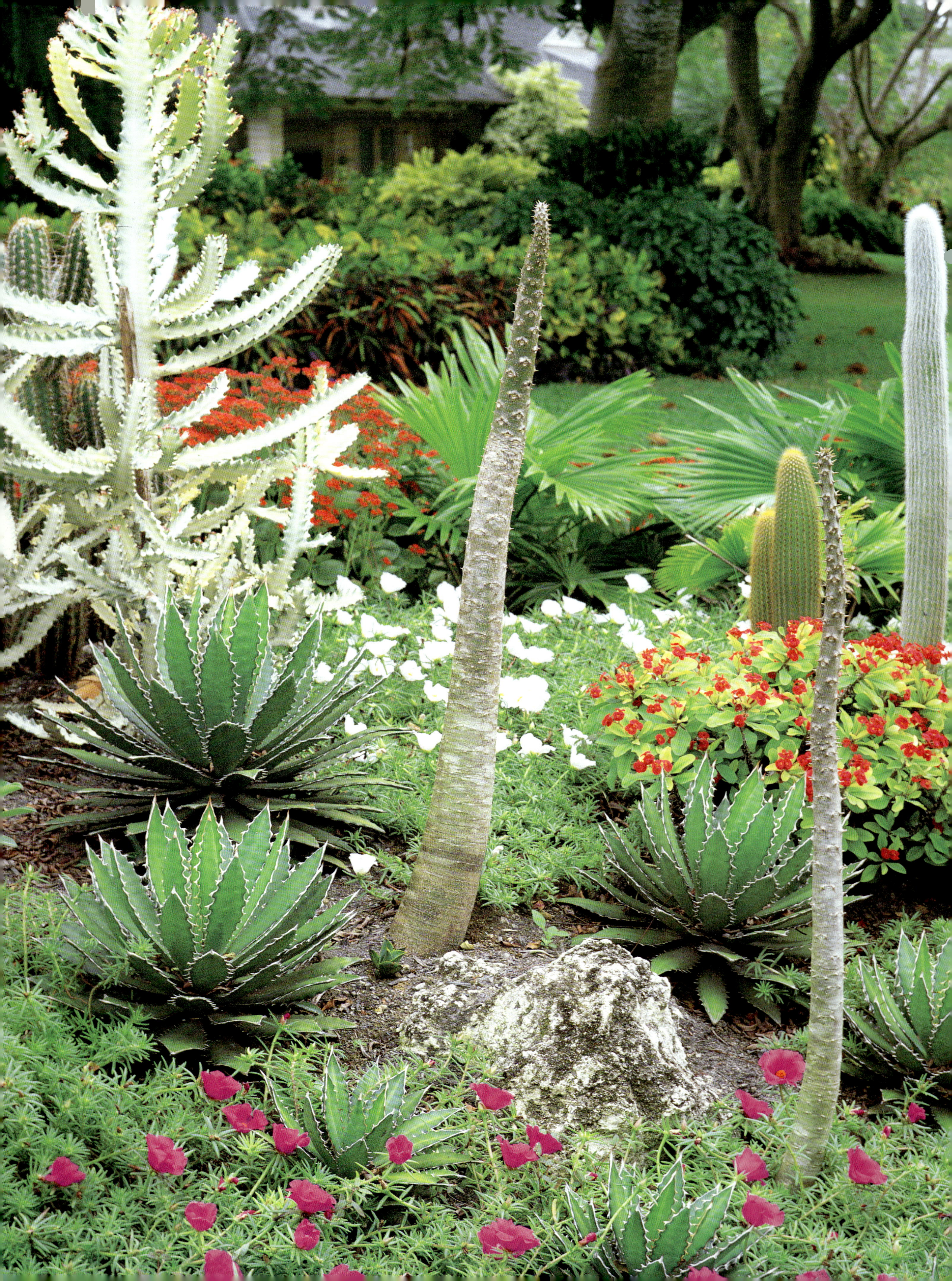

Opposite: A grouping of succulents presents a pleasing variety of shapes and colours. The plants include; a pair of leafless, dormant Pachypodiums rising like sentinels. Top left – Ghost Cactus, *Euphorbia lactea* cv. variegata, in front of red flowers of Kalanchoe, *Kalanchoe blossfeldiana*; Lower centre – Agaves, *Agave horrida*, from Mexico; Foreground and centre – Purple and white varieties of Portulaca, *Portulaca grandiflora*; Right of centre – Red flowers of Crown of Thorns, *Euphorbia milli*. • **Above**: Mauritius Hemp, *Furcraea foetida*, which is used in Mauritius in the commercial production of fibre for ropes, sits in the midst of other succulents including Purple Portulaca, *Portulaca grandiflora*, red and cream flowering varieties of Crown of Thorns, *Euphorbia milli*, and three Golden Barrel Cactus specimens, *Echinocactus grusonii*.

Above: Virgin or Nun Orchids, *Diacrium bicornutum*, growing on a stump • **Opposite**: Orchids, *Vandaceous spp*

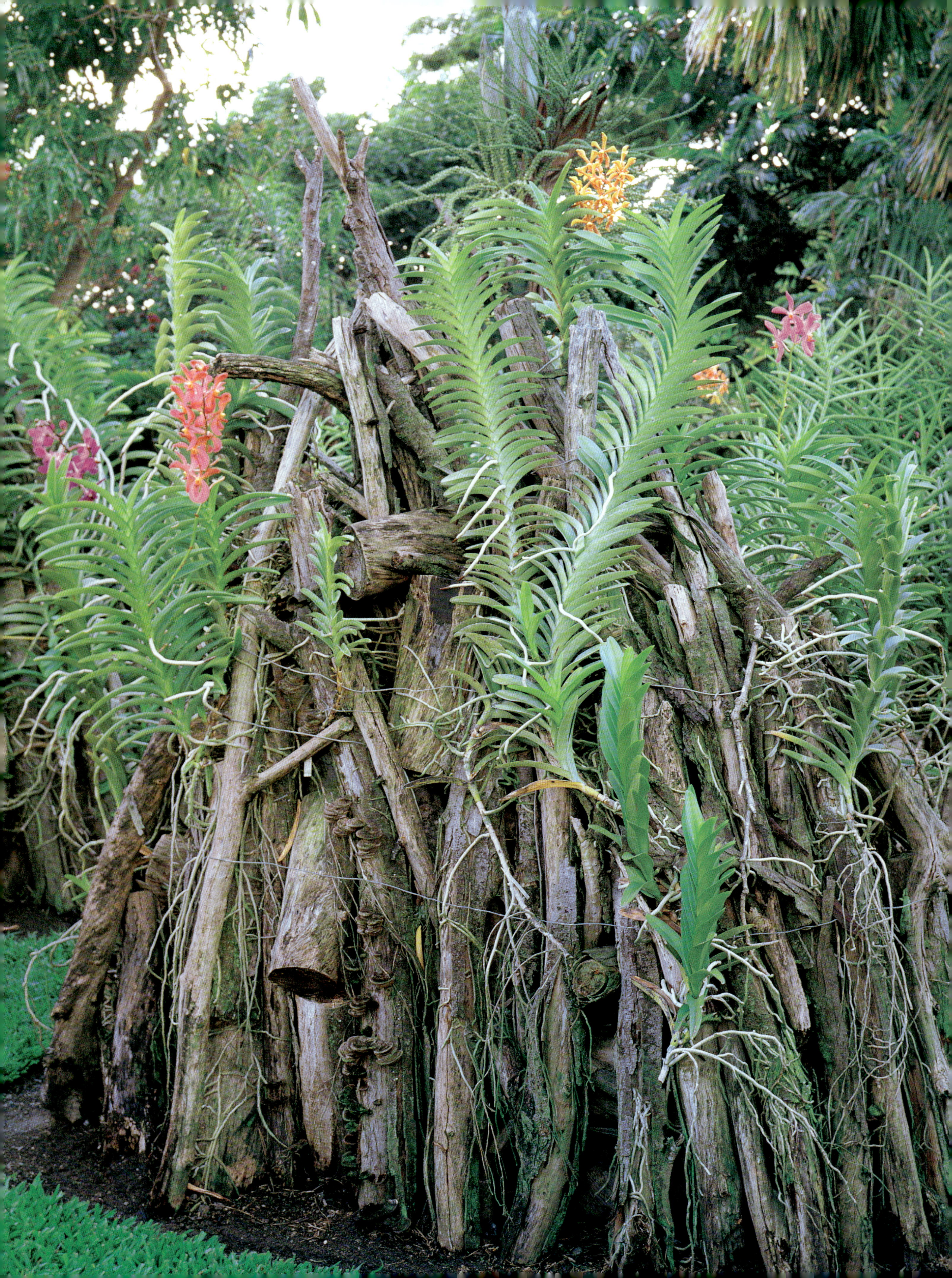

CALYPSO COTTAGE

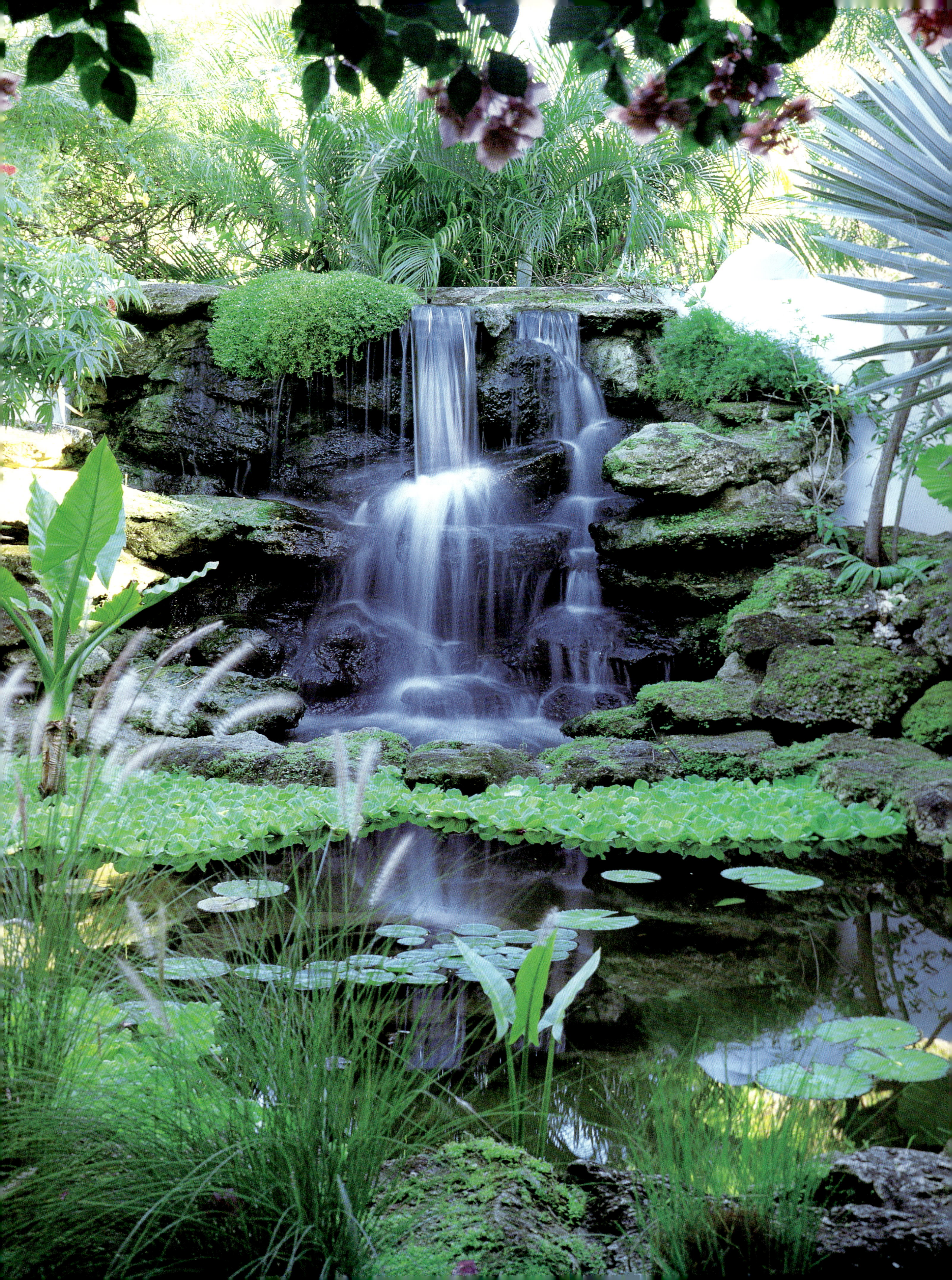

Opening page: Upper left – Coral Plant, *Jatropha multifidia*; Middle left – *Typhonodorum lindleyanum*; Lower left – Feather Grass; Top centre – Flowers of Burgendy Allamanda, *Allamanda violacea*, with a Golden Palm, *Dypsis lutescens*, seen behind waterfall; Upper right, next to the waterfall – Asparagus Fern, *Asparagus densiflorus* cv: *sprengerii*; In the pond, at the base of the waterfall – Water Lettuce, *Pistia stratiotes*; Bottom centre – *Portulacca grandiflora florepleno* • **Above**: This photograph is dominated by a trio of Bismarck Palms, *Bismarckia nobilis*, with an *Alocasia macrorrhiza* cv: 'Rubra' in the bottom left and Water Lettuce, *Pistia stratiotes*, growing in the pond. Bougainvillea, *Bougainvillea spectablis*, cascades down to the left of the centrally located Bismarkia Palm •
Opposite: Mature Coconut Trees, *Cocos nucifera*, tower above newly planted coconuts, with Sea Grape bushes, *Cocoluba uvifera*, visible between them. The Sea Grape, a beautiful and versatile tree with round, attractive leaves, is widely used in Barbados for coastal hedging, as indoor potted plants and to provide welcome seaside shade. The "sea grape" fruit is edible and popular with locals, but may be considered an acquired taste. The lawn is planted with Savannah Grass, *Anoxopus compressus*.

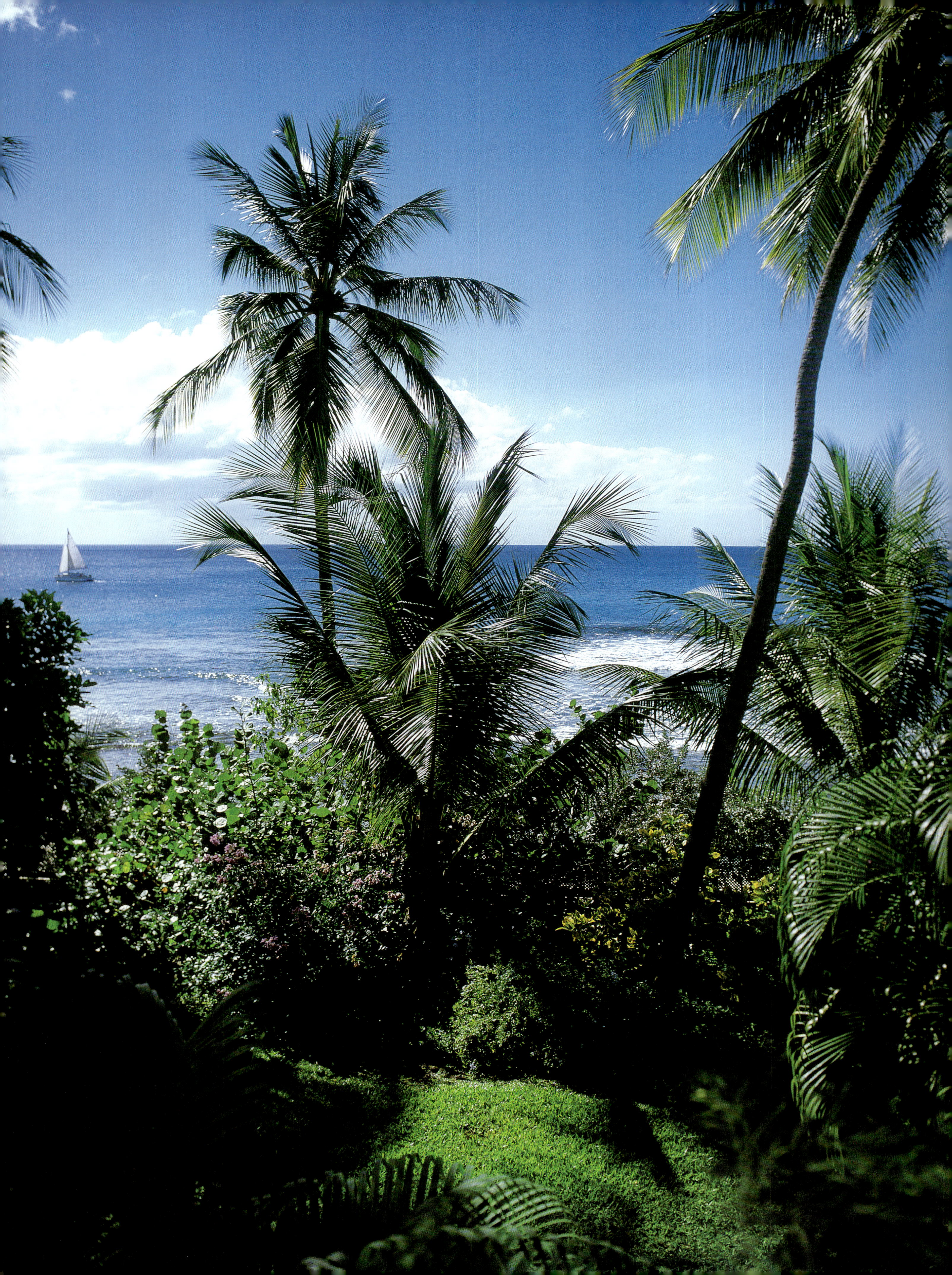

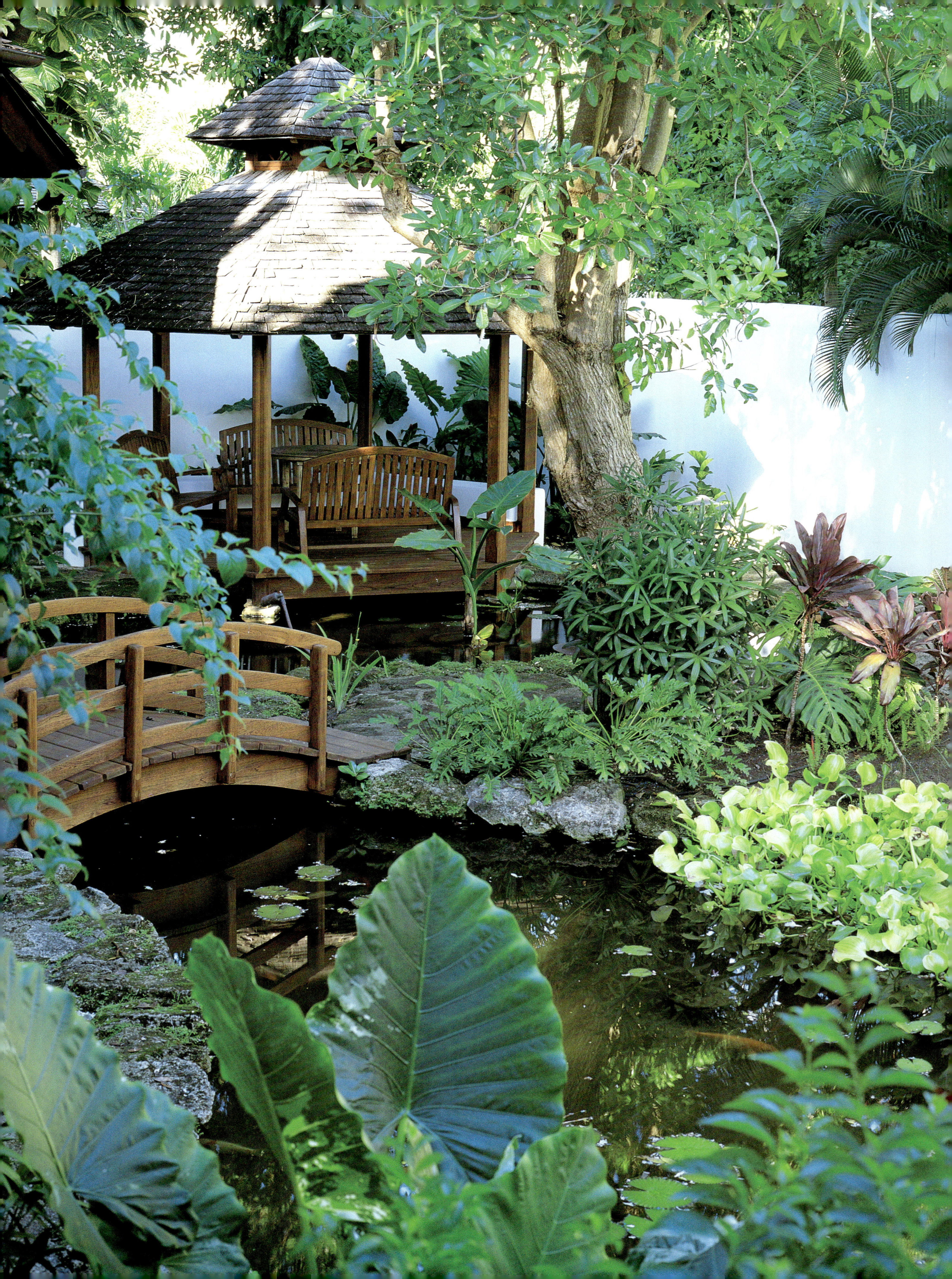

Opposite: Bottom left – Elephants Ear, *Alocasia macrorhiza*, seen below hanging branches of Chinaman's Hat or Cup and Saucer plant, *Holmskioldia sanguinea*; Top Centre – A Whitewood Tree, *Tabeuia pallida*, which was probably at one time the most common tree in the wilds of Barbados. The wood of the Whitewood was used in the construction of fishing boats. At the base of the Whitewood tree is a clump of Lady Palms, *Rhapis excelsa*, and to the right is a Red Dracena, *Cordyline terminalis* cv: 'Firebrand'. In front of the Lady Palm is a self-heading Philodendron, *Philodendron xanadu*; Lower right, growing in the pond – Water Hyacinth, *Eichhornia azurea* • **Above**: Blue Latan Palms, *Latania loddigessii*, standing over a Ponytail Plant, *Beaucarenea recurvata*, in the lower centre foreground, and a Variegated Corkscrew Ginger, *Costus speciosus* 'Variegata', to the right.

Above clockwise from top left: Water Hyacinth, *Eichhornia azurea*, and Papyrus, *Cyperus papyrus* • Desert Rose, *Adenium obesum* • Next to the pond, a Bottlebrush Tree, *Callistemon viminalis*, creates a soft, Willow-like effect with its trailing branches and fine leaves. The bottle brush shaped, red infloresence adds interest and attracts birds and bees. In contrast to the Bottle Brush Tree, the *Alocasia macrorhiza*, seen at the lower left, is bold and upright and distinctly tropical in both appearance and effect. In the foreground there is Boston Fern, *Nephrolepis exaltata* 'bostoniensis', while to the right we see a Bamboo Palm, *Chamaedorea seifrizii*. • Water Lillies, *Nymphaea caerulea*, with Koi swimming in the pond • **Opposite**: The play of sunlight on tropical greenery. A close up of *Alocasia macrorhiza*

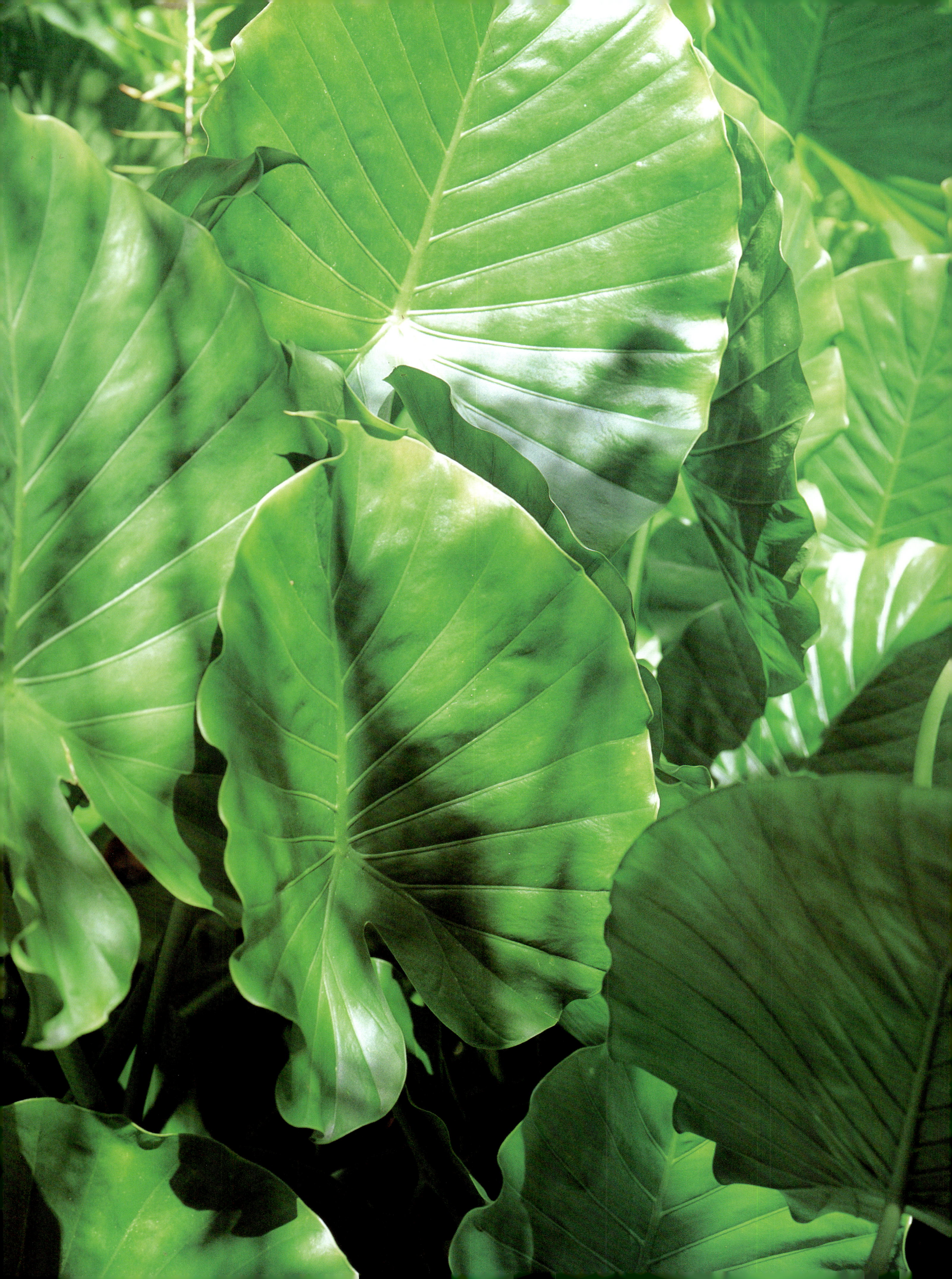

Olive Wood

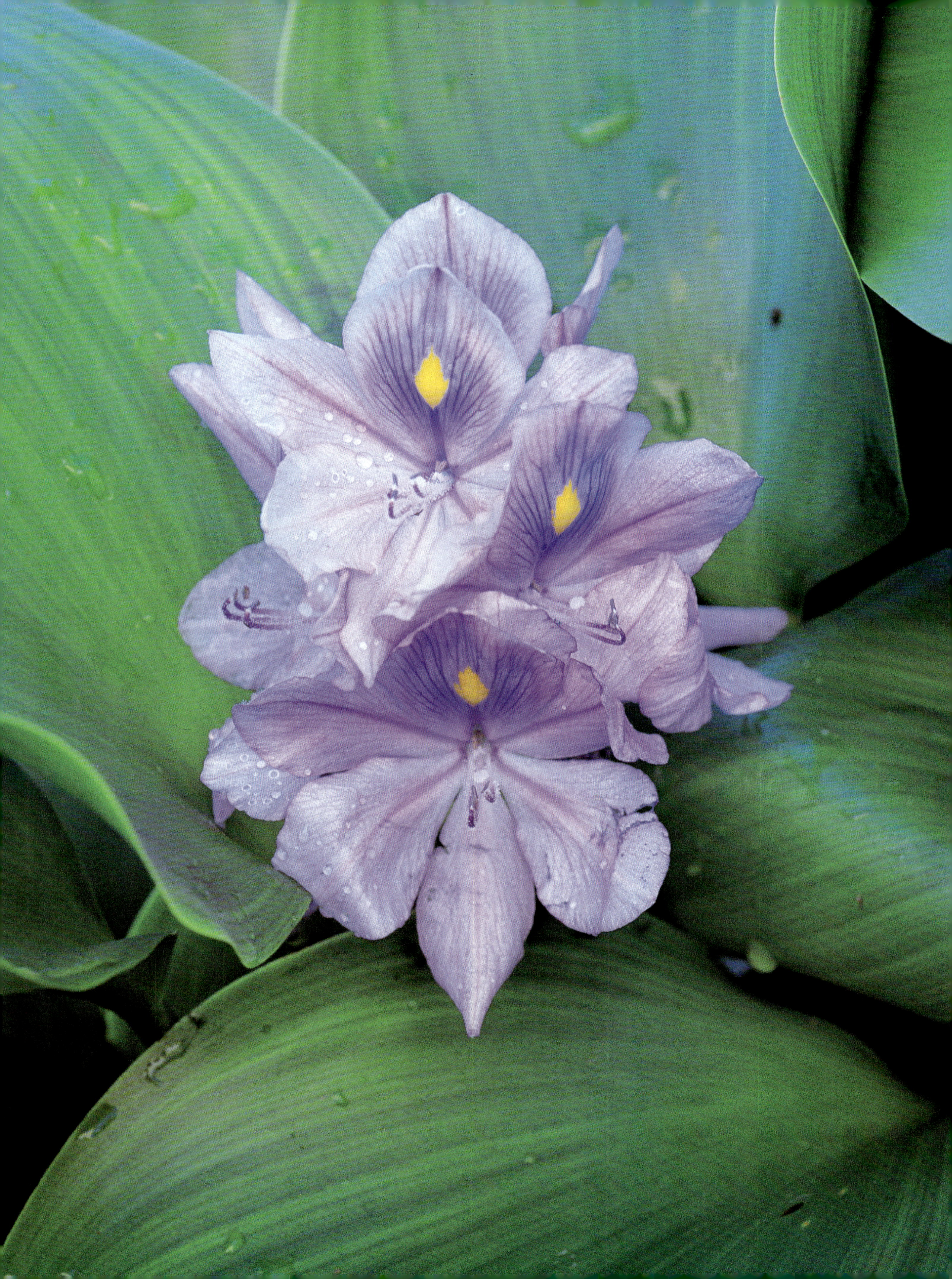

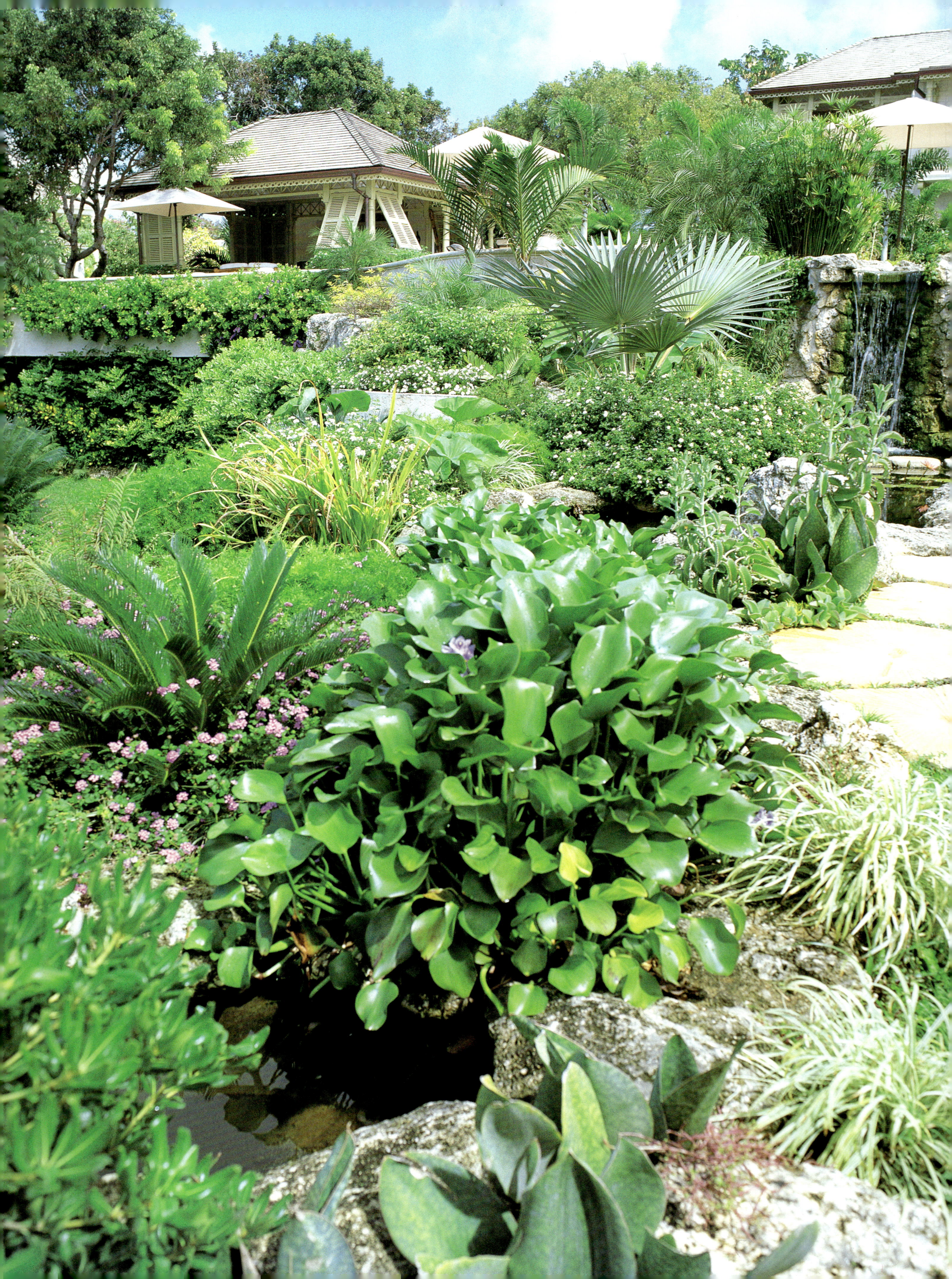

Opening page: Close up of Water Hyacinth, *Eichhornia crassipes* • **Opposite**: Upper right – Waterfall; Lower centre – Water Hyacinth, *Eichhornia crassipes*; Bottom right – Coral stone boulders; Left centre – Sago Palm, *Cycas revoluta*, surrounded by Lilac Sage flowers, *Lantana montevidensis*, as ground cover • **Above**: Foxtail Palms, *Wodyetia bifurcata*, gracefully frame an entranceway. Foxtail Palms, from Northern Australia, are a comparatively recent addition to the palms used in landscaping worldwide, having only been discovered in the 1970's, but they have rapidly become one of the world's most popular landscape palms. They are undeniably beautiful palms when used in odd numbered groupings in the landscape.

Above: Close up of Dwarf Sago Palm, *Cycas revoluta*, entwined with Lilac Sage, *Lantana montevidensis*. •
Opposite: A Young Flamboyant, *Delonix regia*, rises from the middle of a grouping of Crotons, *Codiaeum variegatum*, and Dwarf Sago Palm, *Cycas revoluta*. *Pilea microphylla* borders the plantings. In the background are several Fiji Fan Palms, *Pritchardia pacifica*, a very fast growing fan palm from Tonga, considered by many to be the most beautiful fan palm and the epitome of a tropical environment.

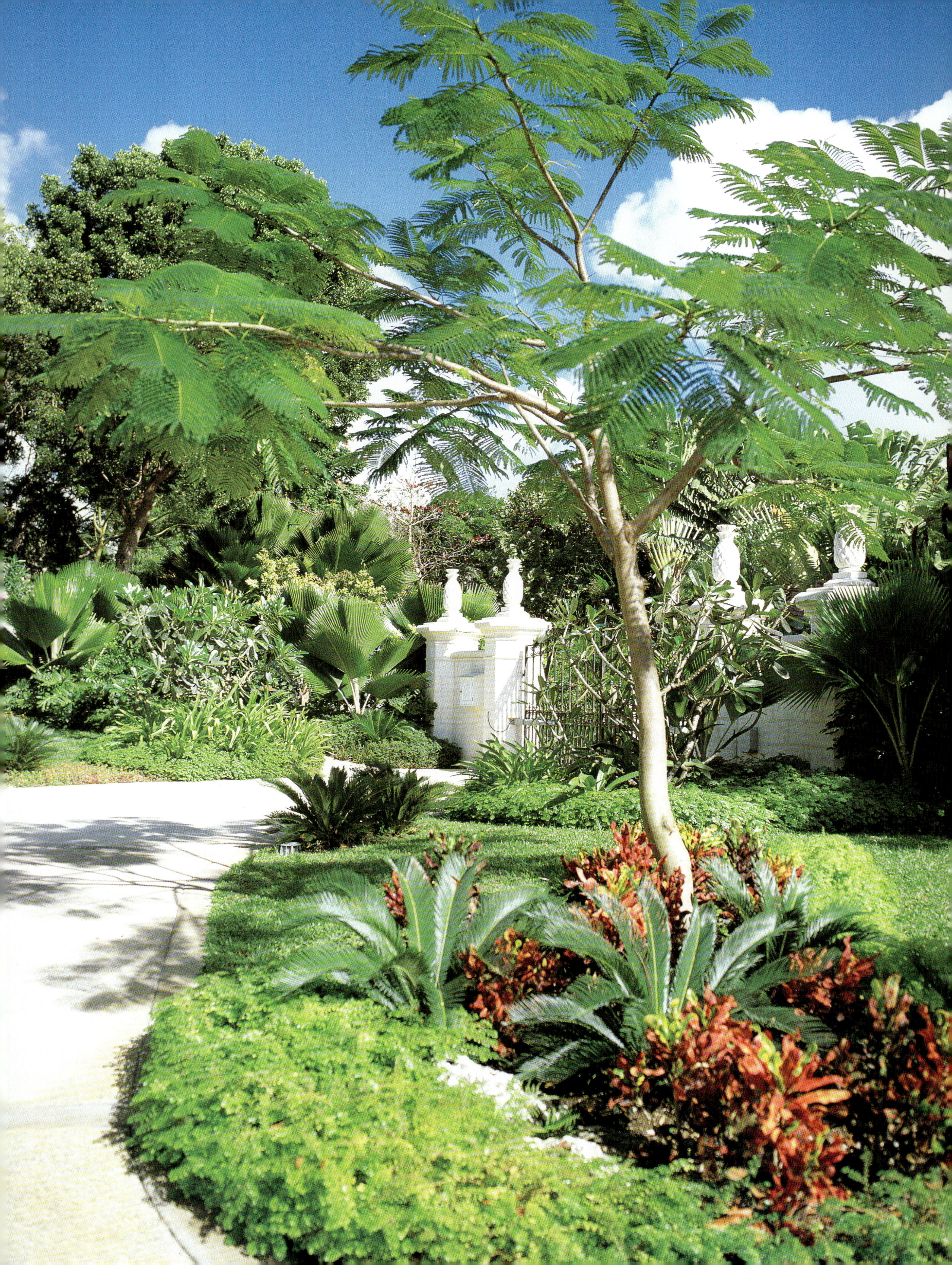

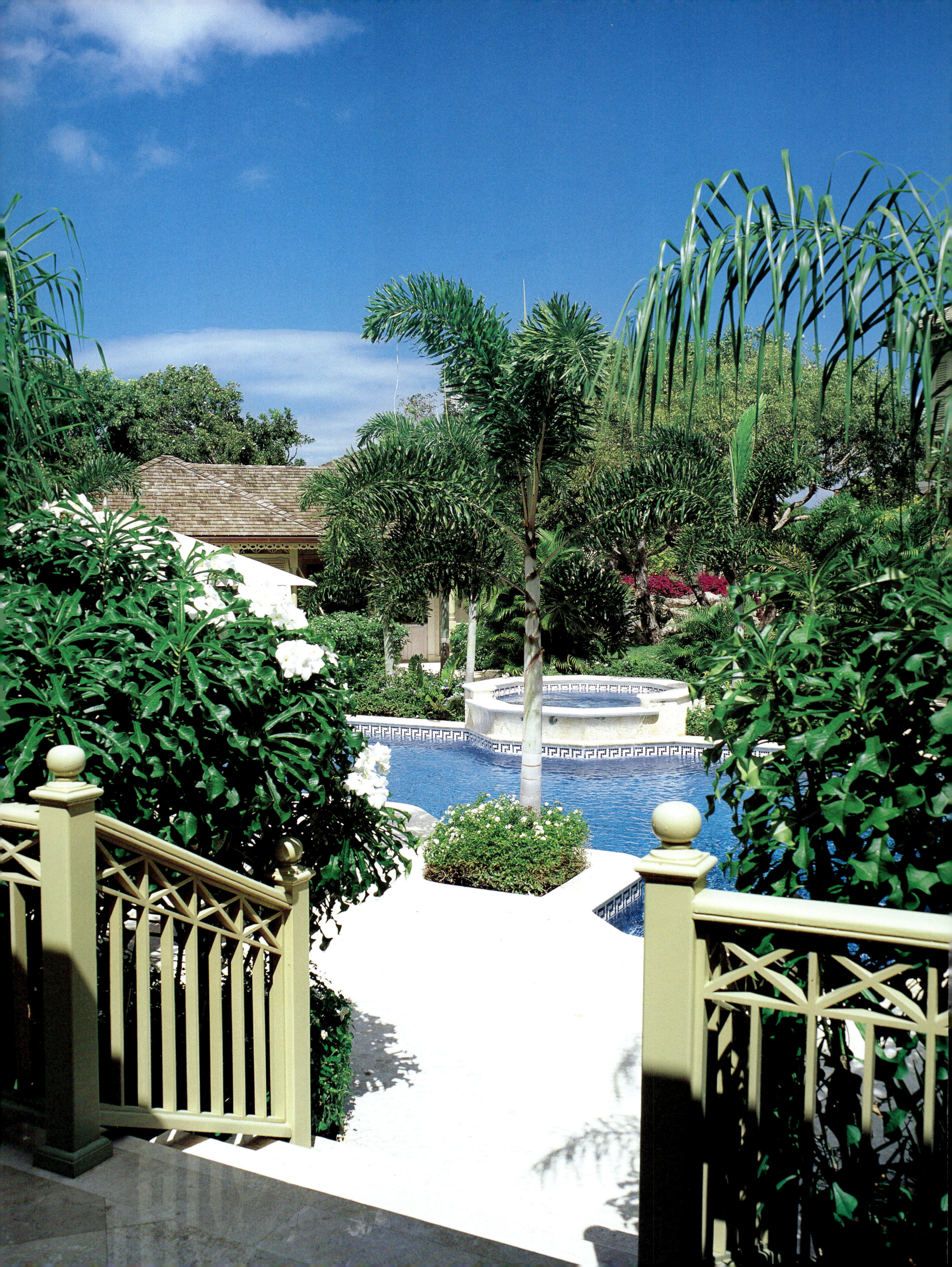

Opposite: Bridal Bouquet Plumeria, or Puerto Rican Frangipani, *Plumeria pudica*, border the steps descending to the pool, with a Foxtail Palm, *Wodyetia bifurcata*, centrally located at the edge of the pool. Bridal Bouquet is a recent addition to landscapes in Barbados. It is grown for its form and foliage as much as for its flowers. Unlike other Plumerias which undergo much horizontal branching, Bridal Bouquest produces dense vertical branching, resulting in a much more compact, dense and vertically oriented shape. Also, where other Plumerias shed their leaves in October, and remain leafless until about April, Bridal Bouquet is an evergreen. Once planted in a sunny location, large clusters of white flowers with yellow centres are produced year round at the top of the plant, giving the appearance of a bridal bouquet sitting on the top of the plant. The leaves are deep green, glossy and very attractive and unusually shaped, resembling an arrowhead or spear point. Periodic pruning ensures that the plant retains its shape, density and continues to flower profusely. • **Top**: Coral boulder retaining walls are used to create cost effective and natural looking terraces that blend perfectly with the landscape. A grove of Mahogany, *Swietenia mahogoni*, is in the background. Mahogany was, and still is, a very important tree in Barbados, having been first introduced to the island in 1763, and the wood subsequently used to produce much of the furniture produced on the island. The majority of traditional items of antique furniture available on the island, handed down through generations, are made from Barbados Mahogany and are treasured as the supply of Barbados Mahogany is now very limited. Also, over the years, these older pieces of furniture have acquired an incredible patina and depth of colour that is virtually impossible to achieve with the younger lumber that is available. • **Above**: Foxtail palms, *Wodyetia bifurcata*, surround the pool.

Above clockwise from Top left: Coleus, *Plectranthus scutellarioides* hybrid • Purple Fountain Grass, *Pennisetum setaceum* cv: 'Purpureum' • Beefsteak acalypha, *Acalypha wilkesiana* cultivar • Bottom left - Ornamental grass, *Panicum virgatum*, in flower • **Opposite**: *Hibiscus rosa-sinensis*

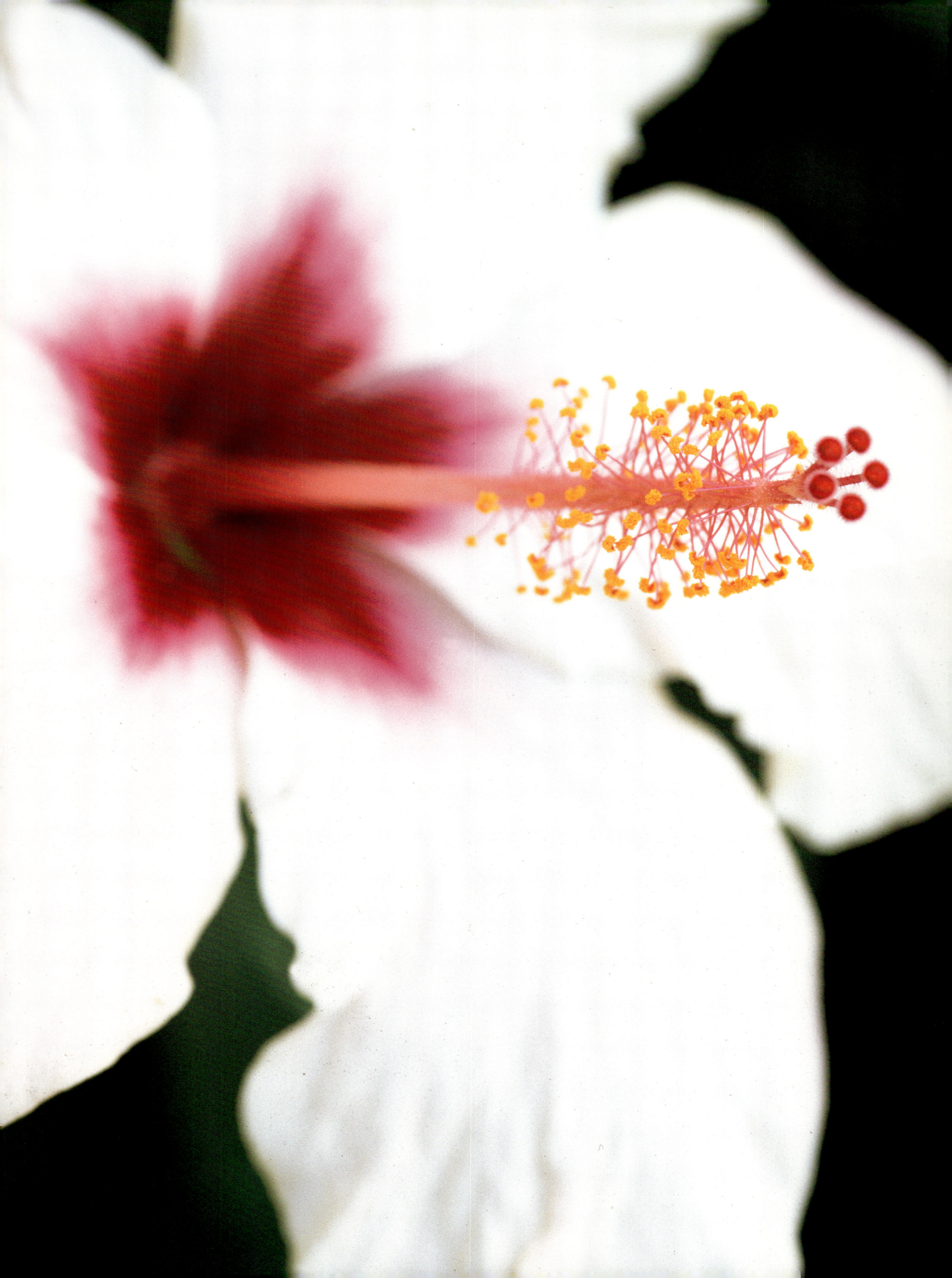

LAZYBONES

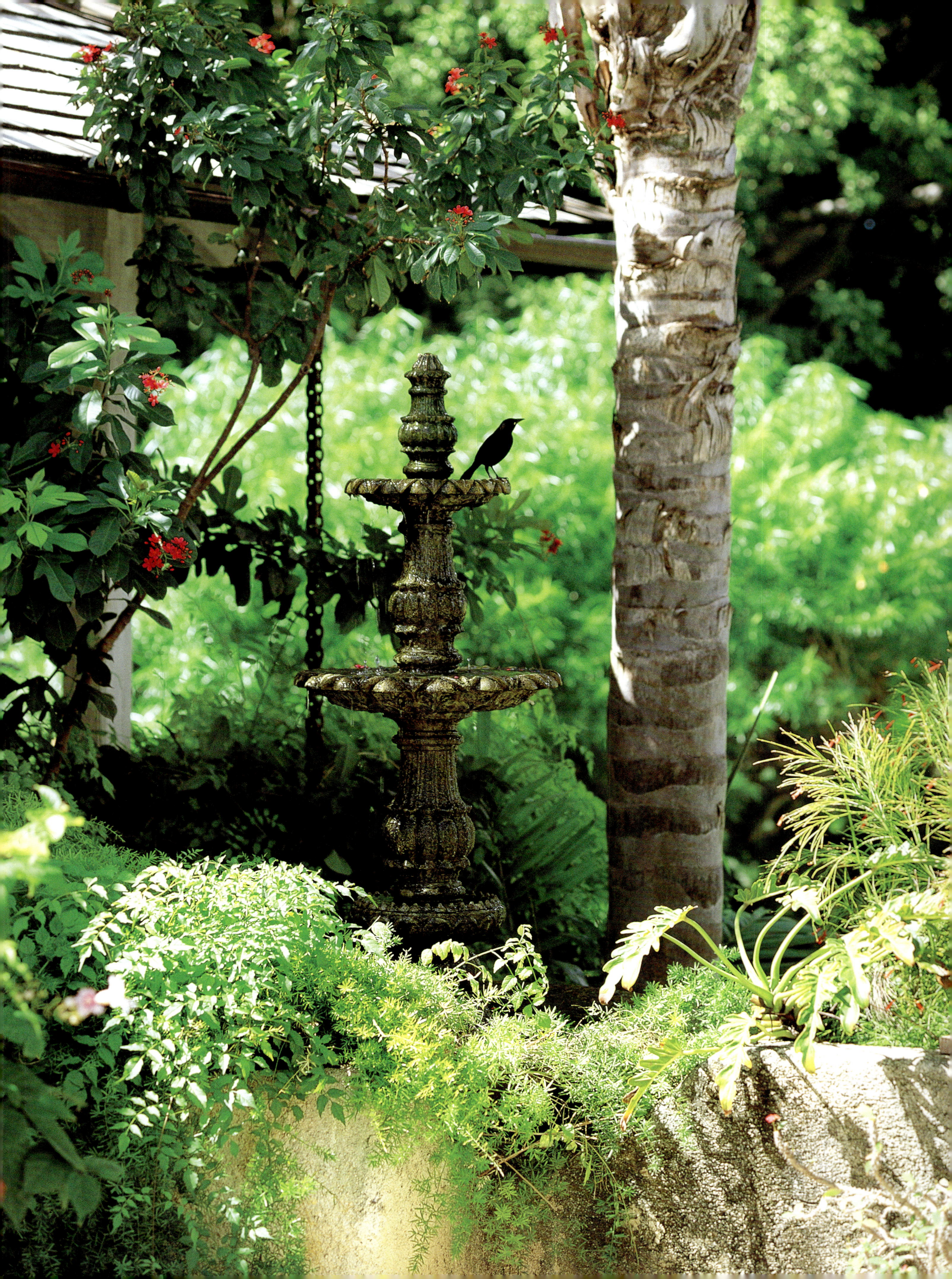

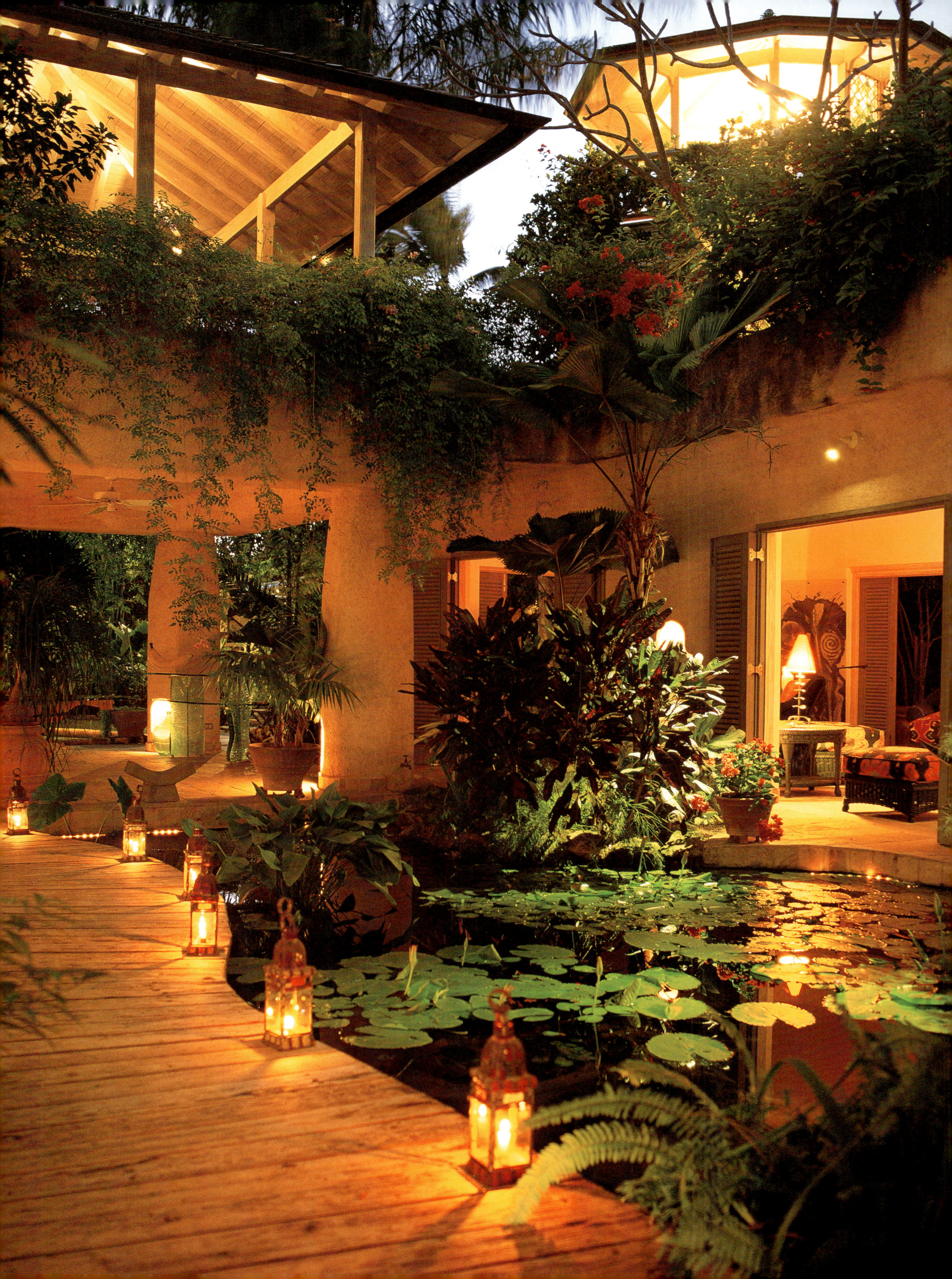

Opening page: A Carib Grackle, or Blackbird as it is locally known, surveys the beautiful gardens from his perch on the fountain; Upper left – *Jatropha integerrima*, a very hardy plant, a member of the *Euphorbiacea* and native to the West Indies, used extensively for borders and as accent plants; Lower centre – Asparagus fern, *Asparagus densiflorus* cv: 'Sprengeri', a native of South Africa, is used extensively as a ground cover and in borders overhanging walls. It is also an excellent container plant, especially in hanging baskets. The Asparagus fern is a member of the *Lilliaceae*, the Lily family; Lower right – Firecracker or Coral plant, *Russelia equisetiformis*, is a favourite with Hummingbirds who flitter back and forth amongst its clusters of red, drooping, firecracker-like flowers. The Firecracker plant, a native of Mexico, requires little care and is a great plant for cascading over walls and boulders and in borders. In sunny locations it flowers extensively year round and guarantees a splash of colour wherever planted • **Opposite**: Lily pond in an inner courtyard • **Above**: Potted Ficus topiaries flanking a doorway

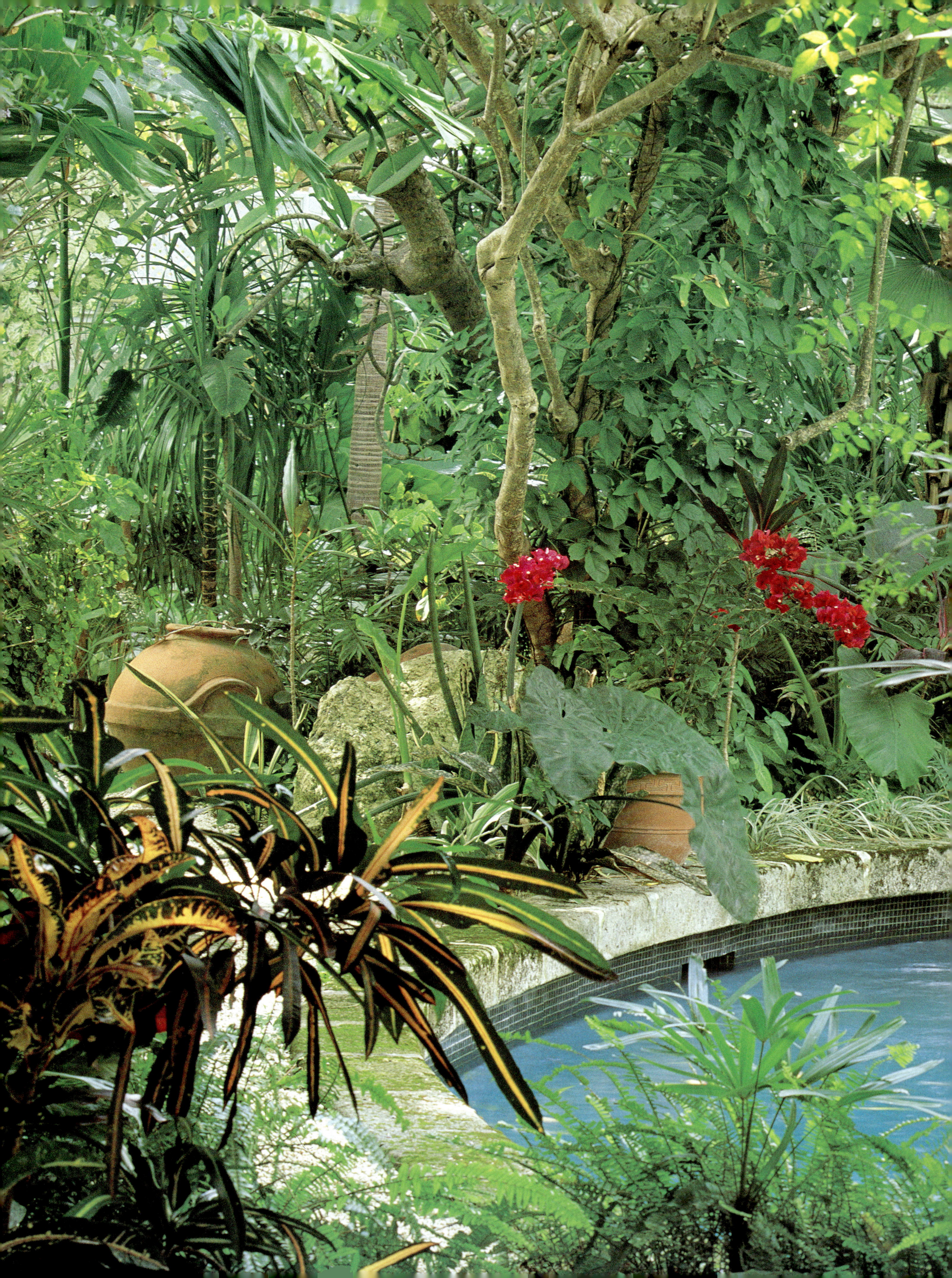

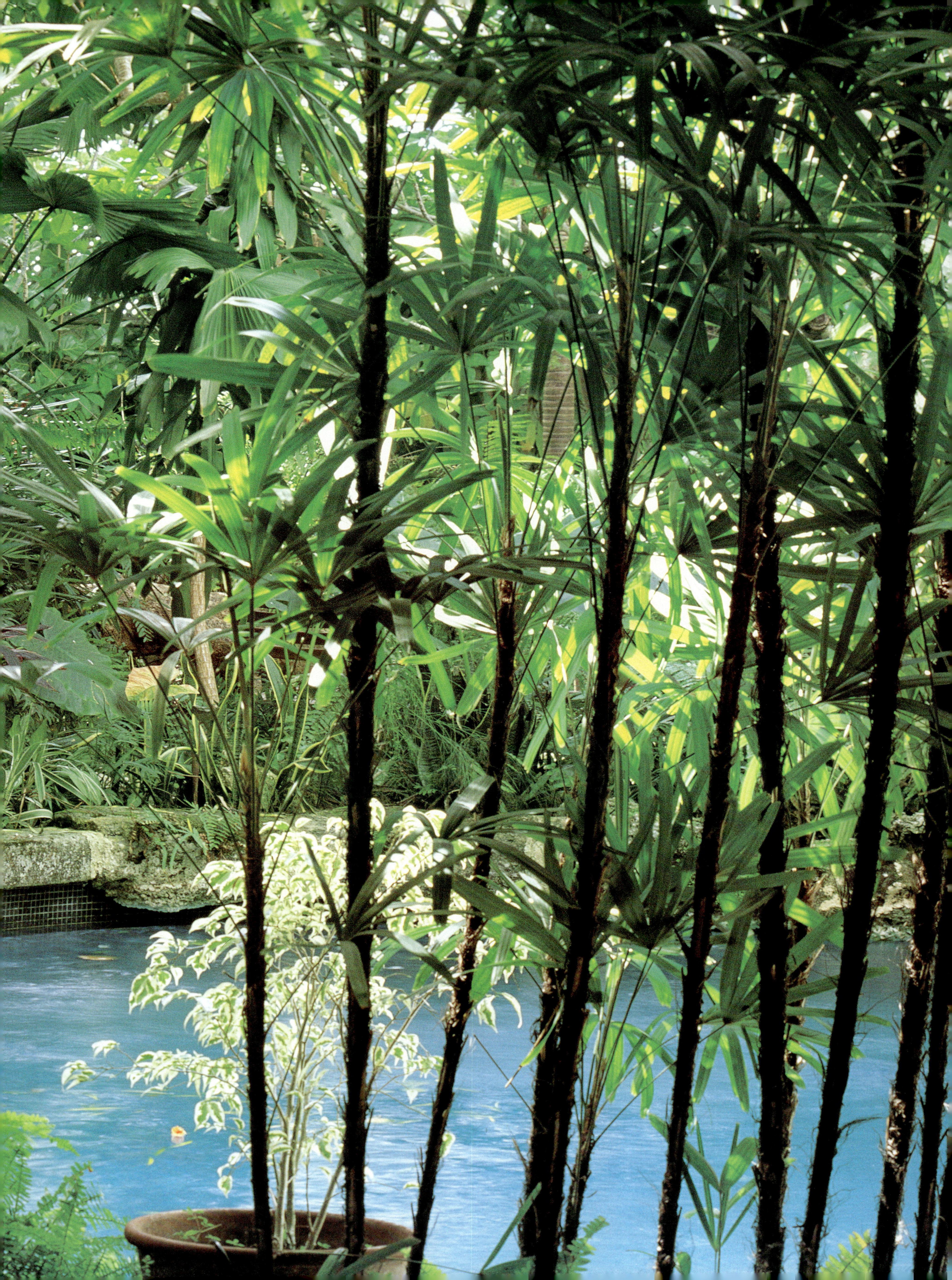

Previous pages: A 'tropical spectacular' encompasses the pool including: From left to right – Croton, *Codiaeum variegatum*, at the pool's edge: *Alocasia macrorrhiza* cv; 'Rubra', Bougainvillea, *Bougainvillea spectabilis*, *Ophiopogon*, Mother-in-Law Tongue or Variegated Snake plant, *Sansevieria trifasciata* cv; 'Laurentii'; background: a Syngonium grows up the trunk of a Frangipani, *Plumeria rubra*, and a *Licuala grandis* palm peeks through the dense planting. Right foreground – A row of Lady Palms, *Rhapis excelsa* • **Above**: Upper left - A Chalice Flower or Cup of Gold, *Solandra maxima*, scrambles over the pergola thereby providing filtered shade for relaxation in the deck chairs below. It is a fast growing woody climber which periodically produces large yellow flowers that are fragrant at night. The Chalice Flower is related to the Angel Trumpets (*Datura* and *Brugmansia*) and like them, has hallucinogenic properties. A large potted specimen of Madagascar Palm, *Pachypodium lamerei*, with three heads, is located behind the deck chairs. The Madagascar Palm is not a palm but a succulent of the *Apocynaceae* family and is native to Madagascar. Its trunk, which under ideal conditions can reach 15 feet, is covered with spines up to about 2 inches long, and has the foliage arranged spirally at the top • **Opposite**: Centre right – Growing at the base of the tree and climbing into its branches is Pothos, *Epipremnum pinnatum* cv:'Aureum'. Pothos is a well known house plant that has small oval leaves that may be patterned in dark green and yellow or all yellow. As a house plant, or when growing on the ground as ground cover, the leaves are small, but once the plant begins to climb they expand to an enormous size (up to 18" in length) and take on a heavily variegated colouration; Bottom – Aglaonemas thriving in the shade. Left centre – a Sygonium grows up the trunk of a Sago palm, *Cycas circinalis*. The Sago palm is not a palm but is actually a Cycad. Cycads are some of the oldest plants growing on earth. The fossil record shows that they flourished during the time of the dinosaurs, being one of the dominant plant species at that time, reaching their peak in the Mesozoic Era some 150 million years ago. Today they are a relatively small plant group consisting of about 185 species in 11 genera.

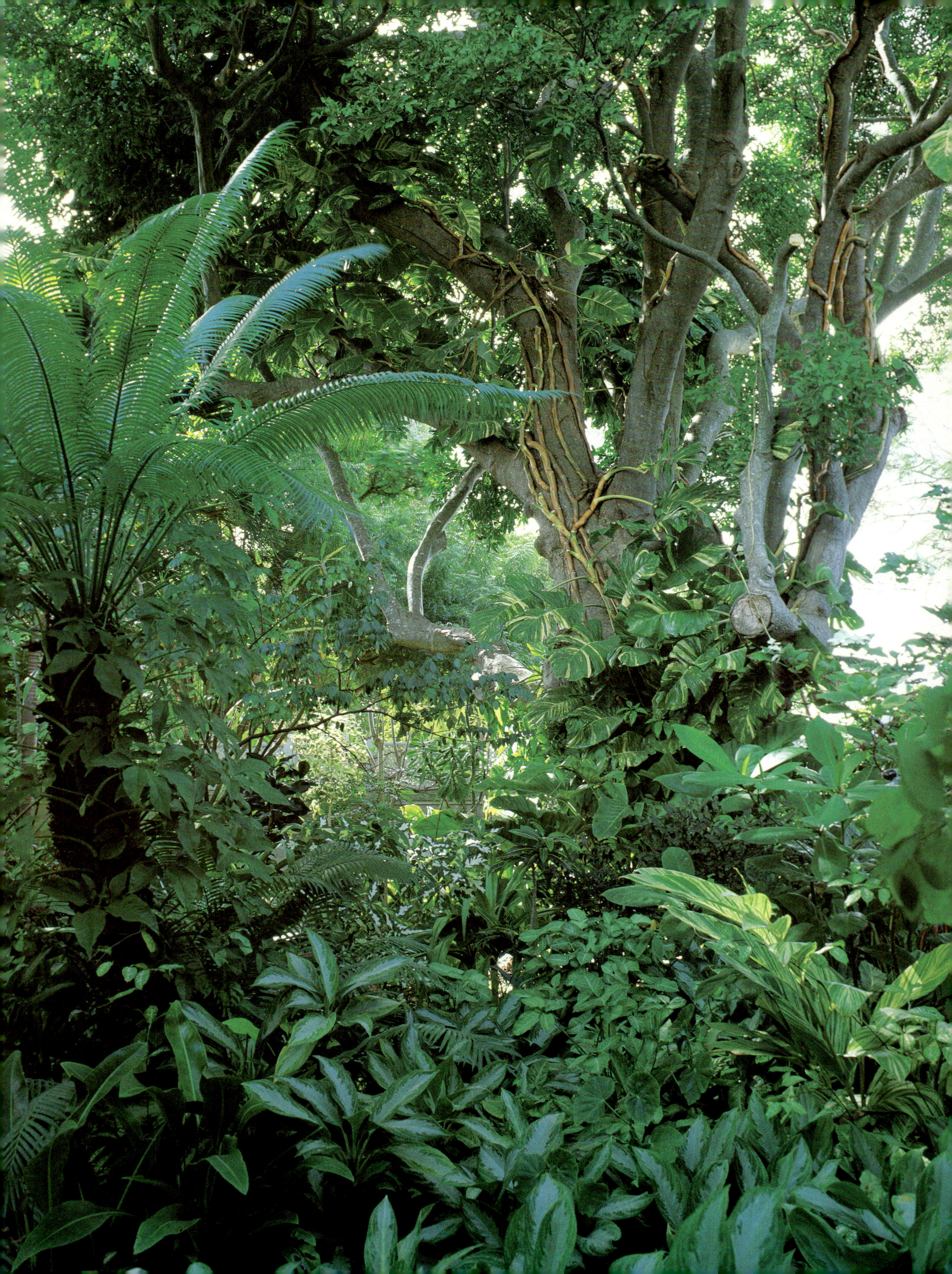

Bellerive

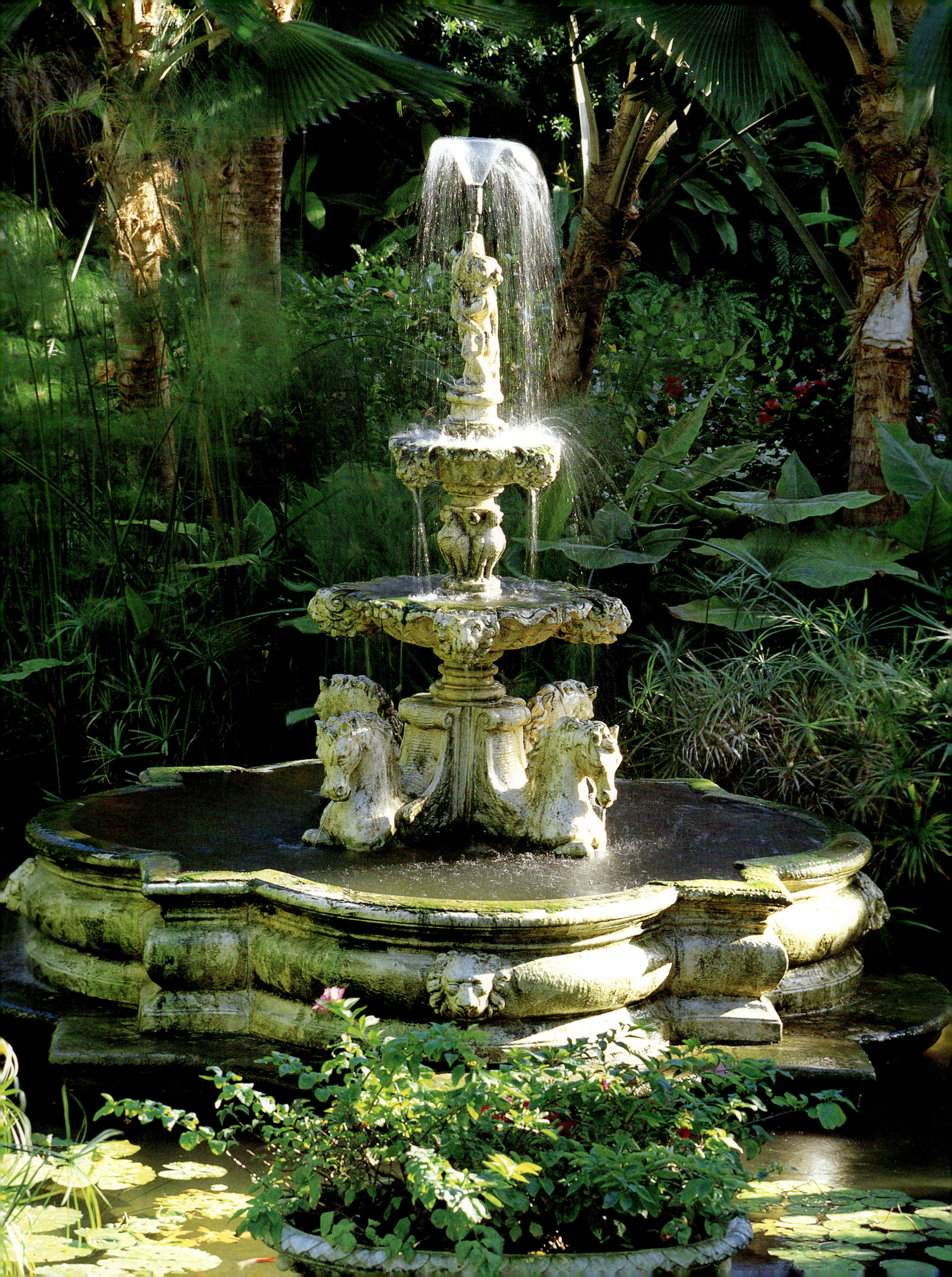

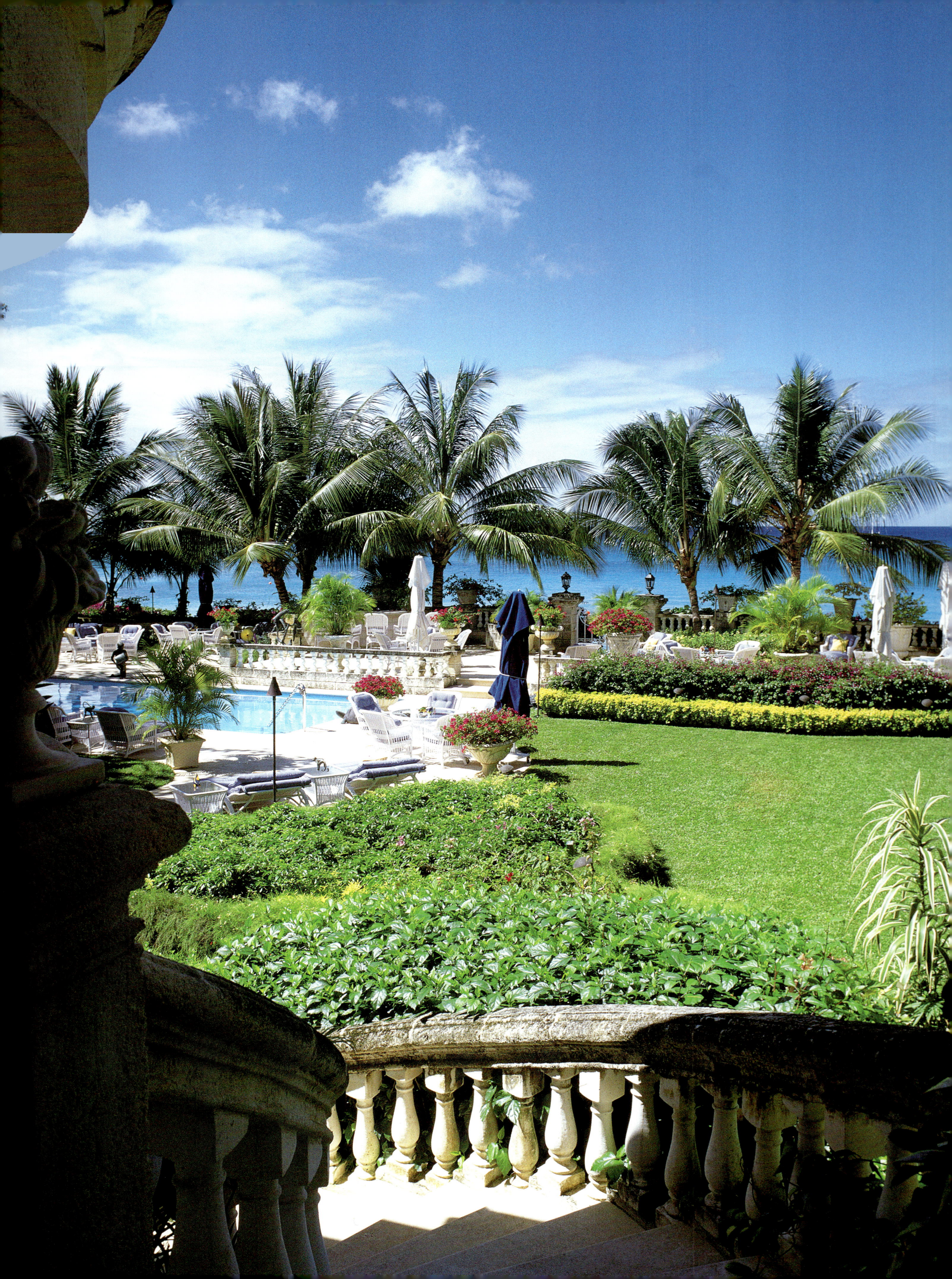

Opening page: A beautiful fountain is positioned against a backdrop of Papyrus, *Cyperus papyrus*, on the left and Umbrella Grass, *Cyperus alternifolius*, on the right. Fiji Fan Palms, *Pritchardia pacifica*, are in the background • **Opposite**: A row of Coconut Palms, *Cocos nucifera*, border the sea side of the garden • **Above**: Fiji Fan Palms *Pritchardia pacifica*, stand as sentinels over a friendly Rhinoceros. Two Traveller's Palms, *Ravenala madagascariensis*, may be seen in the top left.

Above: Top left – Frangipani, *Plumeria Rubra*; Top centre – Fiji Fan Palms, *Pritchardia pacifica*; Middle right - Hibiscus; Bottom left – Bougainvillea in a stone plant pot; Bottom right – Blue Plumbago, *Plumbago auriculata* • **Opposite**: Right – Traveller's Palm, *Ravenala madagascariensis*

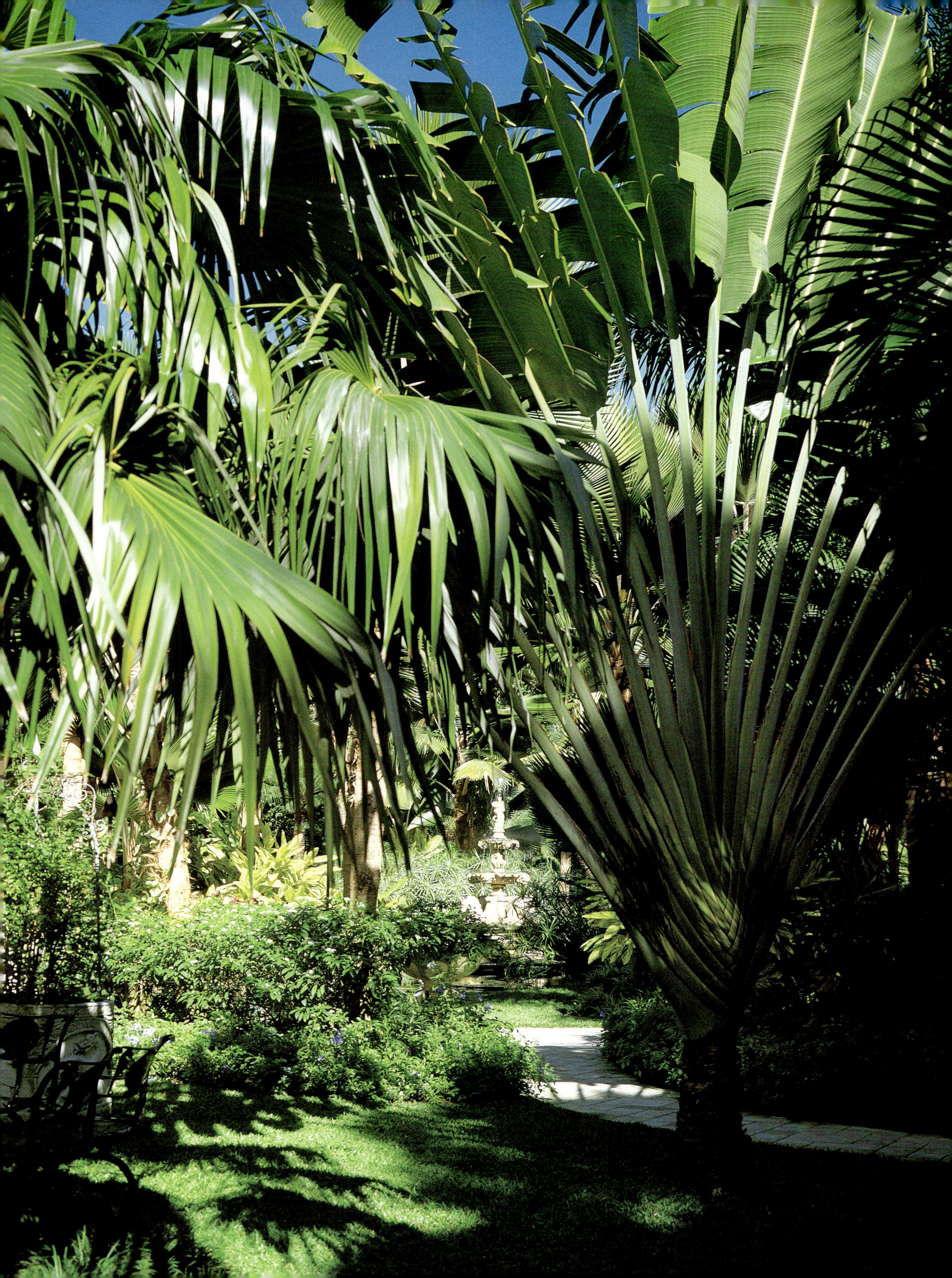

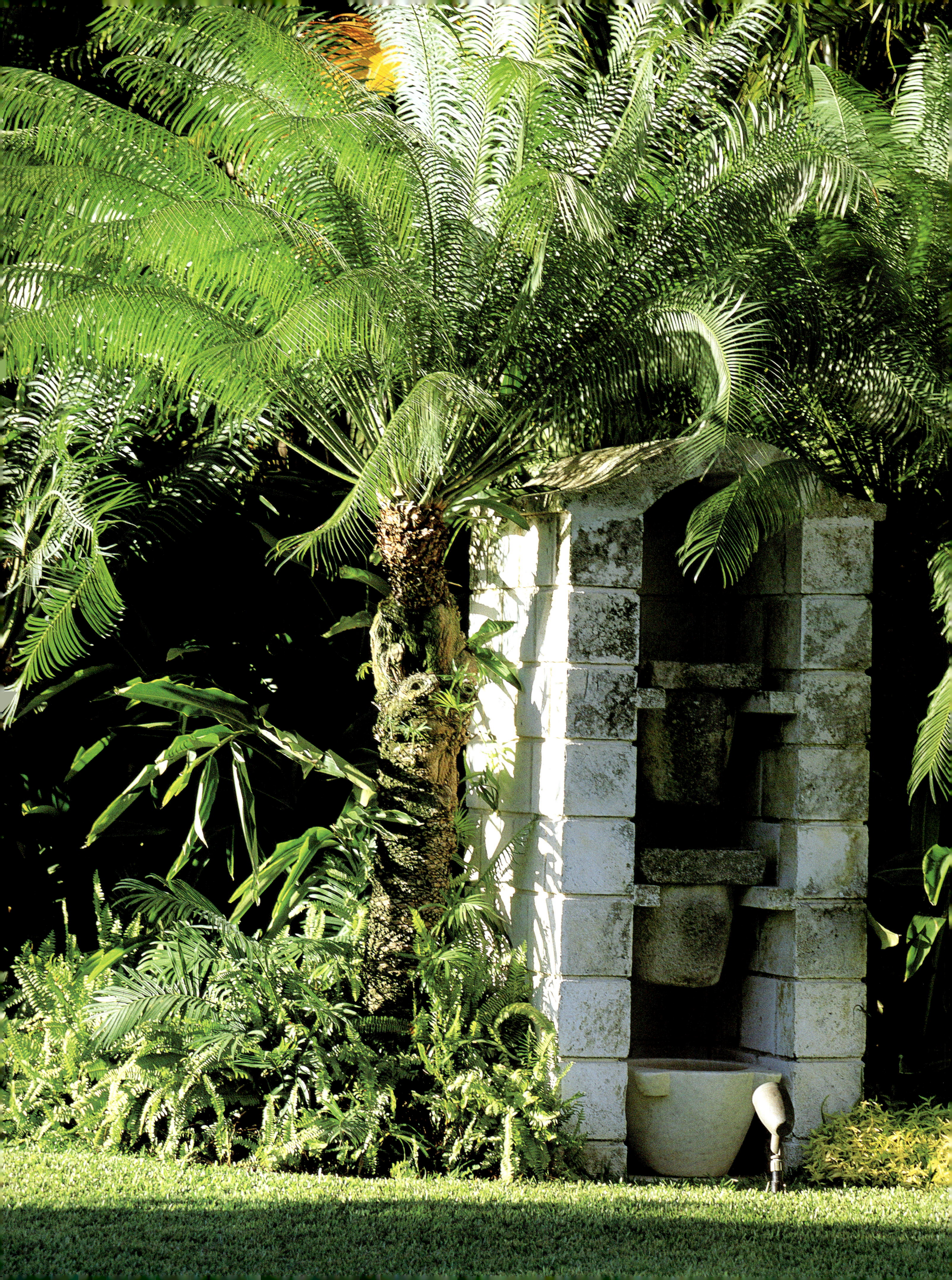

Opposite: A Sago Palm, *Cycas circinalis*, adjacent to a coral dripstone tower. In byegone days, the dripstones were used to collect and filter water for drinking • **This Page**: Natural coral stone has been extensively used as a building material throughout the history of Barbados

MANGO BAY

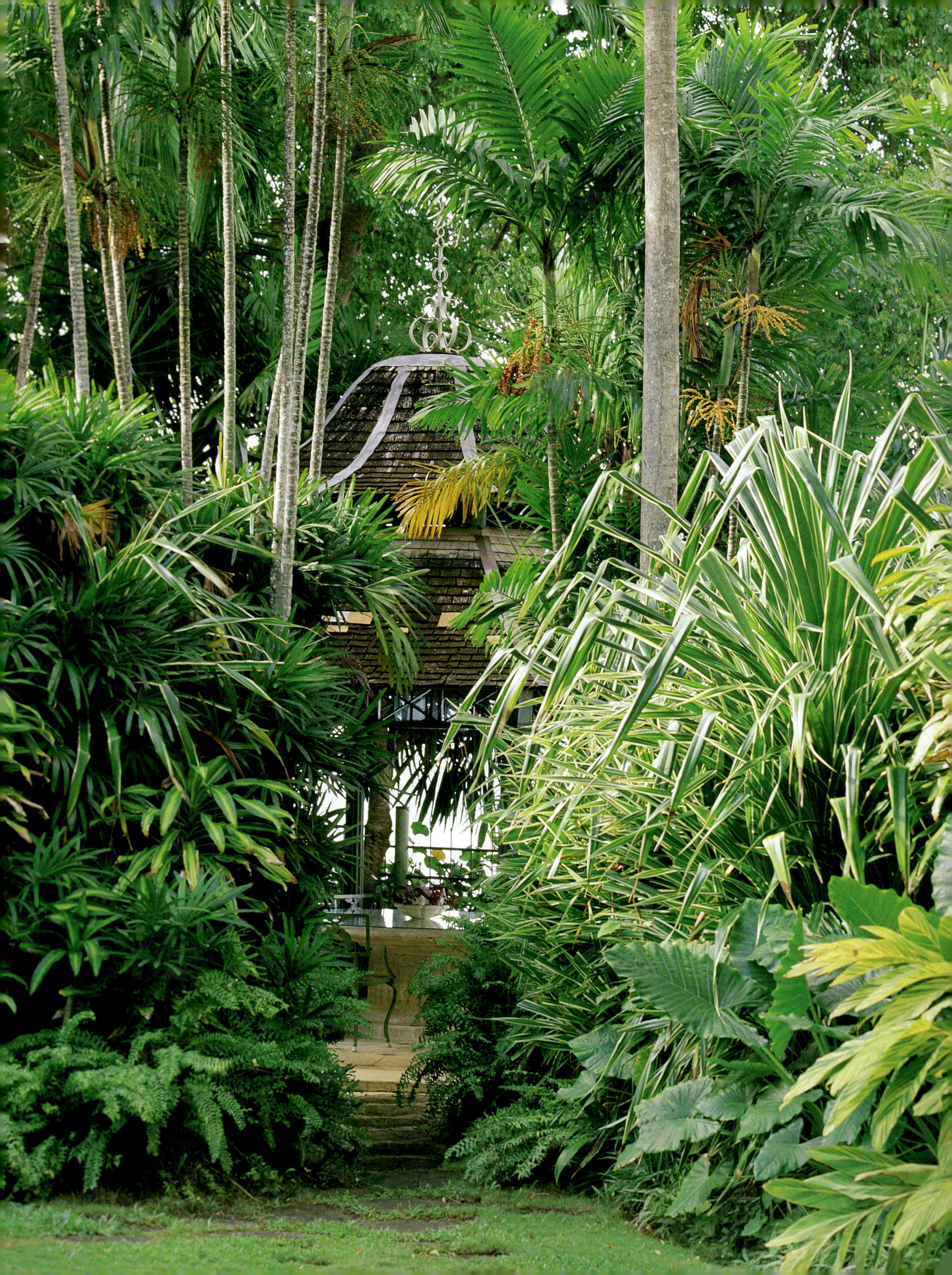

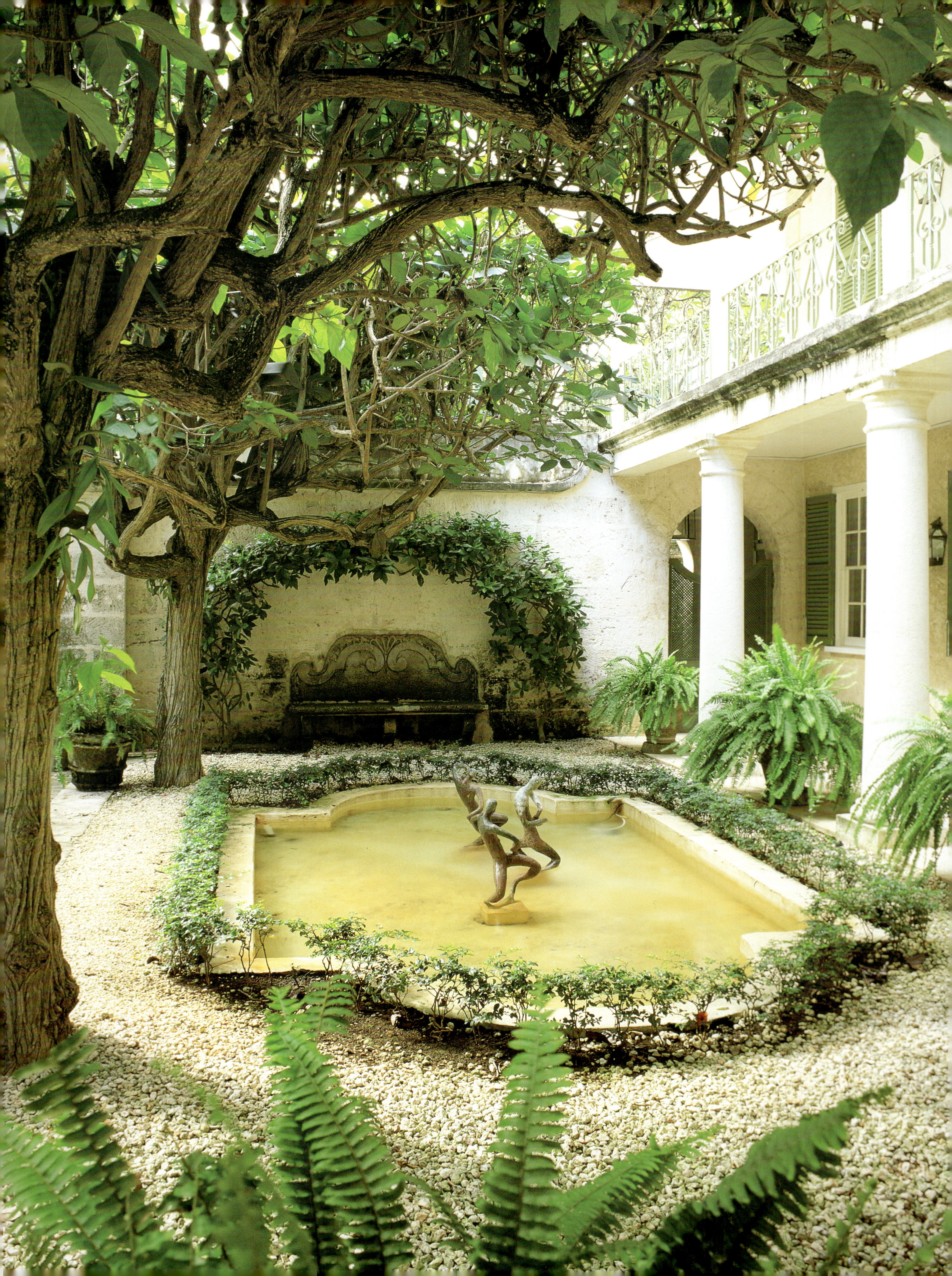

Opening page: Clumps of Macarthur Palms, *Ptycosperma macarthurii*, tower above the mass plantings on either side of the pathway to the gazebo. These plantings include: on the left side, Lady Palms, *Rhapis excelsa*, with Fishtail Fern, *Nephorolepis biserrata* Furcans, at their base; and on the right side, variegated Pandanus, *Pandanus baptistii* cv: Aureus, also with Fishtail Fern at their base • **Opposite**: Gnarled branches of Red Cordia, or Geiger, Trees, *Cordia sebestena*, overhang the pond, which is surrounded with large pots of Boston Ferns, *Nephrolepsis exaltata*. The Red Cordia, an attractive, small tree from the Northern Caribbean, attains a mature height of about 15-20 feet. It bears clusters of reddish-orange flowers, approximately 2 inches across, year round. The upper surface of its leaves are as rough to the touch as sandpaper. It is a plant that is well-suited to beach side planting as it exhibits a very high tolerance to direct sea spray. The wood produced by this tree, although not available in very wide planks, is extremely beautiful due to it being highly figured and its extreme colour contrast, from very dark to very light sections. It is highly prized for the manufacture of furniture. • **Above**: The view from the balcony looks out over a clump of Golden Palms, *Dypsis lutescens*, a Black Pearl or Mgambo, Tree, *Harpullia zanguebarica*, and Boston Ferns, *Nephrolepsis exaltata*. A weathered pot in the foreground sports a Desert Rose, *Adenium obesum*,

Above: Peace and tranquility, surrounded by nature • **Opposite**: Lady Palms, *Rhapis excelsa*, *Asparagus myriocladus*, Boston Ferns, *Nephrolepsis exaltata* and Umbrella Grass, *Cyperus alternifolius*, surround and overhang a tranquil lily pond.

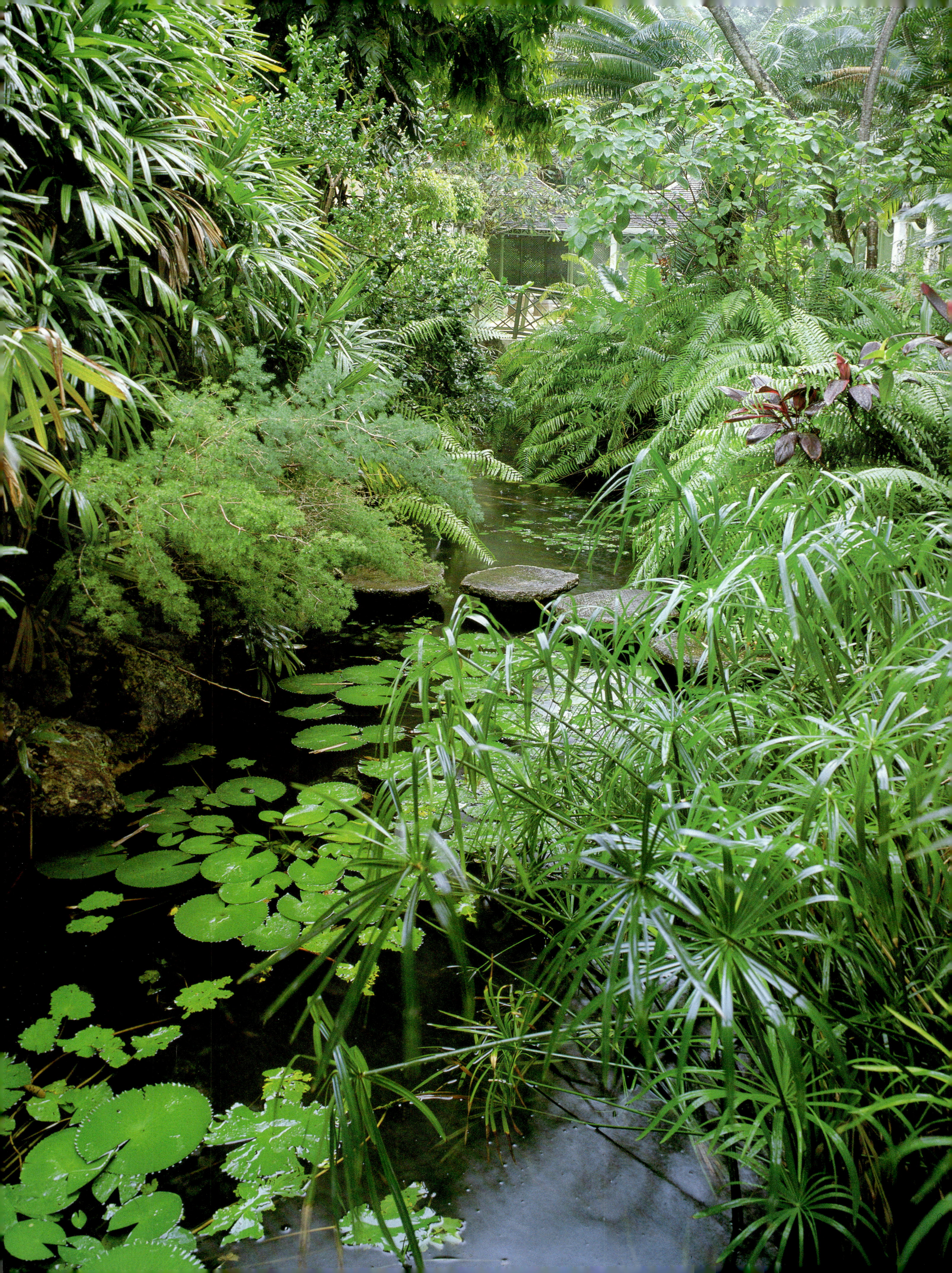

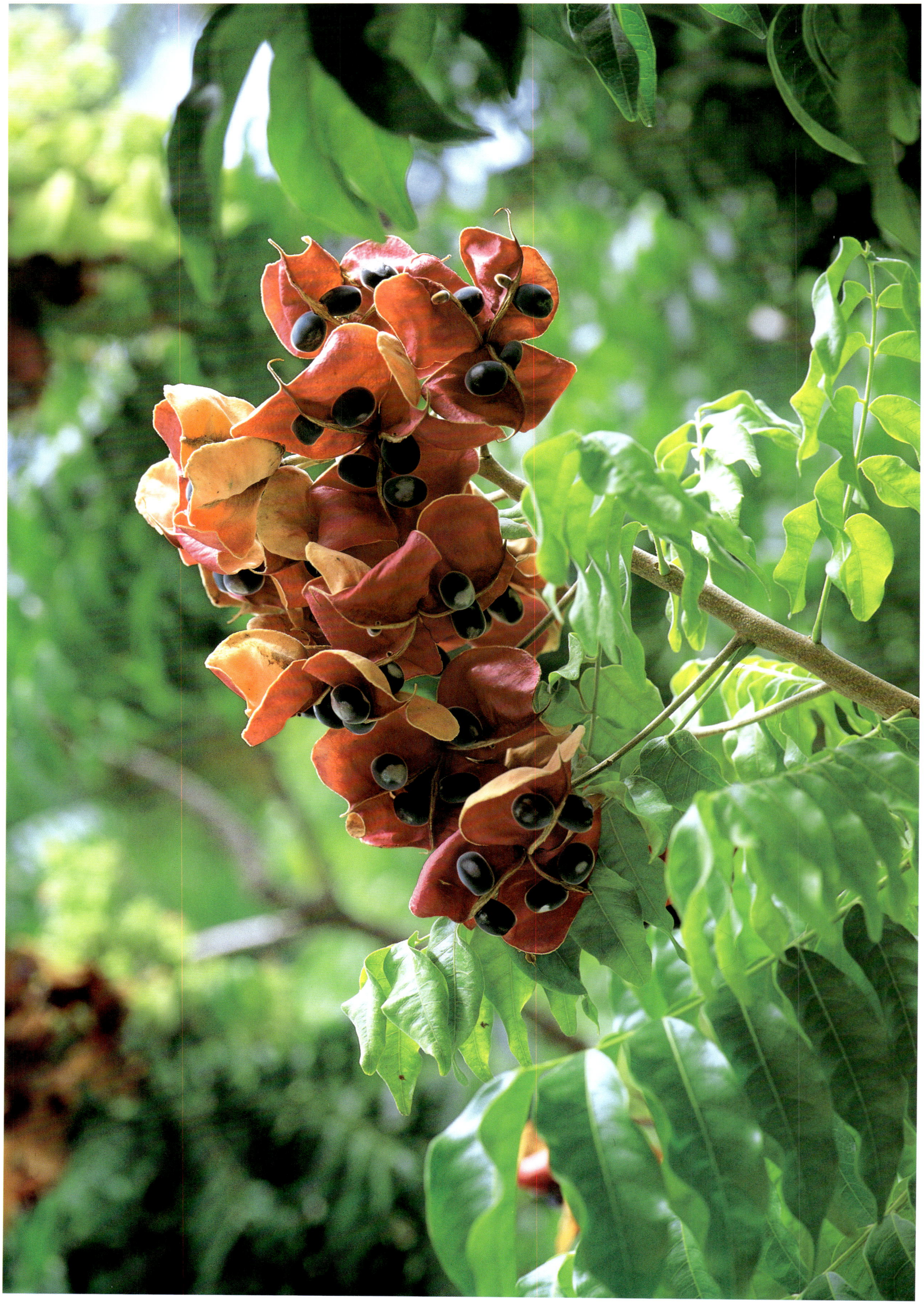

Opposite: Flower of the Black Pearl or Mgambo, tree, *Harpullia zanguebarica*, so named because the velvety seed resembles a black pearl. It is a native of Kenya where it is valued for its wood. • **Above**: Lily pond with Golden Trumpet, *Allamanda cathartica* cv: 'Hendersonii' and Red Ginger, *Alpinia purpurata*, growing in the background.

Dar es Salaam

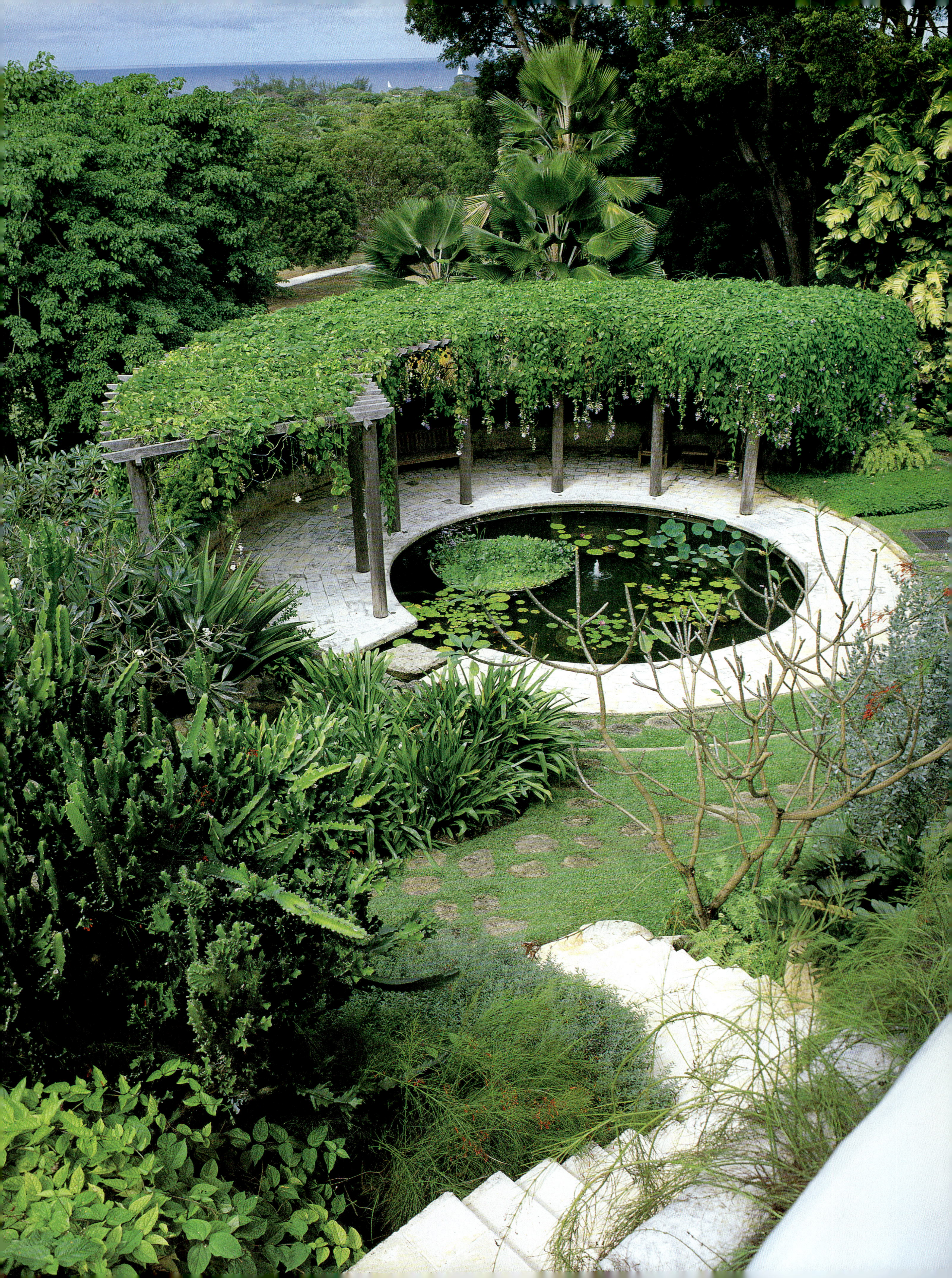

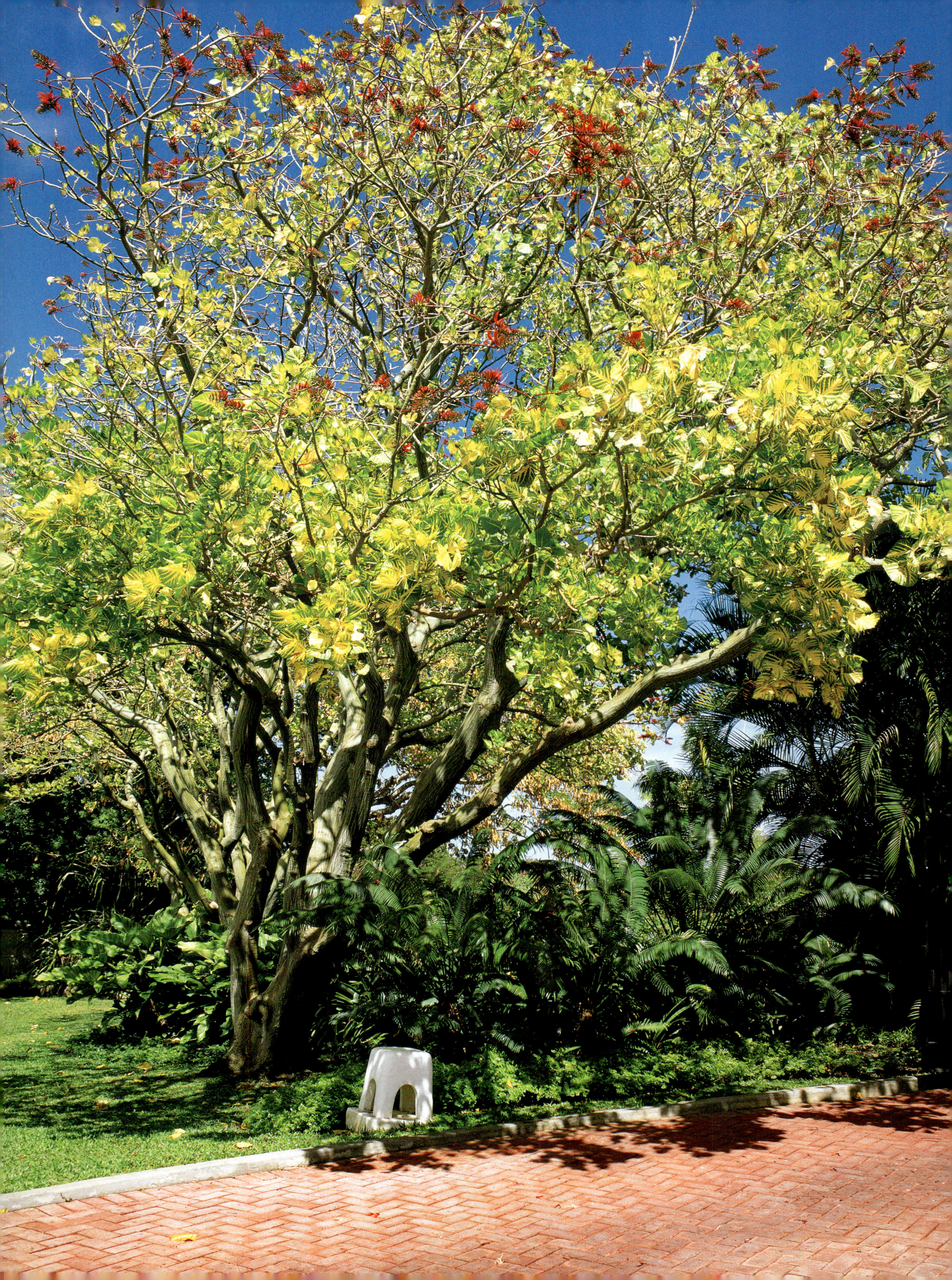

Opening page: A beautifully designed pergola follows the lines of the lily pond and supports a massive vine of *Thunbergia grandifolia*. Centrally, behind the pergola, is a grouping of Fiji Fan Palms, *Pritchardia pacifica*, and to the right a Pothos, *Epipremnum pinnatum* cv: 'Aureum' climbs the trunk of a tree. In the right foreground, a bare Frangipani, *Plumeria rubra*, whose leaves have been shed prior to flowering, presents a fascinating sculptural form • **Opposite**: A Coral Tree, *Erythrina variegata*, with its large spreading branches and bright crimson flowers dominates the landscape. The Coral Tree, a native of Tropical Asia, is a very fast growing tree attaining a height of 60-80 feet and width of 40 feet. Its trunk and branches are armed with curved black thorns. The Coral Tree is both drought and salt tolerant and is therefore a valuable landscape tree in coastal areas and areas where water is in short supply. • **Above**: Clockwise from top left - *Pseuderanthemum carruthersii*; *Thunbergia grandiflora*; Local Gardenia, *Tabernaemontana divaricata*; A pair of Christmas Palms, *Adonidia merrillii*, dominate the background of the lounging area.

Top: Bottom centre - Cochineal Plant, *Nopalea cochenillifera*; Bottom right – Dracaena, *Dracaena marginata* cv. Tricolor; Top right – *Yucca gloriosa* • **Above**: Upper left – Sago Palm, *Cycas circinalis*; Bottom left – *Philodendron melinonii*; Bottom right – *Begonia semperflorens* • **Opposite:** A beautiful *Thunbergia grandifolia* vine hangs from a pergola next to the lily pond.

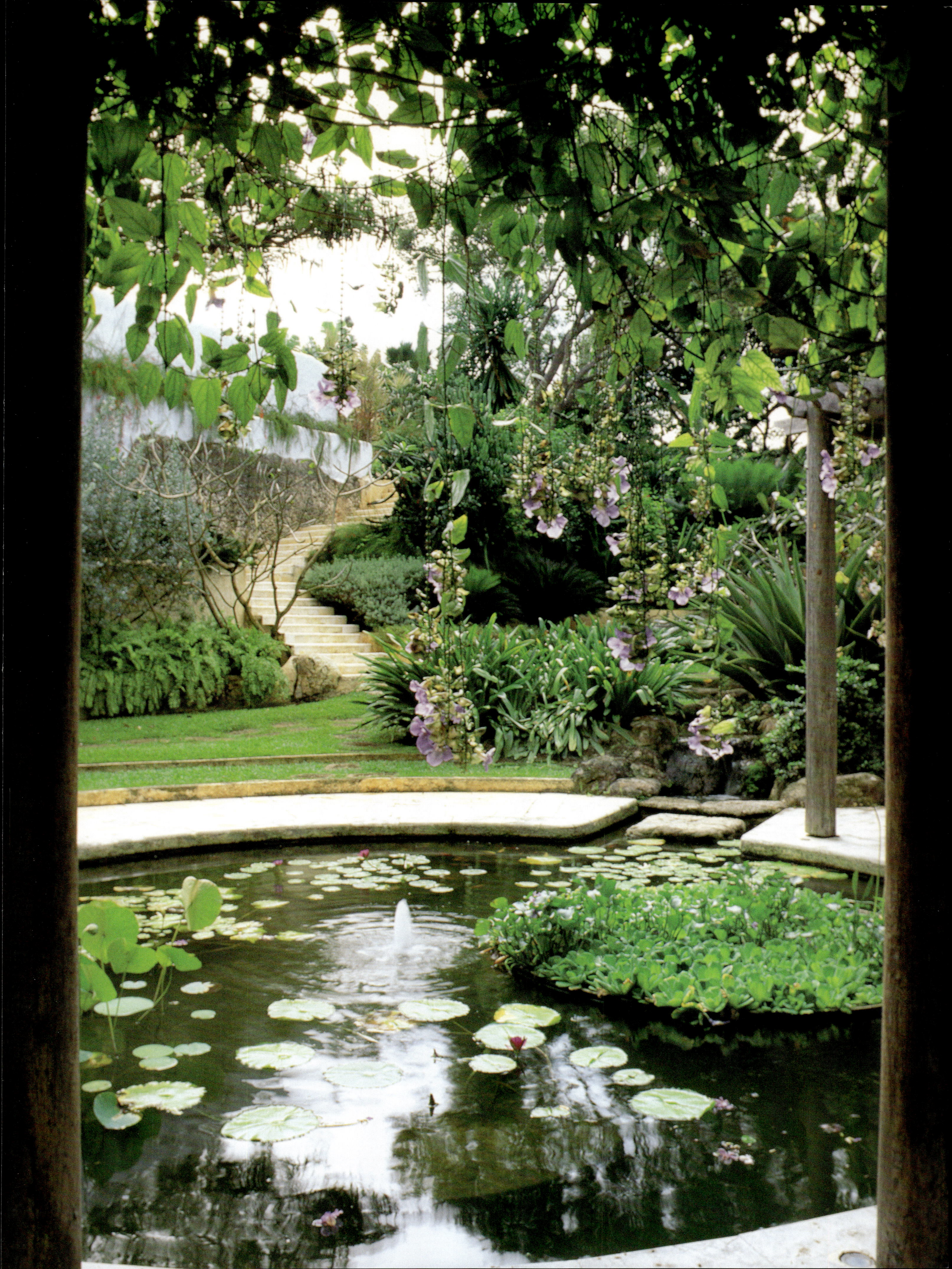

Bachelor Hall

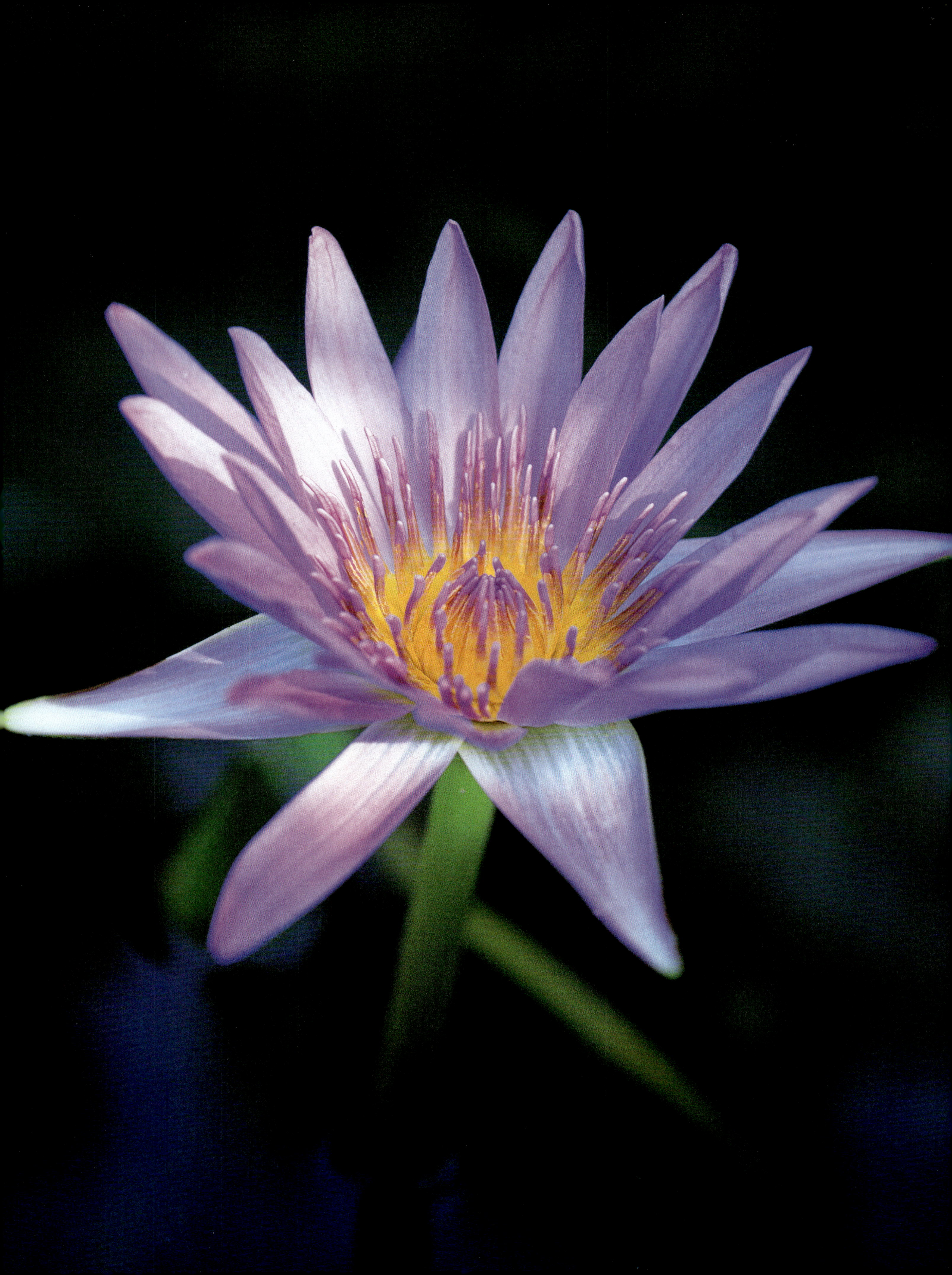

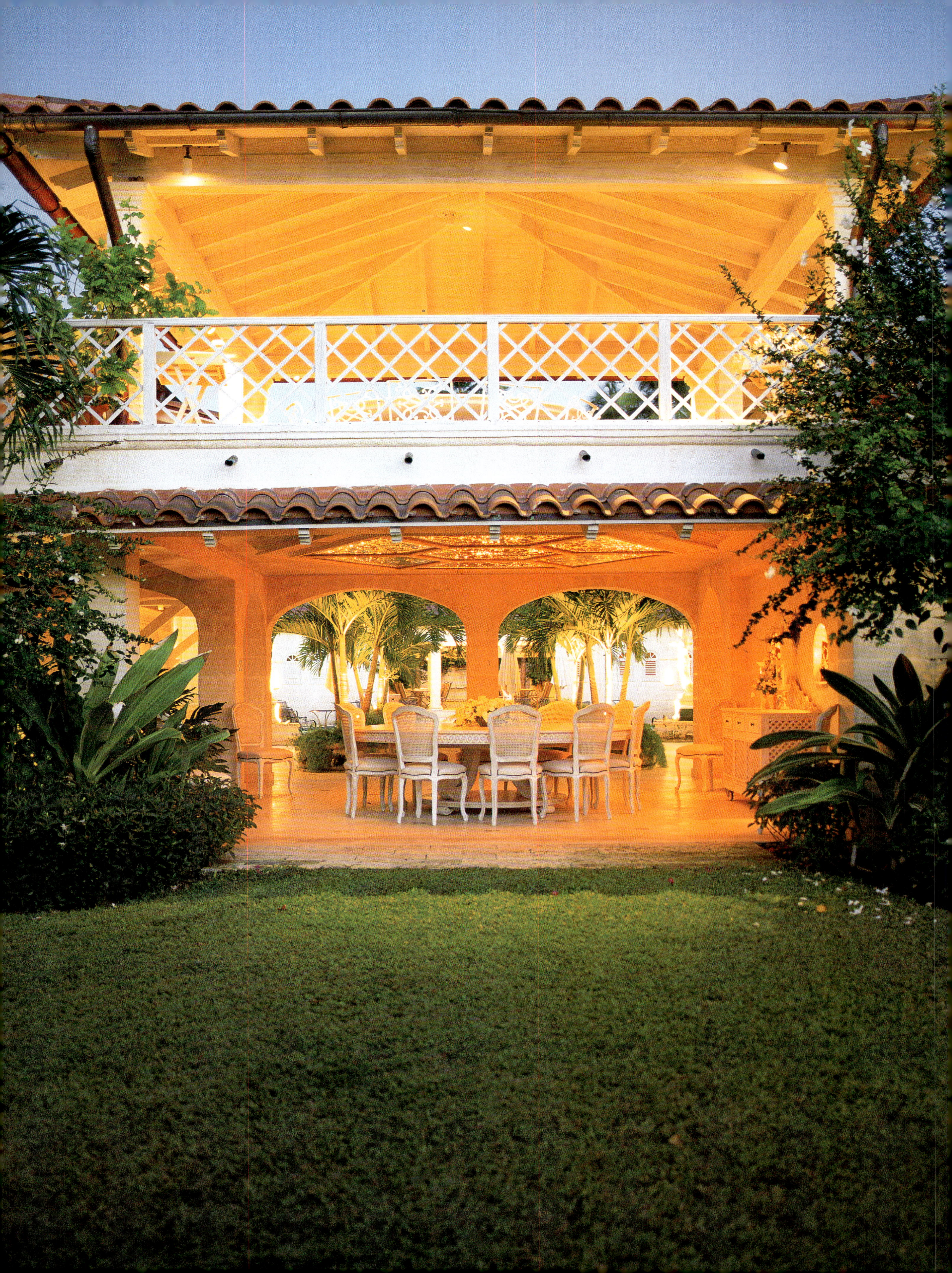

Opening page: Close up of a Water Lily • **Above**: Flowers of *Thunbergia fragrans*

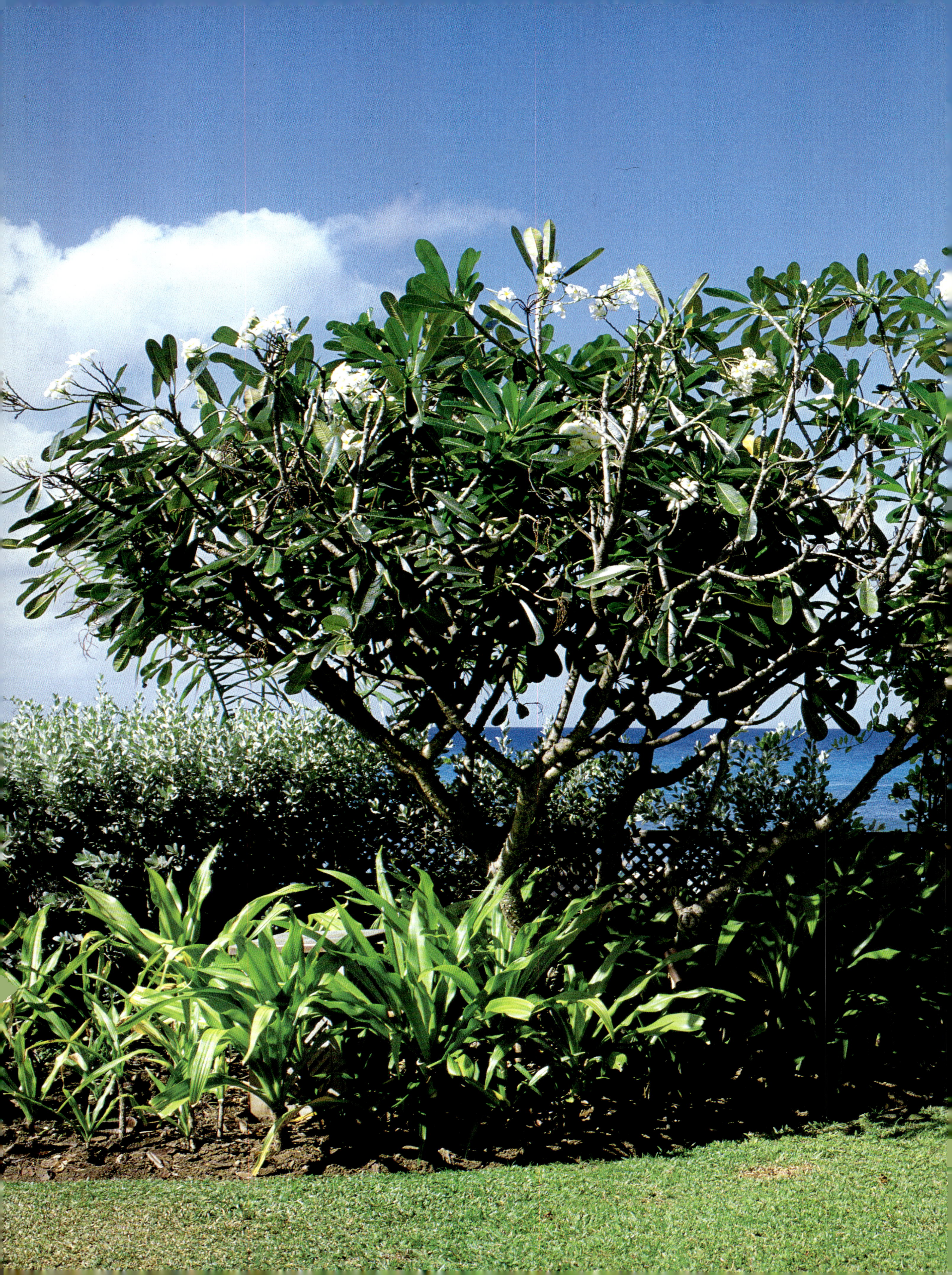

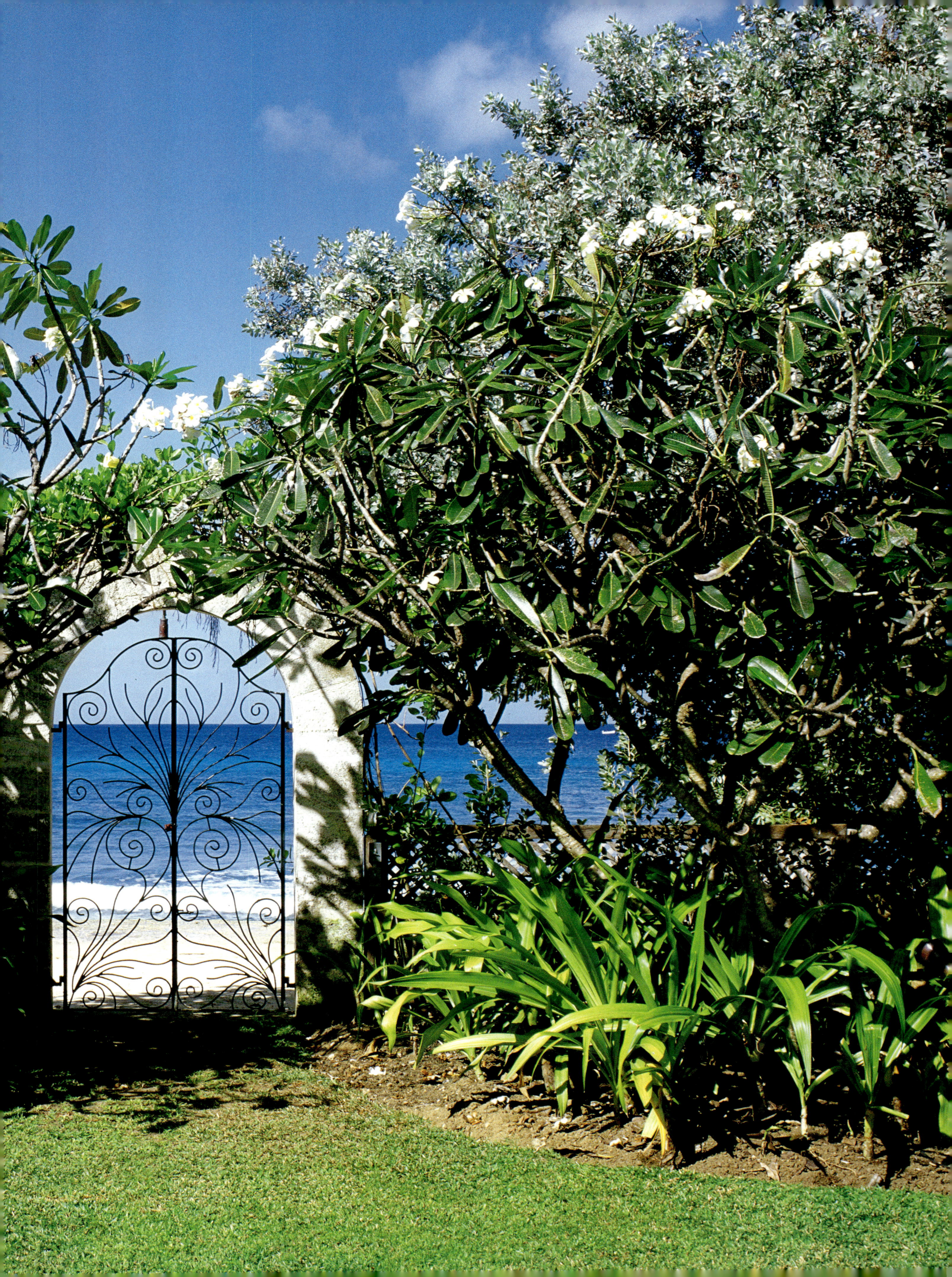

Previous pages: *Plumeria obtusa* frame a garden gate leading to the beach • **Above**: Yellow Mandevilla, *Pentalinon luteum* sprawls its way over the pergola • **Opposite**: Pride of Barbados, *Caesalpinia pulcherrima*, the National Flower of Barbados

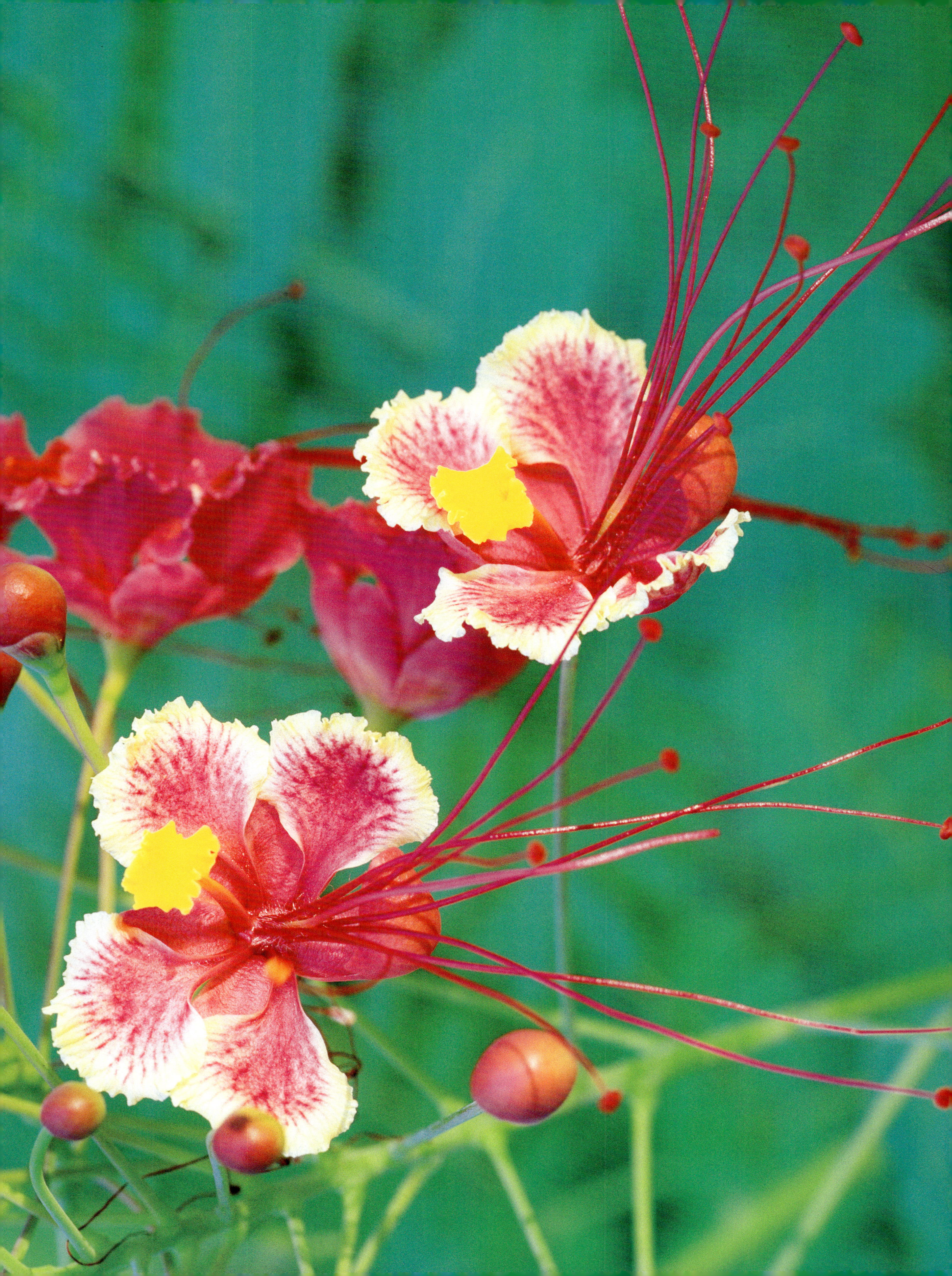

Tanglewood

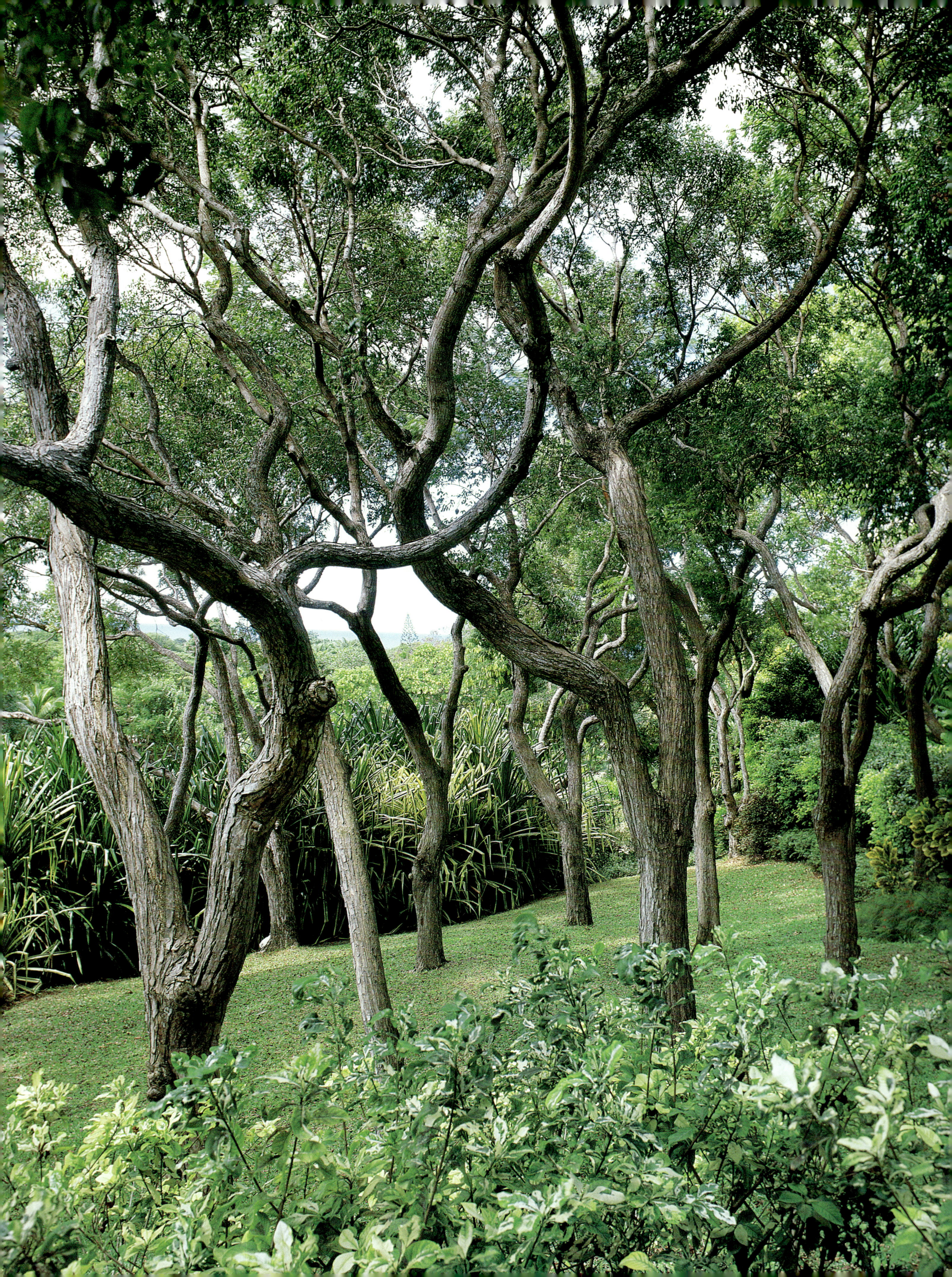

Opening page: A grove of Mahogany trees, *Swietenia mahagoni*, creates an image of 'tangled wood'. In the background can be seen Screw Pine, *Pandanus baptistii* cv; 'Aureus' • **Above**: Middle left and right – Bougainvillea, West Indian Royal Palms, *Roystonea oleracea*, and Mahogany groves; Bottom – *Stemmadenia galeottiana* • **Opposite**: Top – *Pandanus* species; Middle - *Ixora* species; Bottom – *Setcreasea purpurea*

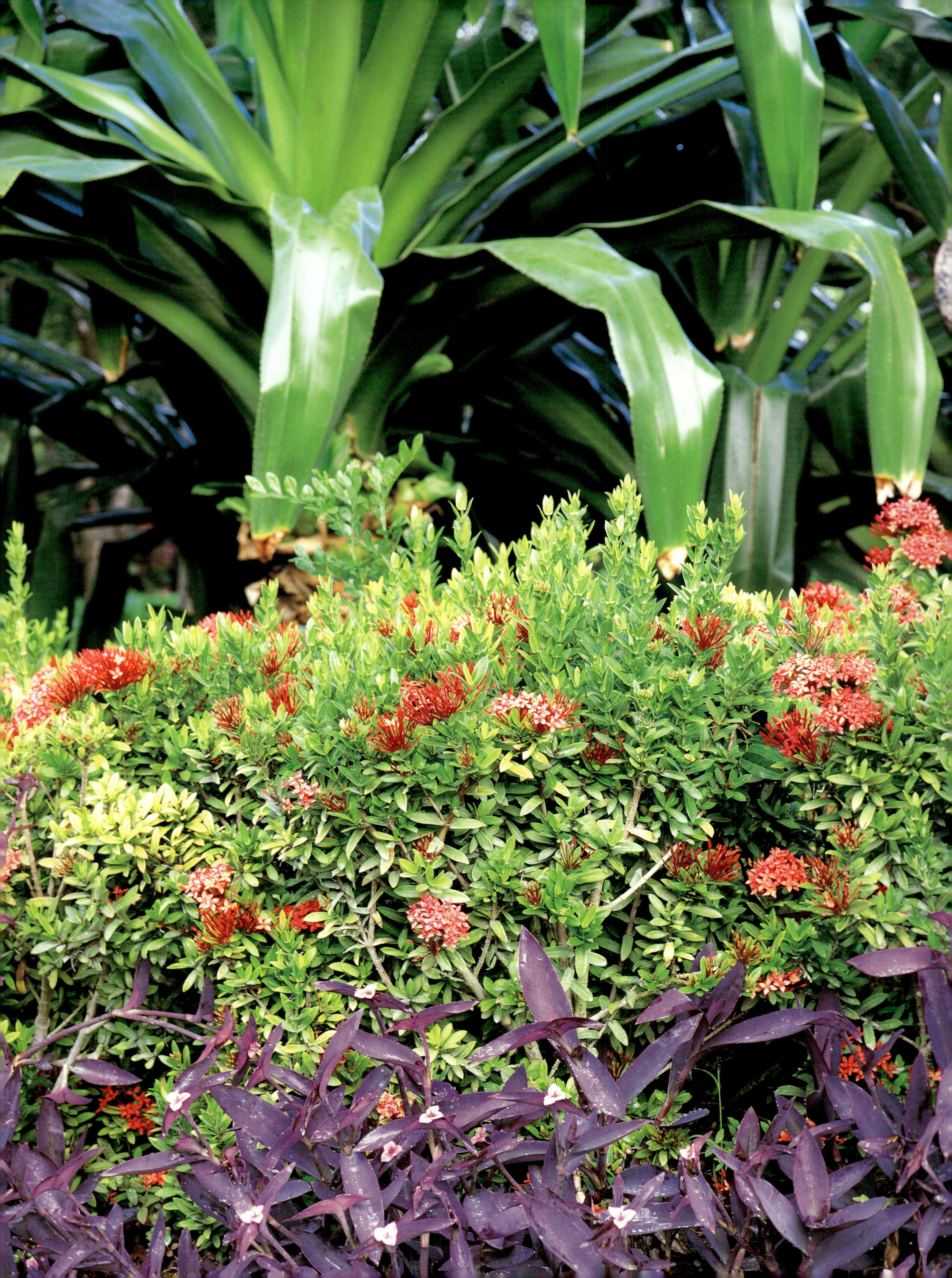

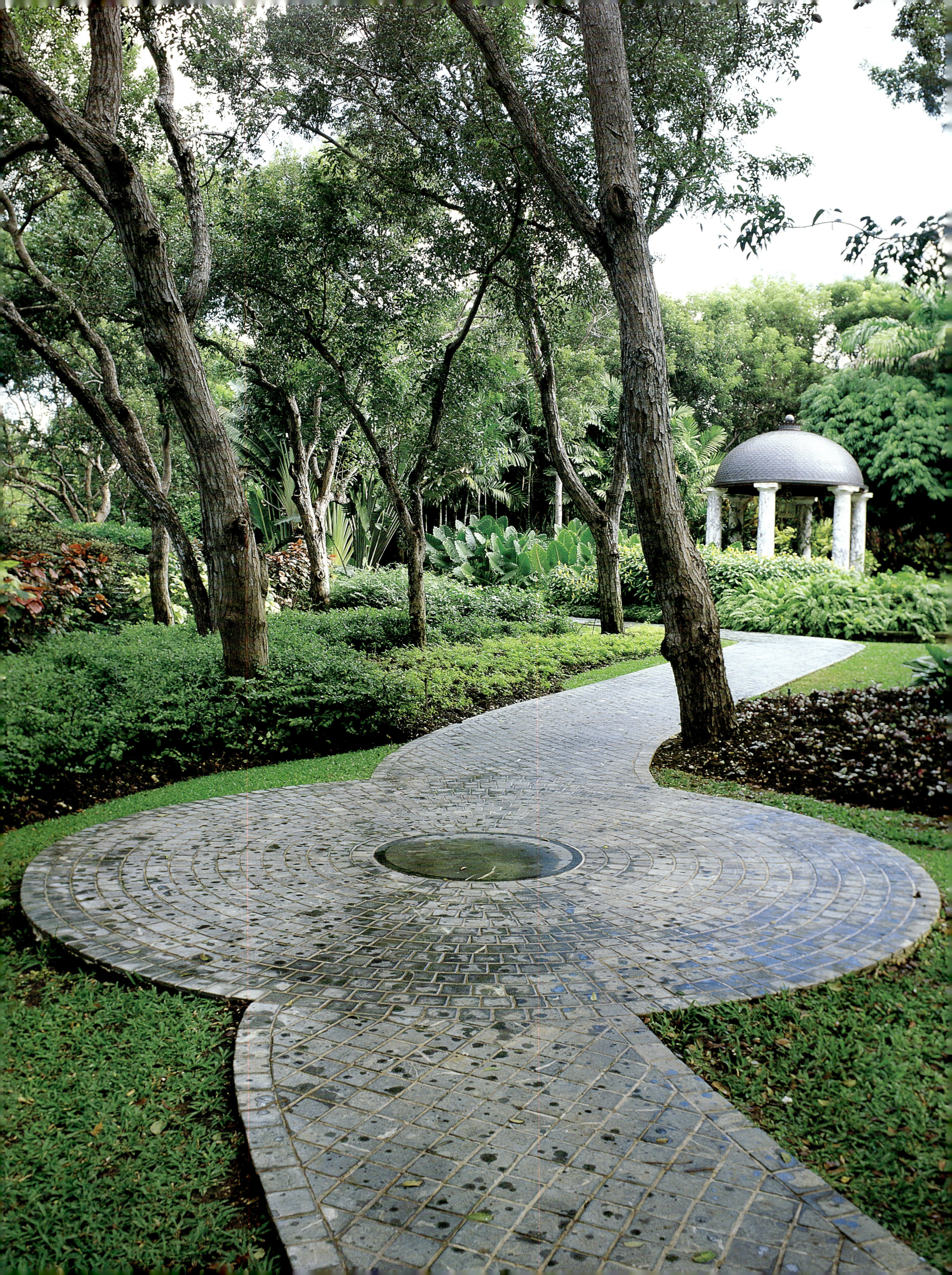

Above: A close up of the flower of *Spathiphyllum* species

Above: *Zebrina pendula* planted as ground cover • **Opposite**: Water Lily

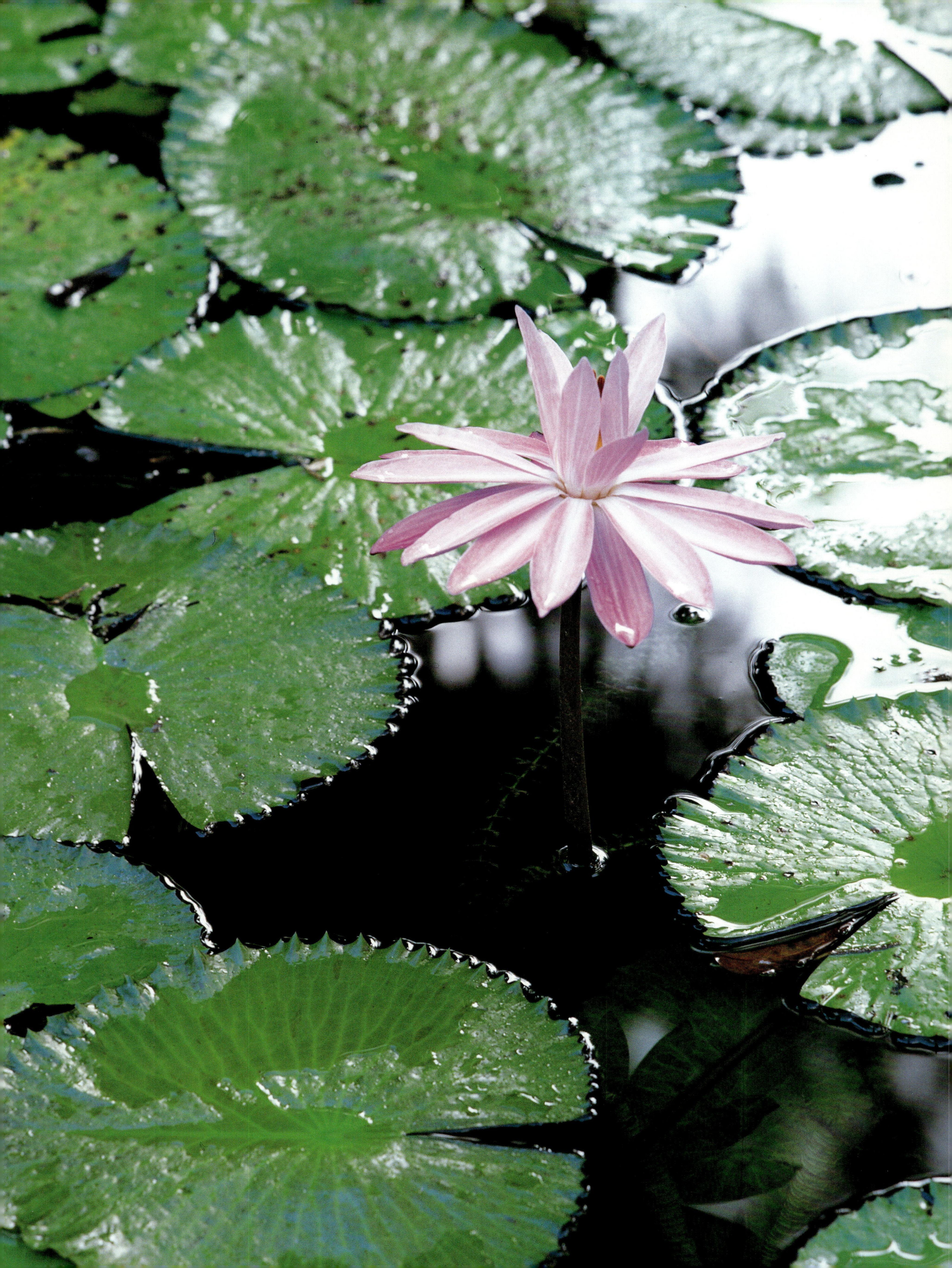

Cane Heaven

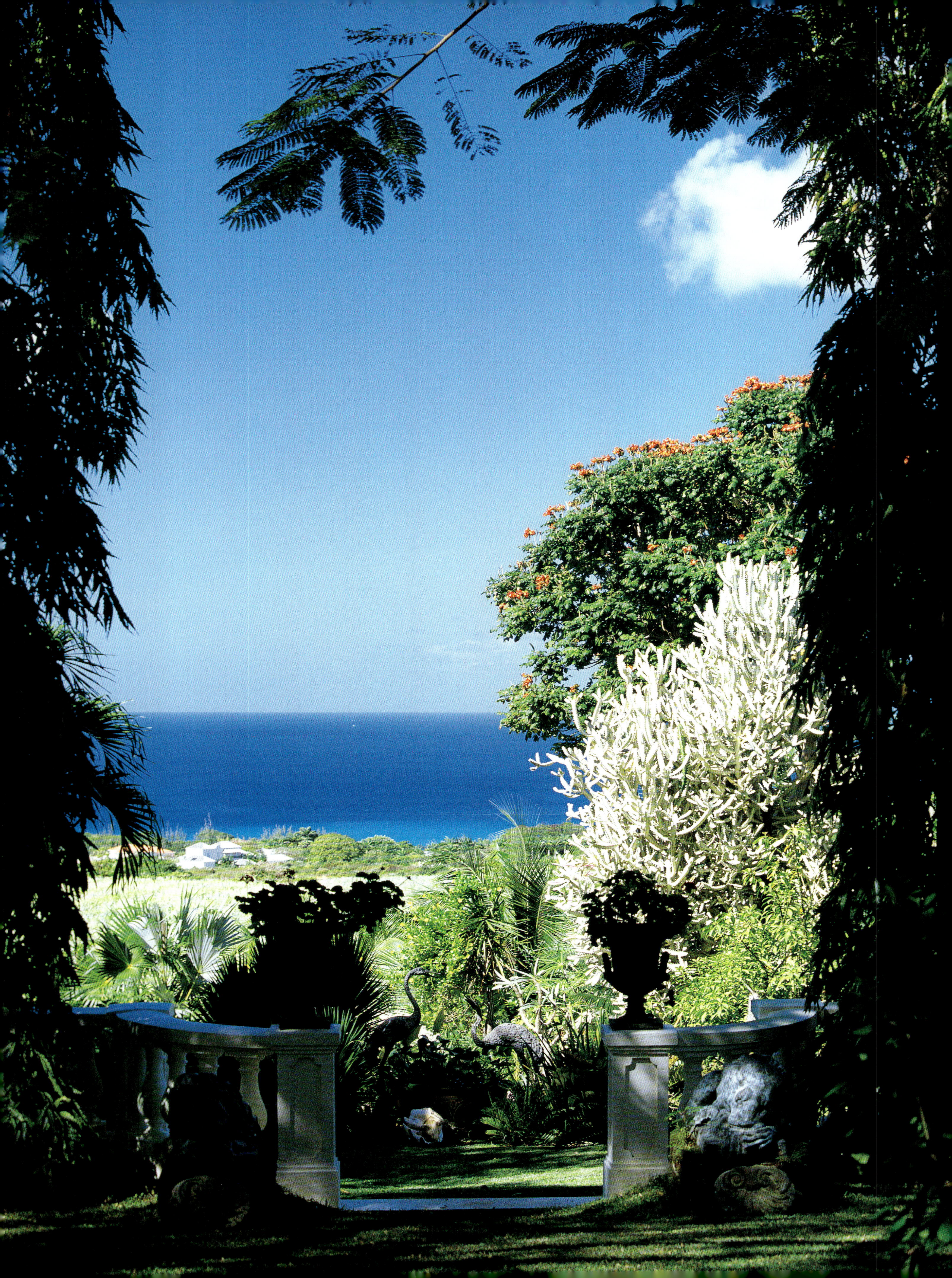

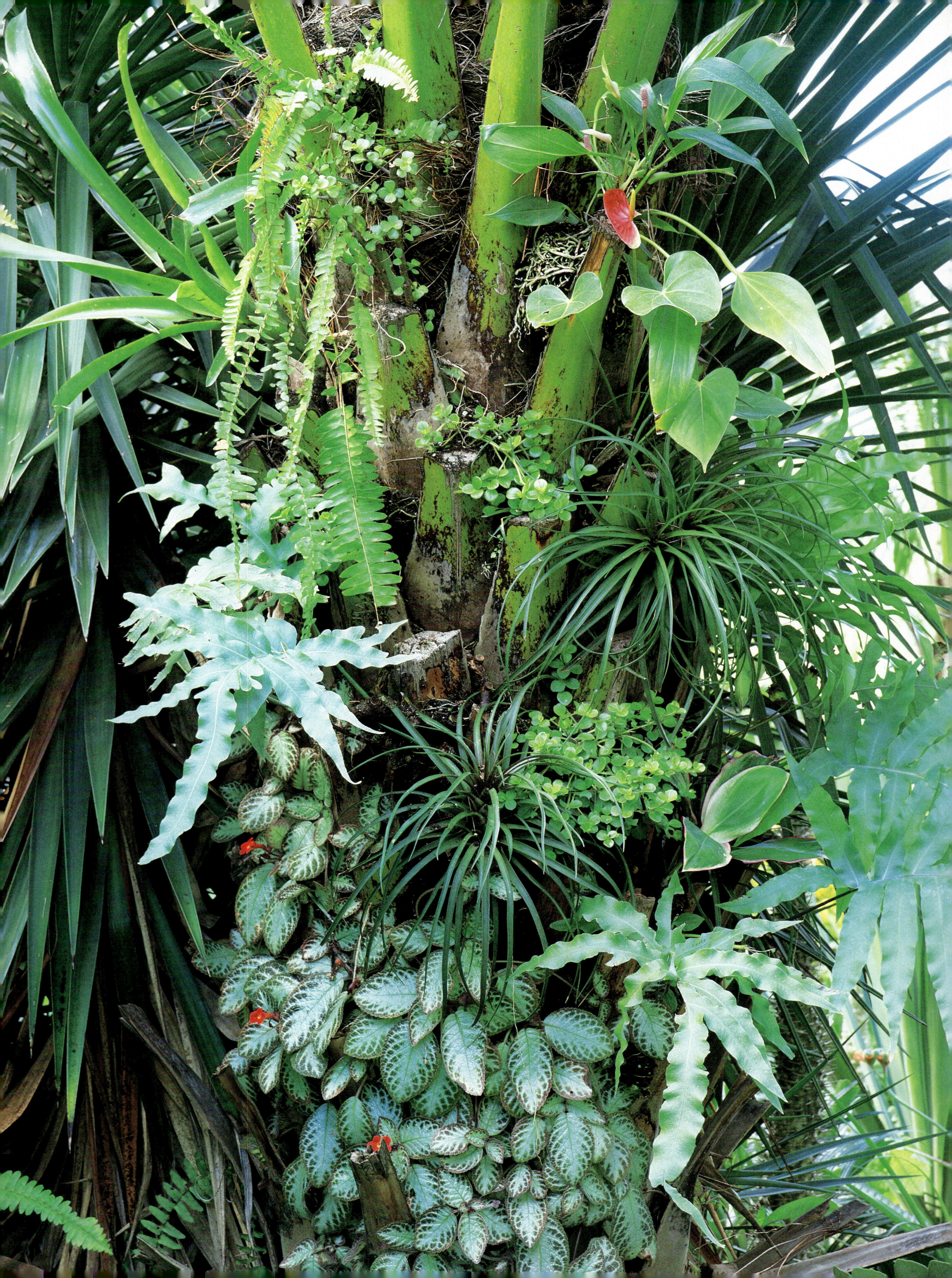

Opening page: The frame for the vista is formed by two Ashoka Trees, *Polyalthia longifolia* cv; Pendula, from the family of *Annonaceae*. These two specimens were brought in from the owner's property in Sri Lanka. The trees are loved by the Hindus and are mainly planted around their temples in Sri Lanka and India. In the centre of the photo can be seen an old Chinese tub hosting Lotus Plants, *Nelumbo species*, and Water Hyacinths, *Eichhornia azurea*, plus two bronze Flamingos from Thailand and a Giant Clam from Cuba. The Ghost Cactus, *Euphorbia lactea* cv: variegata, to the right has grown to a size of approximately 6 meters high and 3 meters wide. To the right in the background, is an African Tulip Tree, *Spathodea campanulata*, showing clusters of its brilliant red/orange flowers • **Opposite:** The trunk of a Canary Island Date Palm, *Phoenix canariensis*, has become home for *Anthurium scherzerianum, Tillandsia cyanea, Fittonia verschaffeltii* and *Polypodium aureum* • **Above**: Clerodendrum "Firework", *Clerodendrum quadriloculare,* in full bloom.

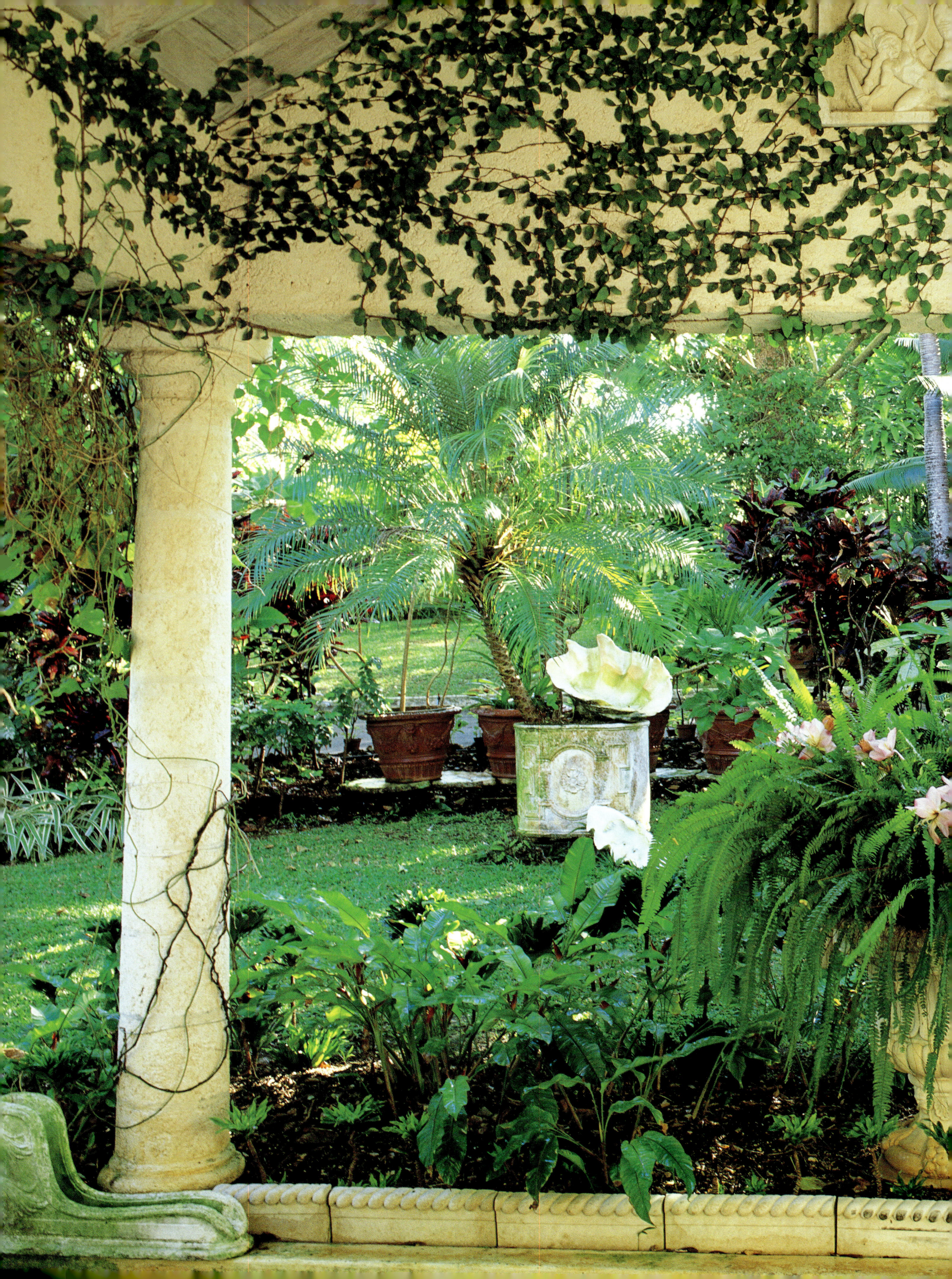

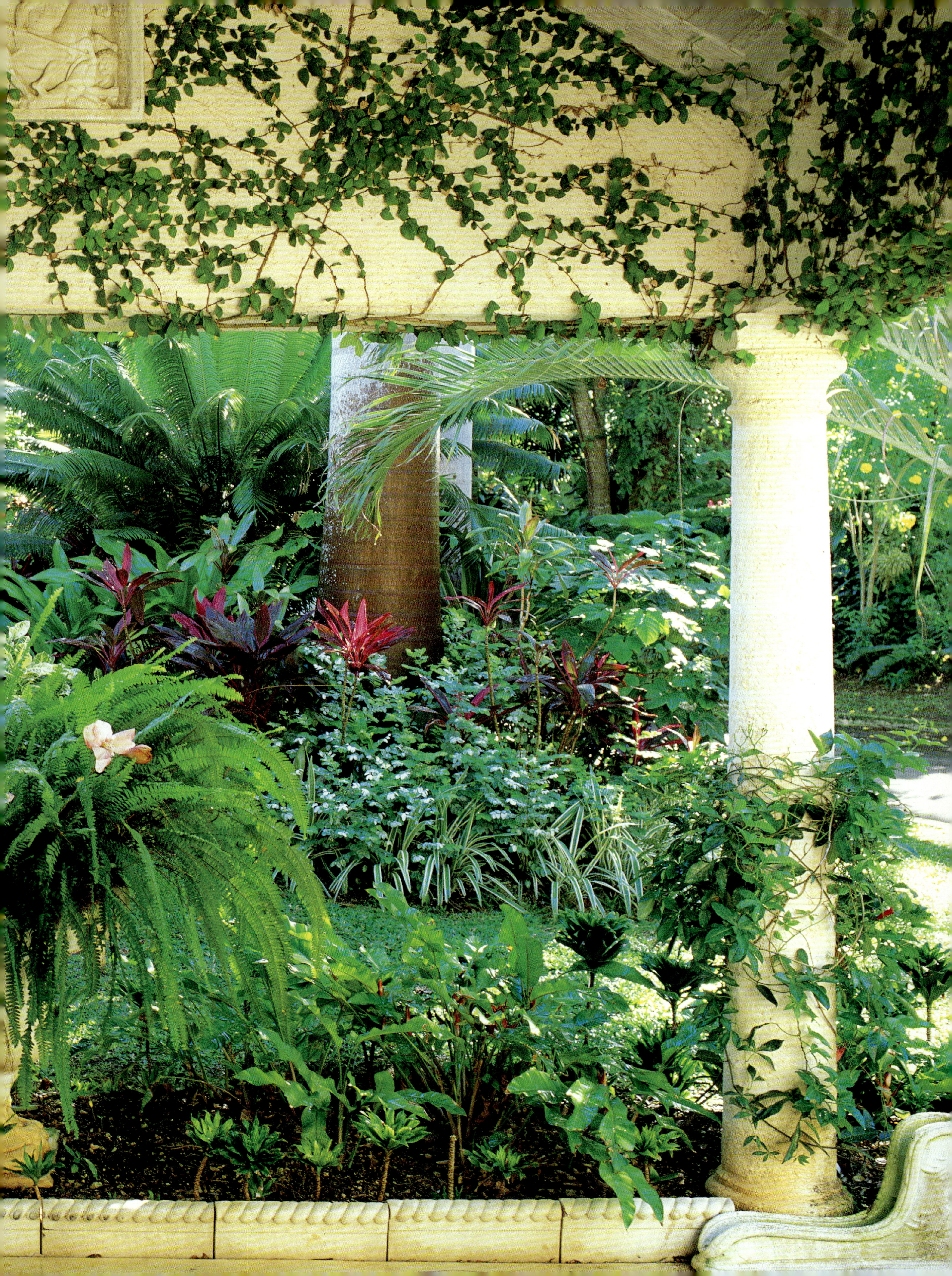

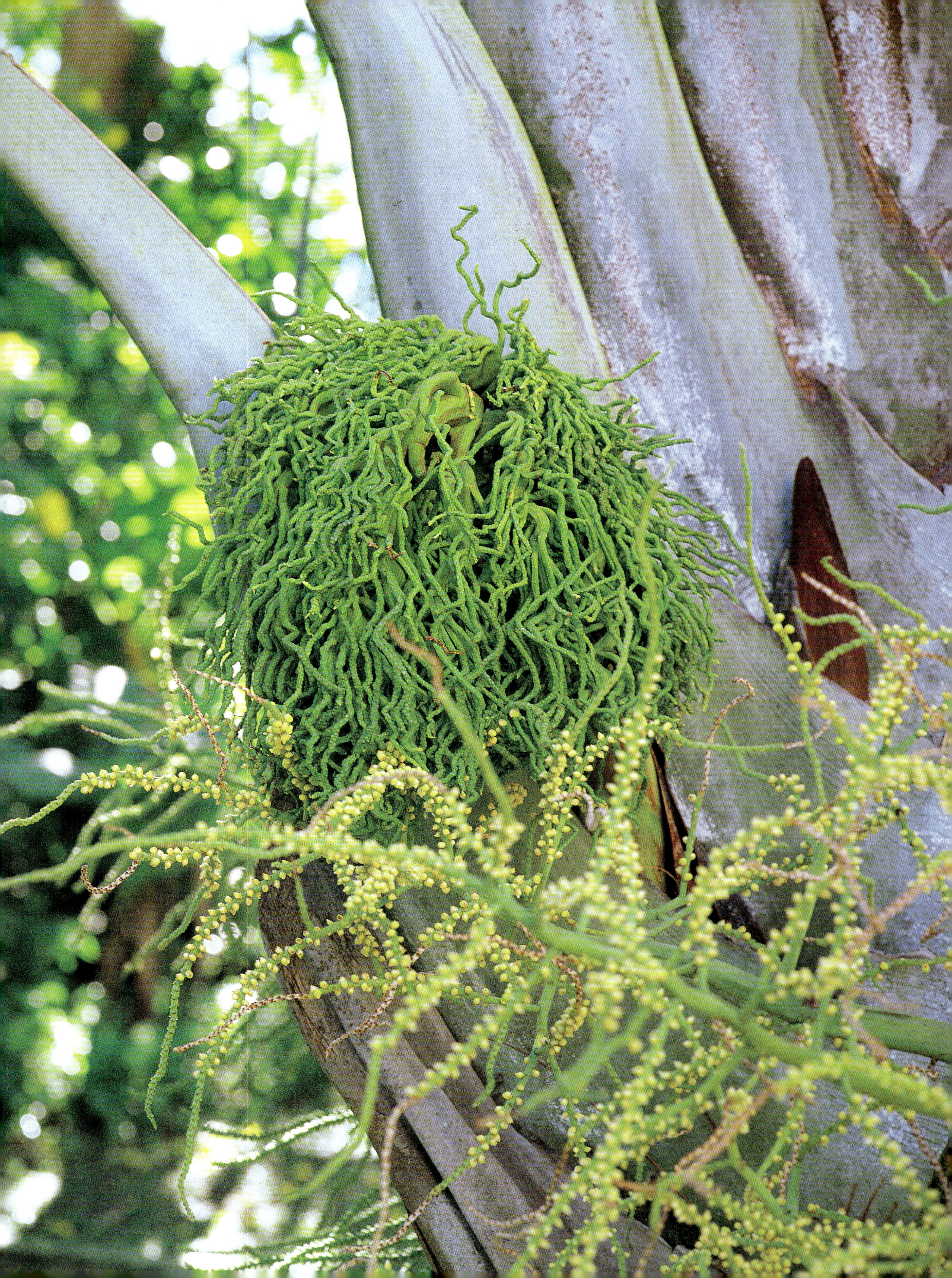

Previous pages: The view from the main entrance to the eastern garden, with creeping *Ficus* on the walls. In the big pot in the front is a Fern, with pink *Curcuma* blooms. In the foreground are miniature Heliconias, In the background behind the fern is a Sago Palm, *Cycas circinalis*; The large Italian pot to the left centre, with a Giant Clam from Cuba, is hosting a Pigmy Date Palm, *Phoenix roebelinii*. The Pygmy Date Palm is a native of Southeast Asia and is one of the most used palms in landscaping in Barbados. It is also an ideal plant for containers and does well in shaded conditions • **Opposite**: Close up of a Triangle Palm, *Dypsis decaryi*, native of Madagascar. The chalky-white bloom, the trunk and the grey leaf bases add to the character of this most unusual palm which we see here in three stages of flower: the young, dark brown emerging inflorescence; unopened inflorescence and one fully opened inflorescence with numerous flowers. • **Top**: A bust of Caesar sits in front of the trunk of a Sandbox Tree, *Hura crepitans*, surrounded by fragrant Lady of the Night, *Brunfelsia americana* and Jasmine, *Cestrum nocturnum*, vines. In the foreground are *Cordylines*, *Begonias*, Ferns and *Alocasias*. • **Above**: The greenhouse is home to a variety of shade loving plants, mainly originating from rainforest areas. The walls and floor are built of solid coral blocks, which retain the moisture and produce greater humidity. In the centre is a classical Italian Pond, which hosts frogs, fish and different water plants.

Above: Front centre - a Chinese pot carrying a 25-year old Desert Rose, *Adenium obesum*, with spectacular root formations; Back centre – a bronze, 18th Century Burmese Buddha, framed by 2 Italian marble columns, planted with Hawaian Pineapple. •
Opposite: This large pond was converted from a former windmill base into a water garden full of exotic water plants, like this *Typhonodorum lindleyanum*. Originating from the Brazilian shores of the Amazon River, this high growing water plant reaches a height of 15 feet (5m) and several times each year it bears a gigantic, white, lily-like flower.

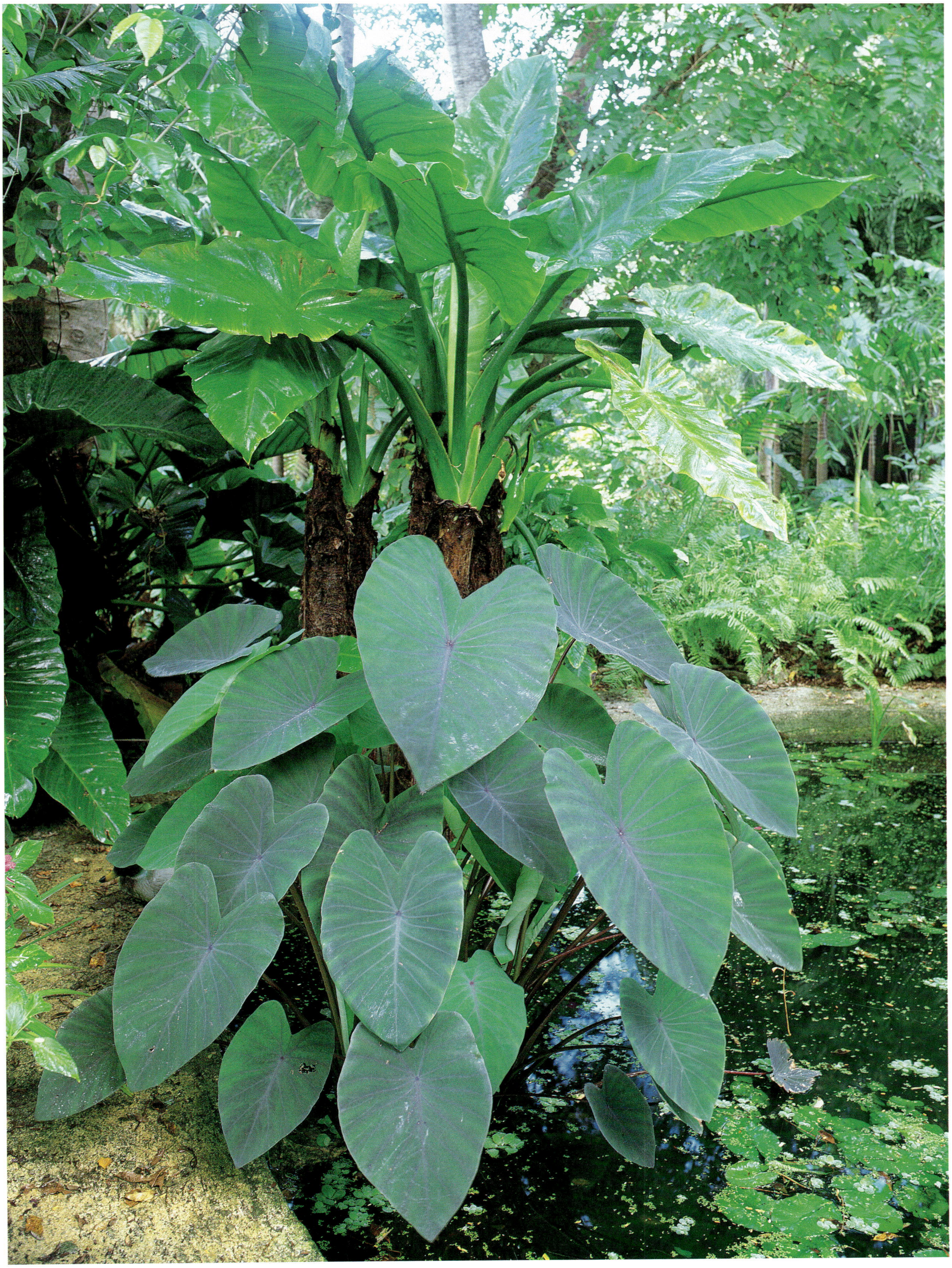

GLENDALE

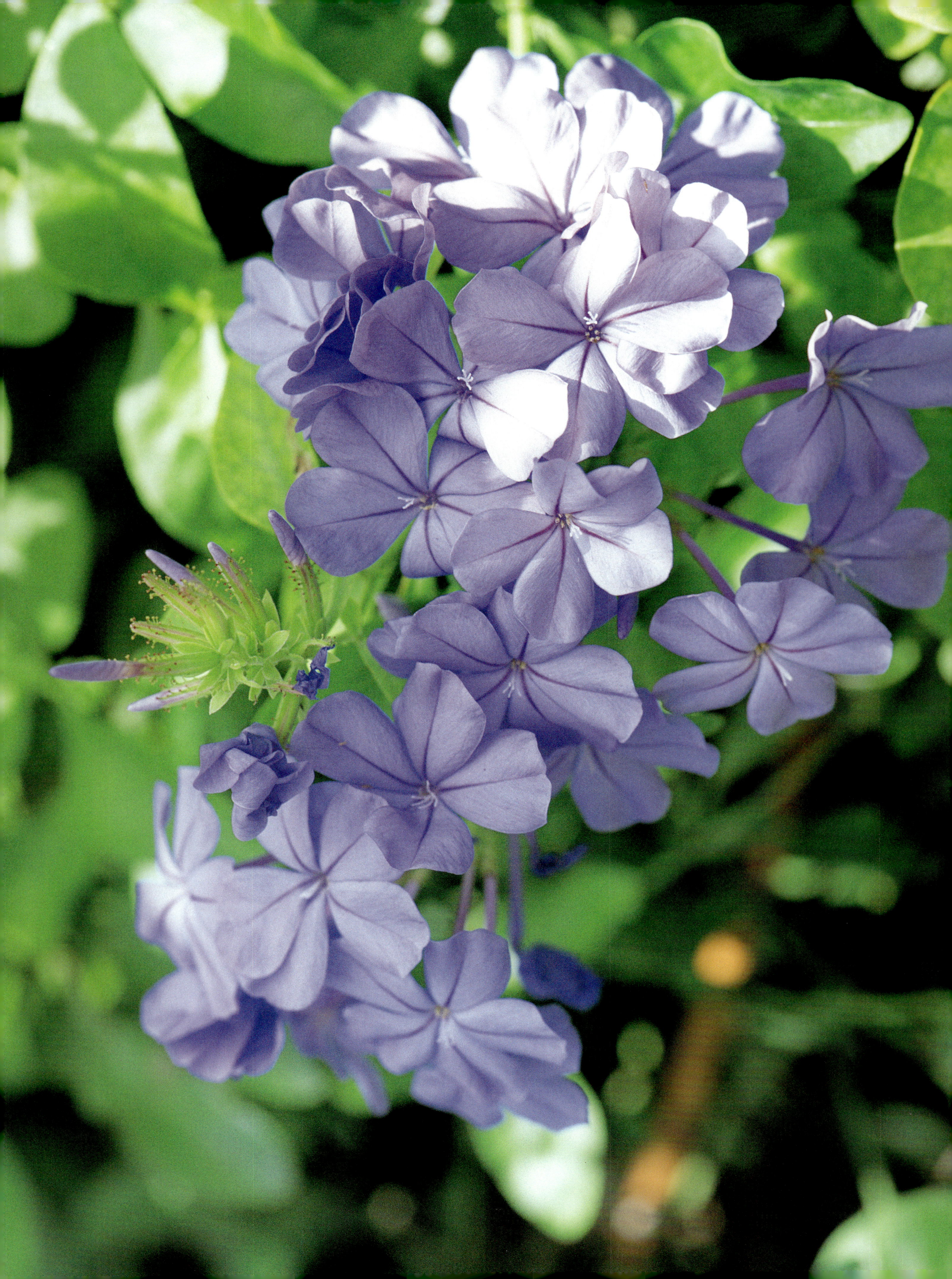

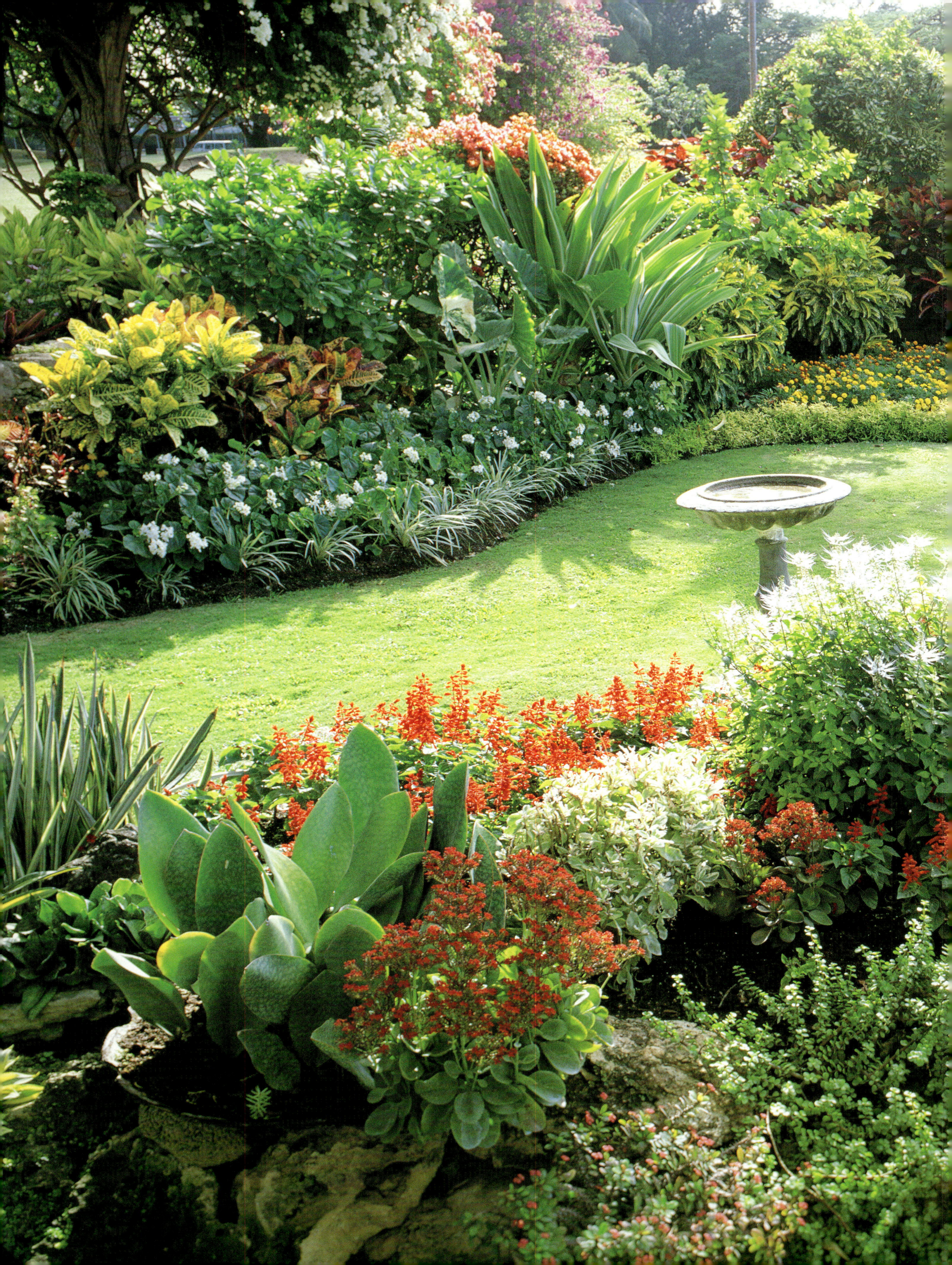

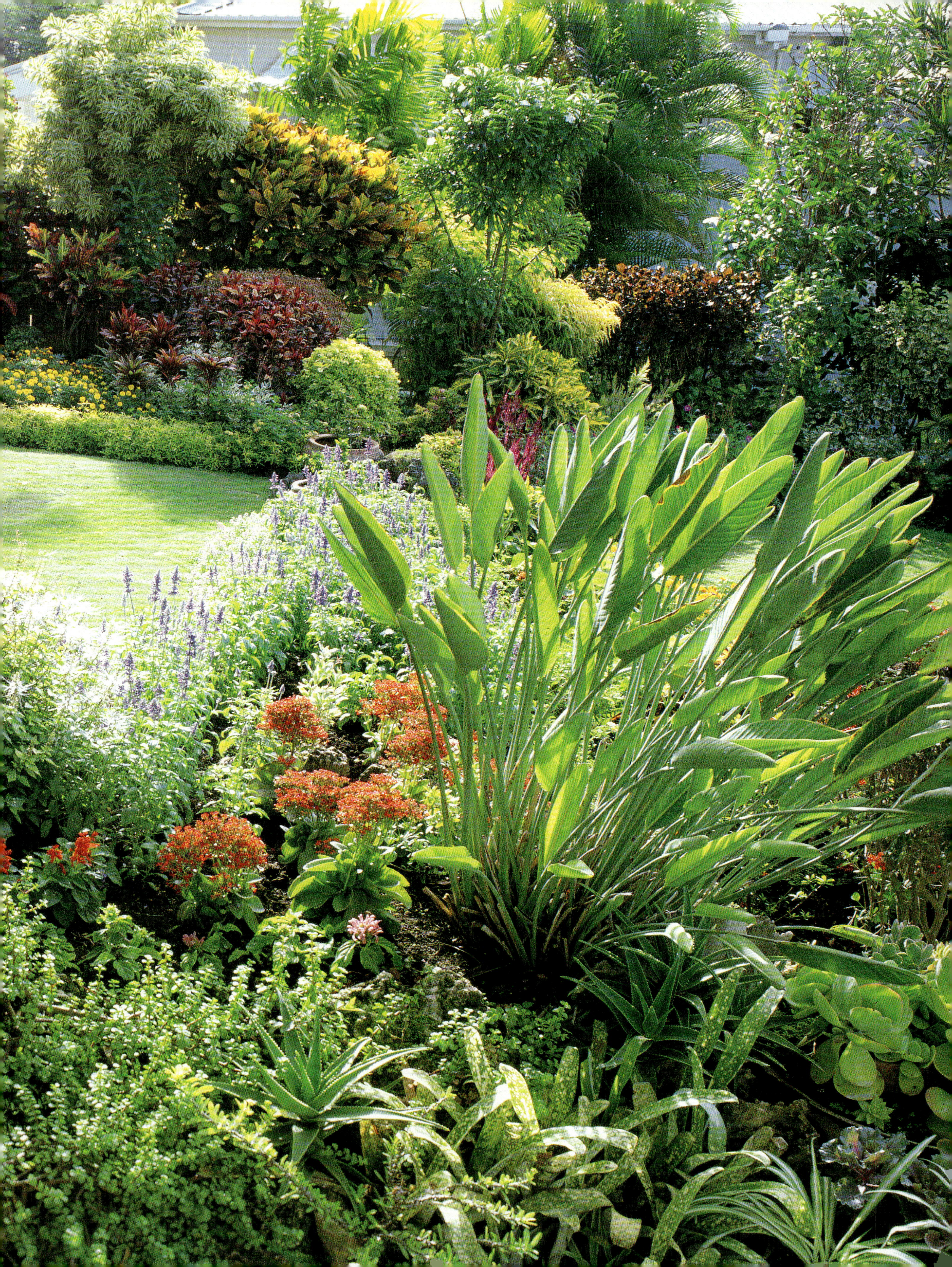

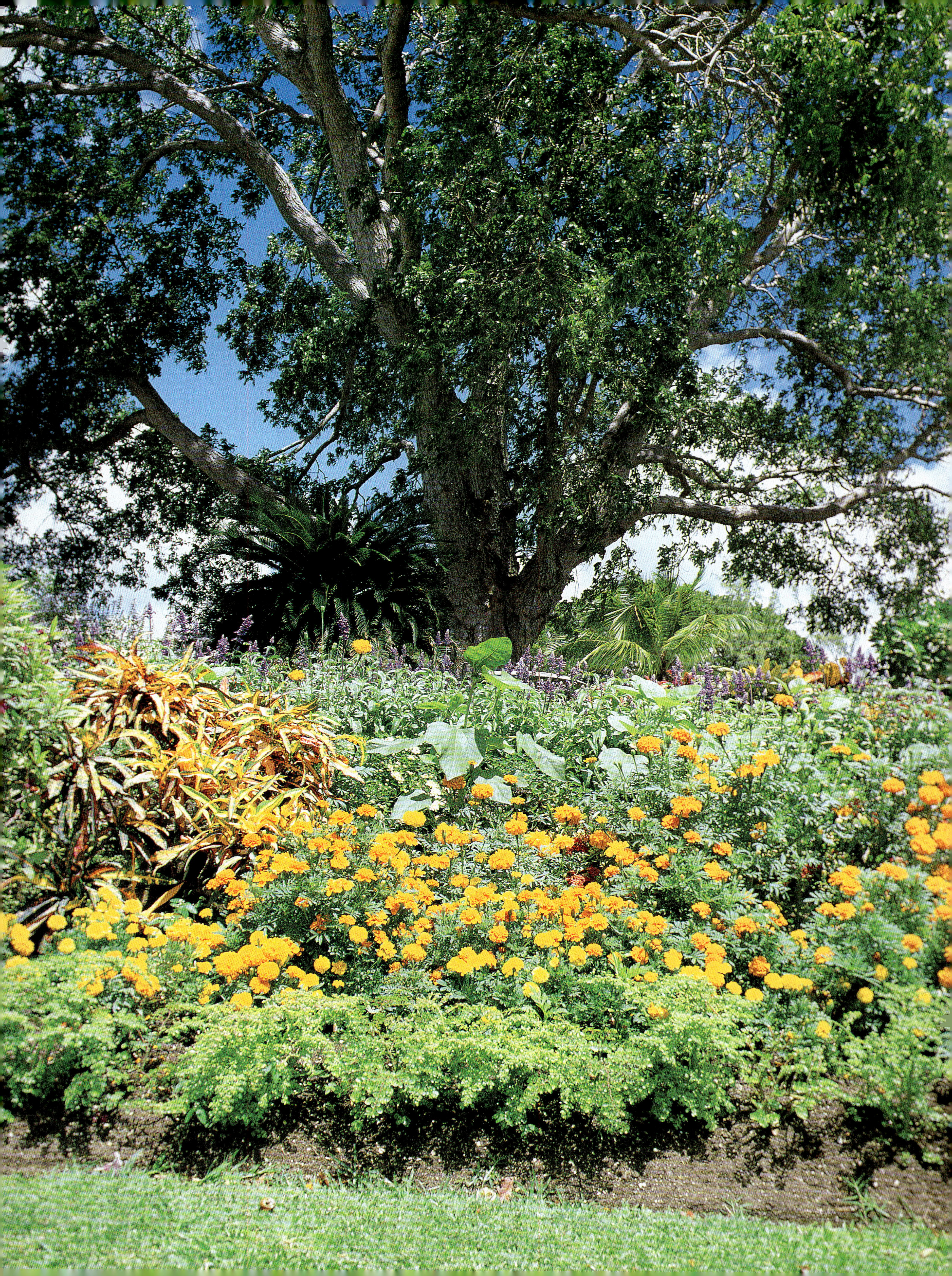

Opening page: Close up of the flower of *Plumbago auriculata*, the dark blue variety • **Previous pages**: A most magnificent garden …… a veritable plant lover's feast. Plants in this landscape include, clockwise from left to right: the border – Begonia semperflorens, Variegated *Ophiopogon*, Tea plant, *Alternanthera bettzickiana*, Marigolds, *Tagates lucida*; behind border plants – Crotons, *Codiaeum variegatum*, Hawaiian Jasmine, *Gardenia taitensis*, *Allocasia macrorrhiza* cv: 'Variegata', Bougainvillea 'Nairobi Orange', variegated Crinum lilies, *Graptophyllum pictum*, Song of India, *Pleomele reflexa* cv: 'Variegata', *Eranthemum andromeda*, Dwarf Cordylines, Bridal Bouquet Plumeria, *Plumeria pudica*, *Polyscias filicifolia*, Beefsteak Acalypha, *Acalypha wilkesiana* cultivar, Golden Palm, *Dypsis lutescens*, Portlandia, Bird-of-Paradise, *Strelitzia reginae*, Blue Salvia, *Salvia farinacea*, Kalanchoe, *Kalanchoe blossfeldiana*, Cat's Whiskers, *Orthosiphon stamineus*, Red Salvias, *Salvia spendens*, Sansevierias, Crown of Thorns, *Euphorbia milli*, Aloe species and Bromeliads, *Billbergia species* • **Opposite**: From bottom up - *Pilea microphylla*, Marigolds, *Tagates lucida*, providing a burst of colour, Croton, *Codiaeum variegatum*, Blue Salvia, *Salvia farinacea*, Dwarf Sago Palm, *Cycas revoluta*, Mahogany Tree, *Swietenia mahogoni*. • **Above:** Well controlled Bougainvillea.

Above: Close up of the leaves of a Croton, Codiaeum variegatum • **Opposite**: Centre – Variegated *Ophiopogun*, *Begonia semperflorens*; Bottom centre – *Ophiopogon* surround a terracotta planter.

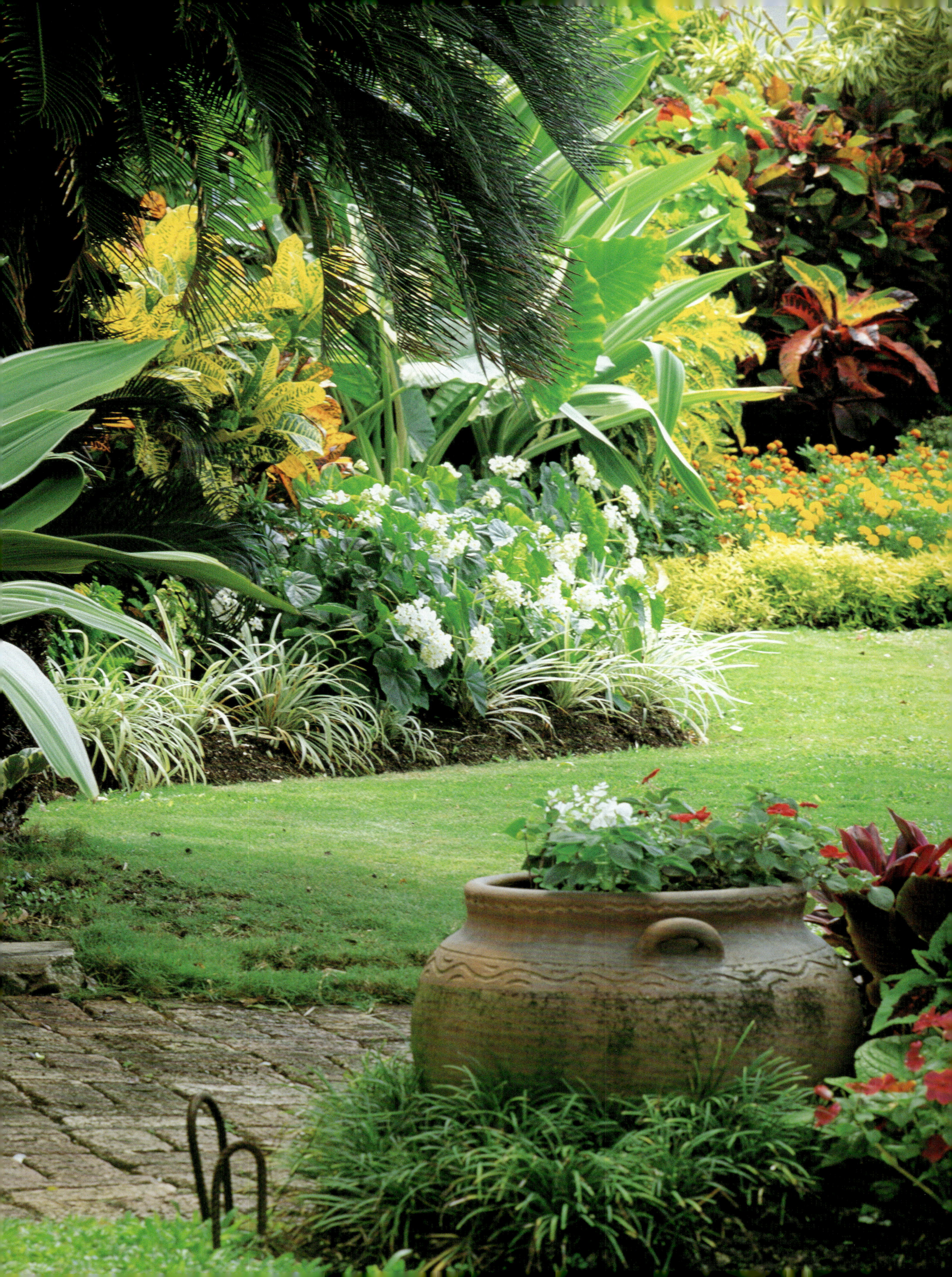

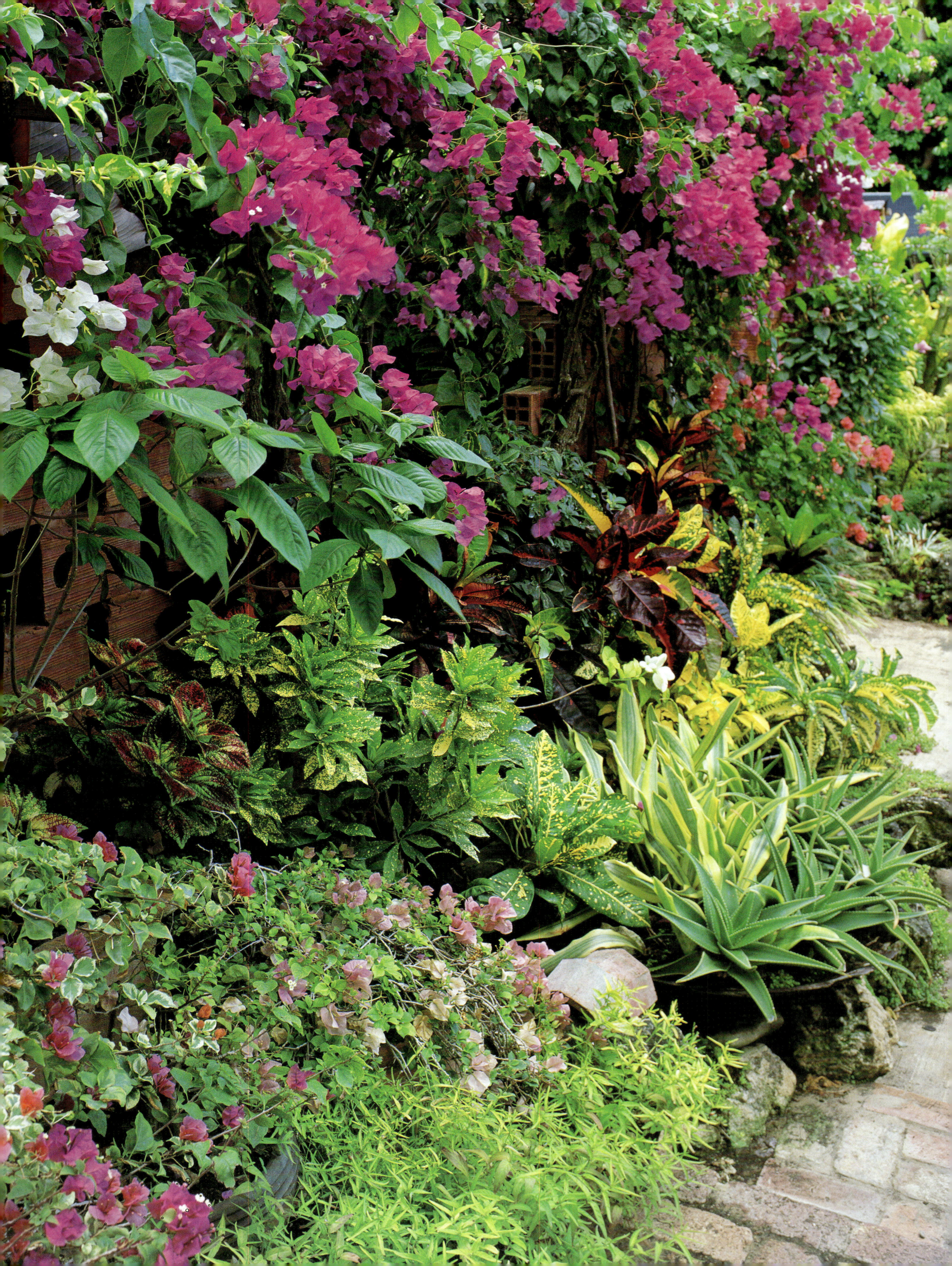

Opposite: Making the most of a small space • **Top**: Shade loving foliage plants. Foreground – Dwarf bamboo, Left centre – *Dracaena godseffiana*, and various ferns and Philodendrons • **Above**: A selection of *Sansevierias*.

EUSTEEN'S GARDEN

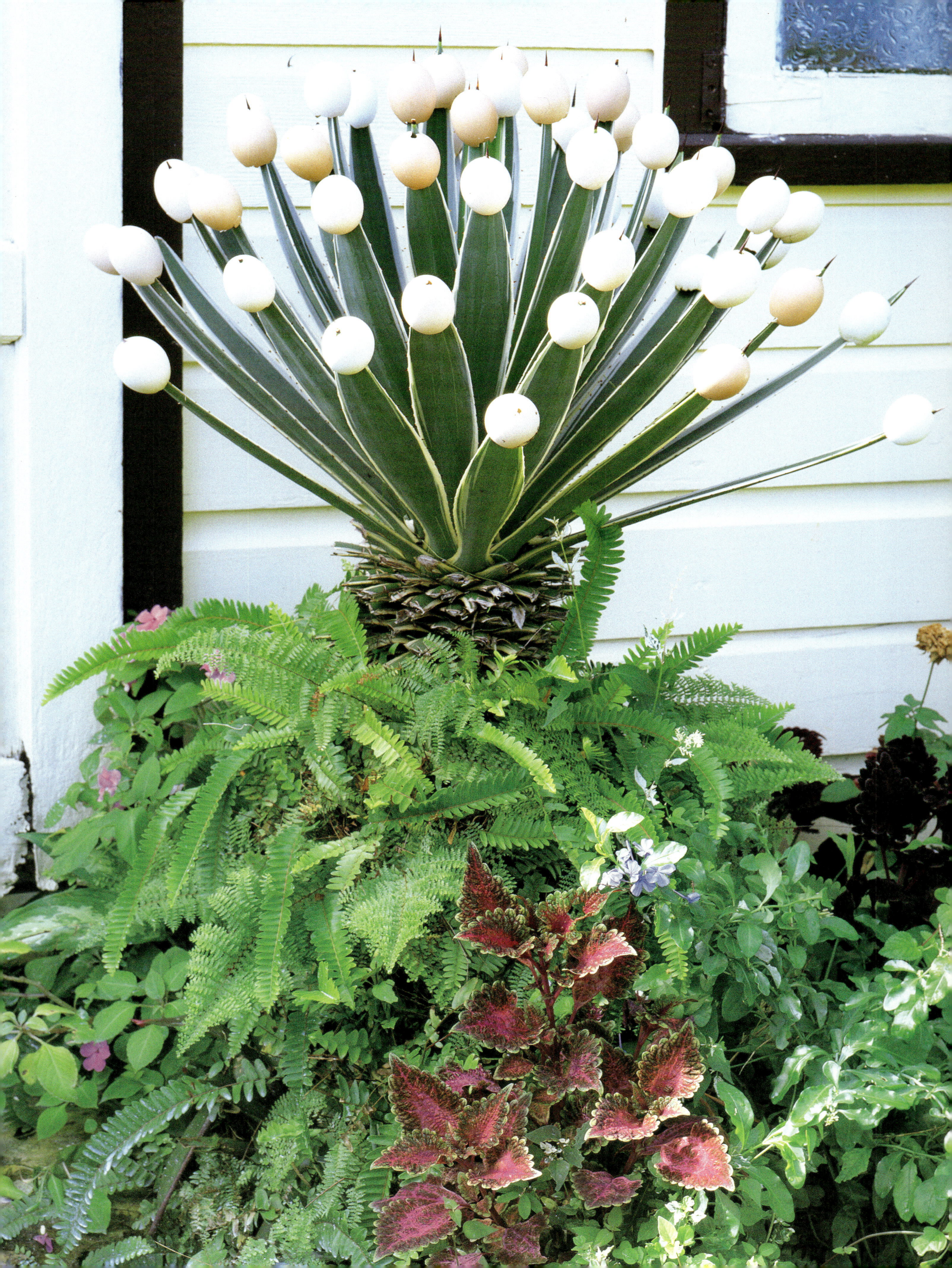

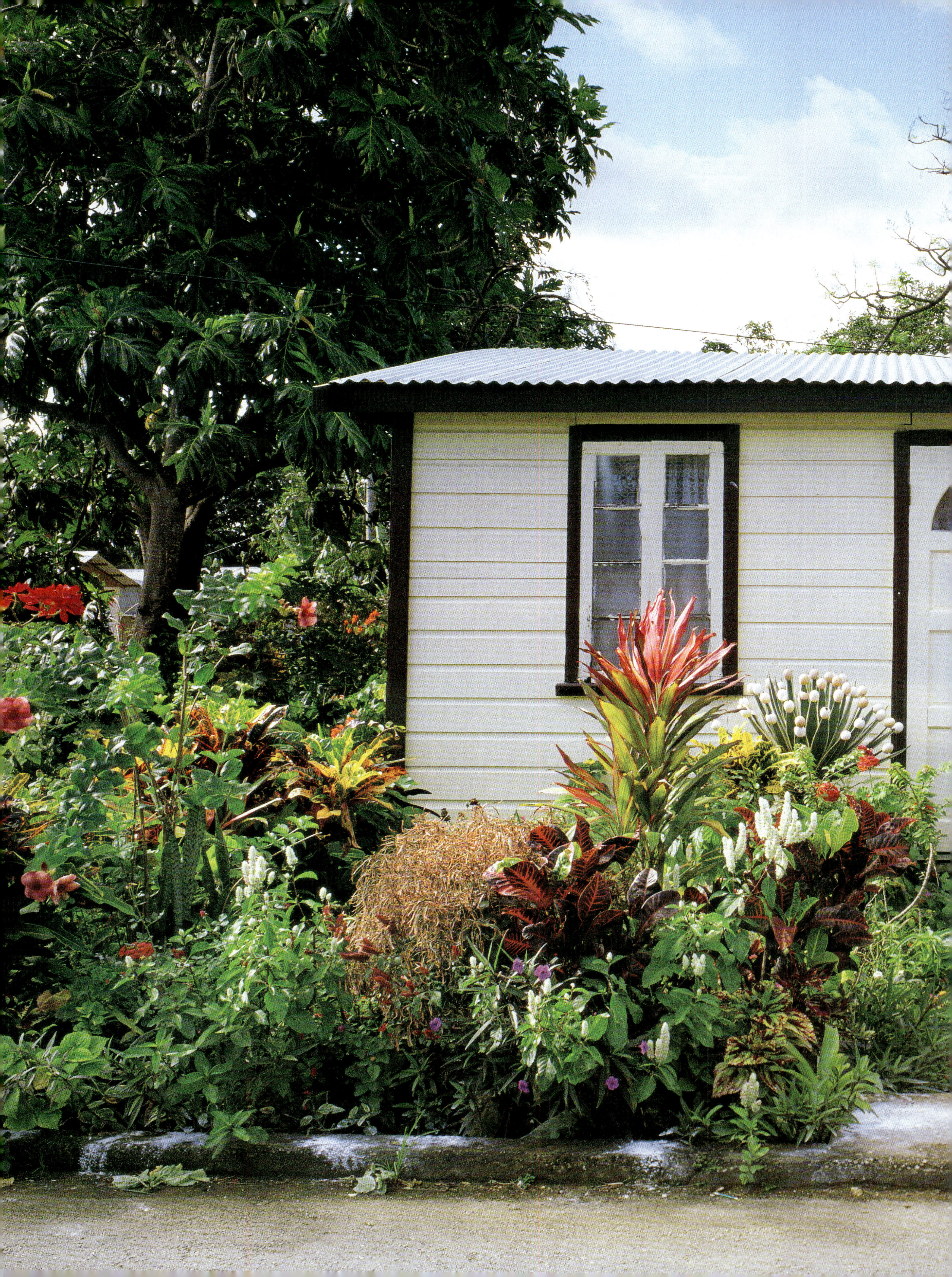

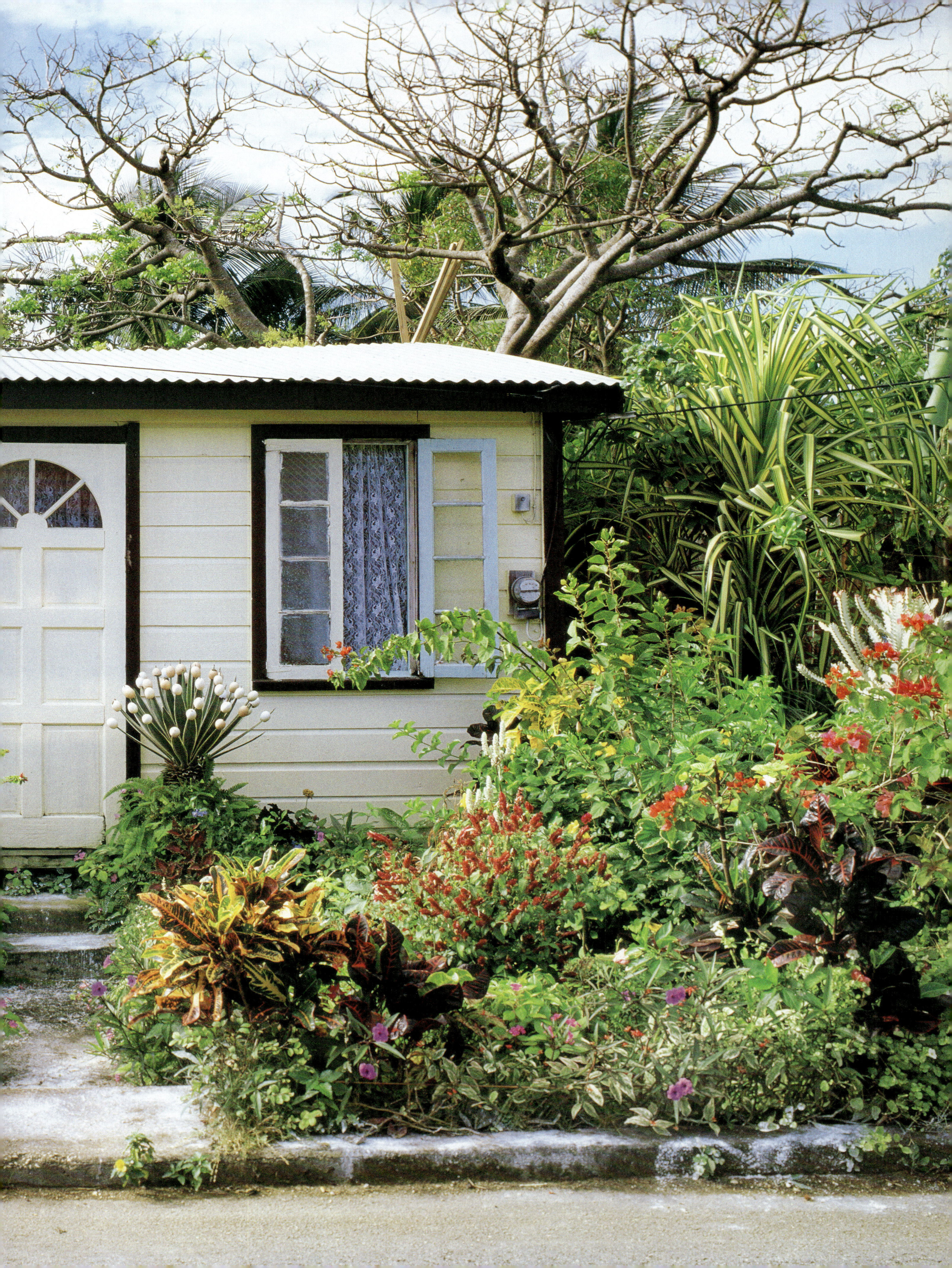

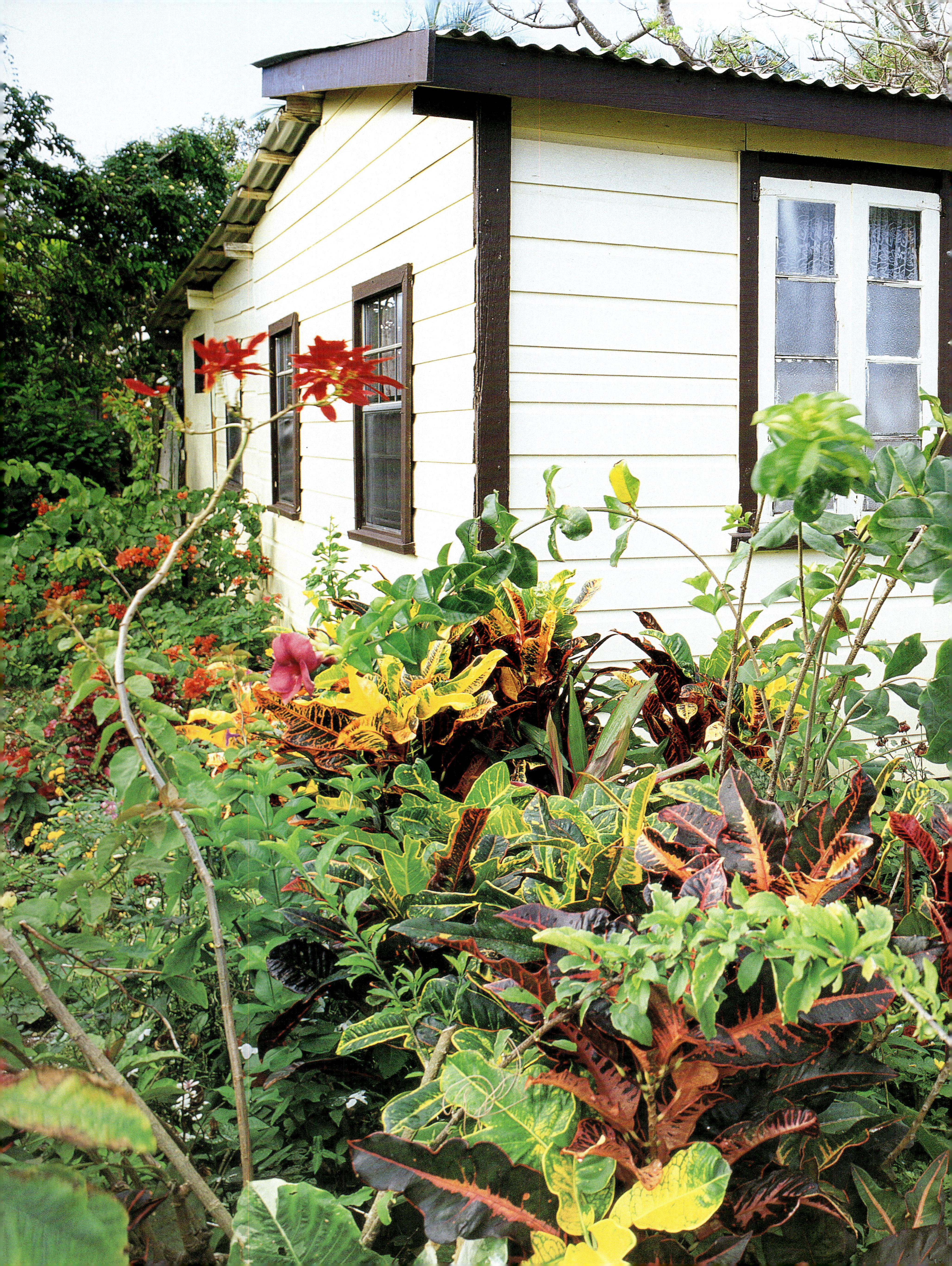

Opening page: Upper Centre – Spanish Bayonet, *Yucca aloifolia* cv. 'Marginata', with egg shells. The name Spanish Bayonet says it all – the tips of the leaves are pointed and sharp and are capable of inflicting painful puncture wounds even through thick clothing. It was traditionally believed in the Caribbean that the presence of egg shells would keep evil spirits away; Lower left – Busy Lizzy, *Impatiens walleriana*, a quick growing flowering shrub that grows to a height of 6"-12", and does well in semi-shade. It grows like a weed in some of the cooler, higher elevation, parts of Barbados. It is available with a very wide range of flower colours ranging from white, all varieties of pink, purple, orange to red. Bottom centre – *Coleus blumei*; Middle centre – Boston Fern, *Nephrolepis exaltata*, and other ferns. • **Previous pages**: Upper left – Breadfruit Tree, *Artocarpus atilis*; Centre left, below the window – Two colour varieties of Ti plant, *Cordyline terminalis*, Croton, *Codiaeum variegatum*, *Acalypha godseffiana*, and, along the kerb - White Shrimp plant, *Justicia betonica*; Upper right – Wild Cane, *Pandanus sanderi*, with a Ghost Cactus, *Euphorbia lactea* cv: 'Variegata', below. Centre right, below the window – Red Shrimp plant, *Justicia brandegeana*. • **Opposite**: Left – Poinsettia, *Euphorbia pulcherrima*; Right foreground – Croton, *Codiaeum variegatum*, Purple Allamanda, *Allamanda violacea* • **Above**: A typical Bajan "Kitchen Garden"

Andromeda Gardens

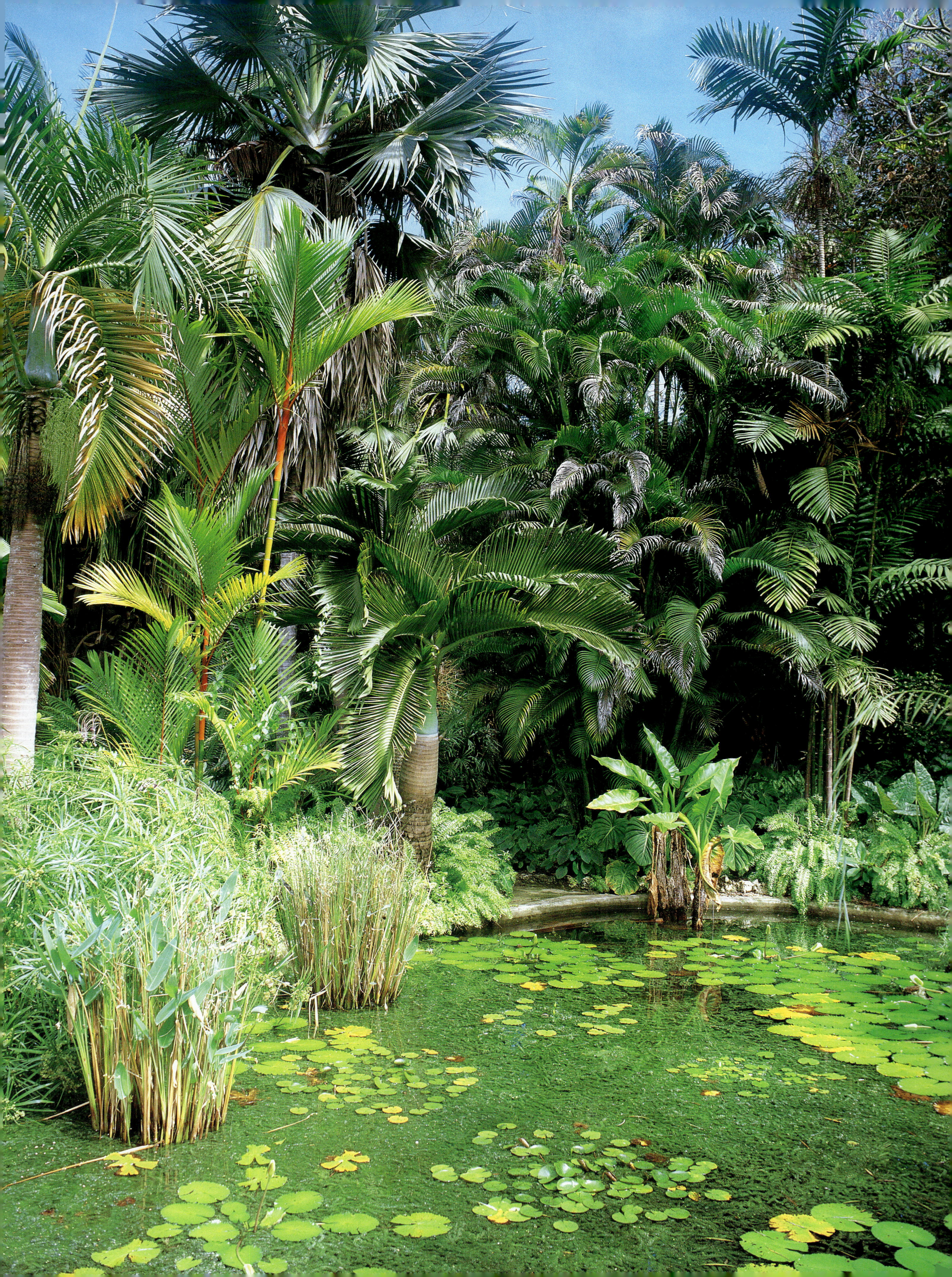

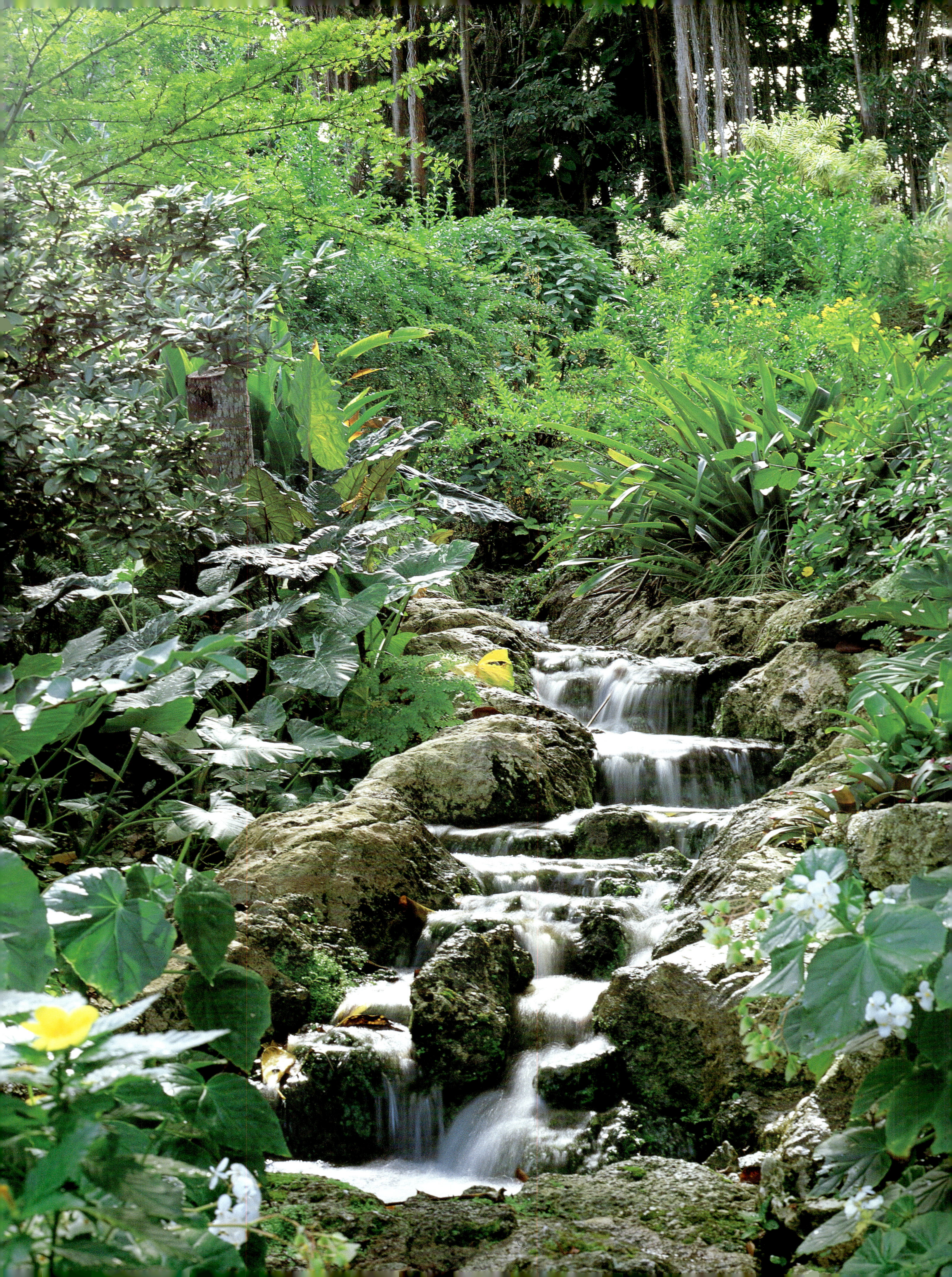

In 1954, on eight acres of land inherited from her mother, Iris Bannochie began to create 'Andromeda'. It is situated on a steep hillside that overlooks the rugged and scenic east coast of Barbados at Bathsheba. Iris chose this site for the stream that cascades through it. The course of the stream forms the main axis of the garden. After heavy wet-season storms and showers, the bed of the stream comes back to life with rushing rainwater runoff.

Porous coral-limestone is the base of most of Barbados. Millennia ago, large blocks of stone broke from the edge of the coral cap at Hackleton's Cliff and slipped downhill, eastward to the Atlantic coast. Large and small, fossil-encrusted coral-stone boulders from the Pleistocene period now litter the landscape. This is the site of Andromeda Botanic Gardens. Here rocks tumble along the valley of the stream to provide rhythm, unity and sculptural beauty. They flow harmoniously throughout the garden and link one area to another. Gardens form between rock outcrops and on top of them. Andromeda Botanic Gardens may be considered a grand rock garden.

They also inspired Iris to name her garden 'Andromeda'. Andromeda was a mythical virgin maiden who, while chained to a boulder near the sea as a sacrifice to the sea-monster, was found and rescued by Perseus and became his wife.

The gardens began at an enormous boulder that bounds the eastern corner of the lawn. Its many pockets and crevices became niches to cultivate rockery plants like Aloe, Haworthia and Kalanchoe. Iris replaced weeds with more decorative plants and this set the tone for the garden. The plant was always the important personality in the garden, with its protection coming first in order to give it every chance to adapt to its new environment.

Today, Andromeda is owned by the Barbados National Trust.

Opening page: A verdant lily pond with *Nymphaea* water lilies and Umbrella Plants, *Cyperus alternifolius*, at the lower left, surrounded by a variety of palms, including from left to right, Spindle Palm, *Hyophorbe verschaffeltii*, Sealing Wax Palm, *Cyrtostachys renda*, in background towering over Sealing Wax palm, Red Latan, *Latania lontaroides*, Bottle Palm, *Hyophorbe lagenicaulis*, Lady Palm, *Rhapis excelsa*, Golden Palms, *Dypsis lutescens*, and Macarthur Palm, *Ptychosperma macarthurii*. The Fishtail Fern, *Nephrolepis biserrata* cv: 'Furcans', grows at the edge of the pond around the base of the Bottle Palm and Macarthur Palm. A giant of the Araceae family, *Typhonodorum lindleyanum*, can be seen growing in the edge of the pond near the centre of the view. Under ideal conditions this plant can exceed 12 feet in height. • **Opposite**: A waterfall cascades through a variety of plants including from left to right: *Alocasia macrorrhiza*, *A. macrorrhiza* cv: 'Variegata', *A. macrorrhiza* cv: 'Rubra', *Pittosporum tobira* cv; 'Variegata', Pink Powder Puff Tree, *Calliandra surinamensis*, Golden Dewdrop, *Duranta repens*, Song of India, *Dracaena reflexa*, Canariensis, *Galphimia glauca*, Bromeliads and Begonias, *Begonia sempervirens*. • **Above**: White Mussaenda, *Mussaenda philippica* cv; 'Aurorae'

Above: A close-up of the menacing spines on the trunk of a Macaw Palm, *Aiphanes minima*. The Macaw Palm is one of a handful of species of palms that are indigenous to Barbados. It is a heavily armed palm with sharp spines on the trunk, petioles and leaves. In its native habitat in the damp, heavily shaded gullies of Barbados it is, in spite of its heavy armament, a very beautiful palm, especially when a mature specimen is viewed form the base of the trunk looking up into its canopy. • **Opposite**: *Furcraea foetida* cv: 'Striata'

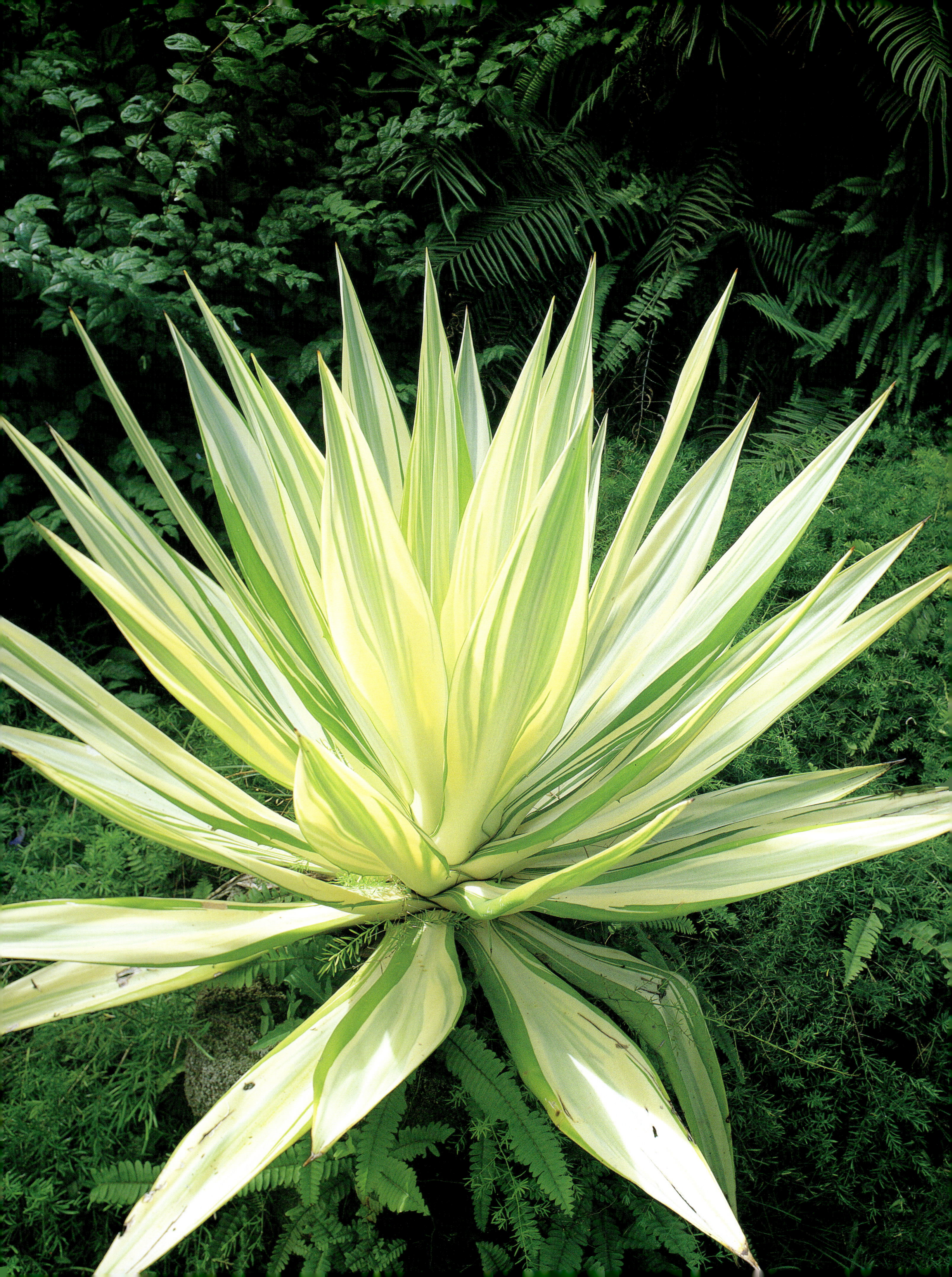

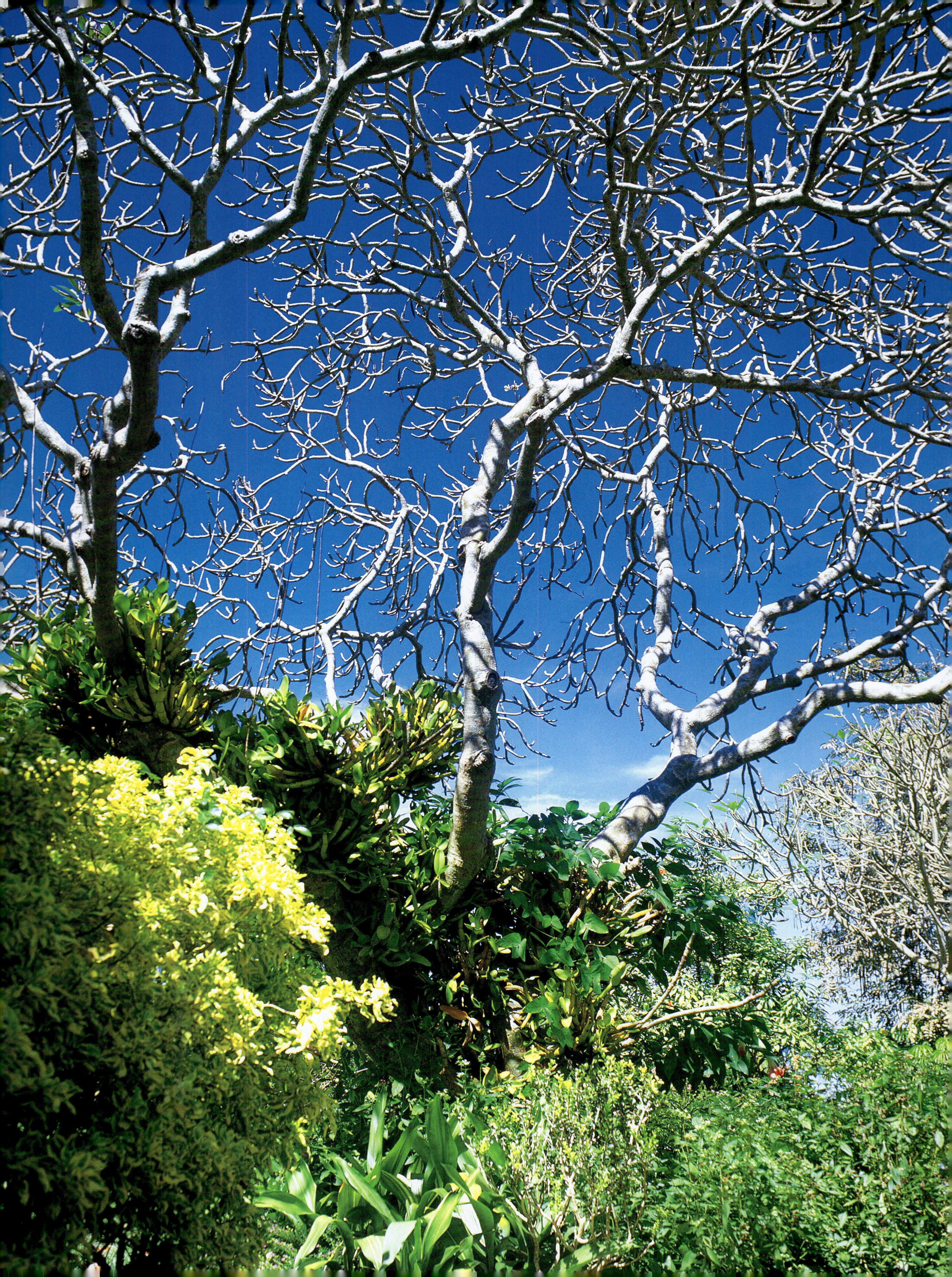

Opposite: Trunks and branches of Frangipani, *Plumeria rubra*, seen here without leaves prior to flowering, on which orchids are growing • **Top**: The Pink Powder Puff Tree, *Calliandra surinamensis*, a member of the *Leguminosae*, is a medium sized tree with low spreading branches. It is grown as an ornamental primarily because of it preponderance of fluffy pink and white flowers that resemble a powder puff. It also makes a good container plant • **Bottom**: Red Powder Puff, *Calliandra haematocephala*

Welchman Hall Gully

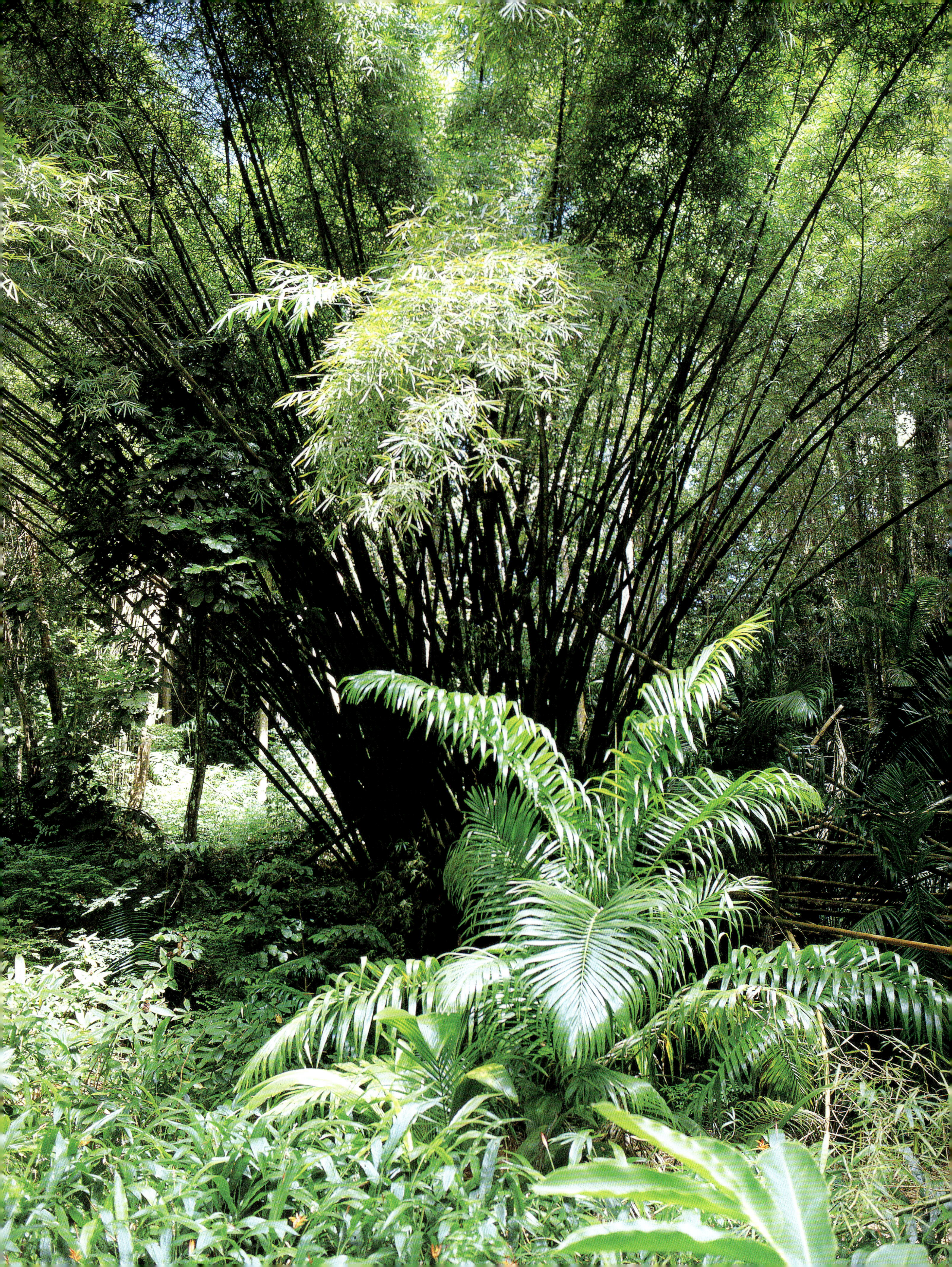

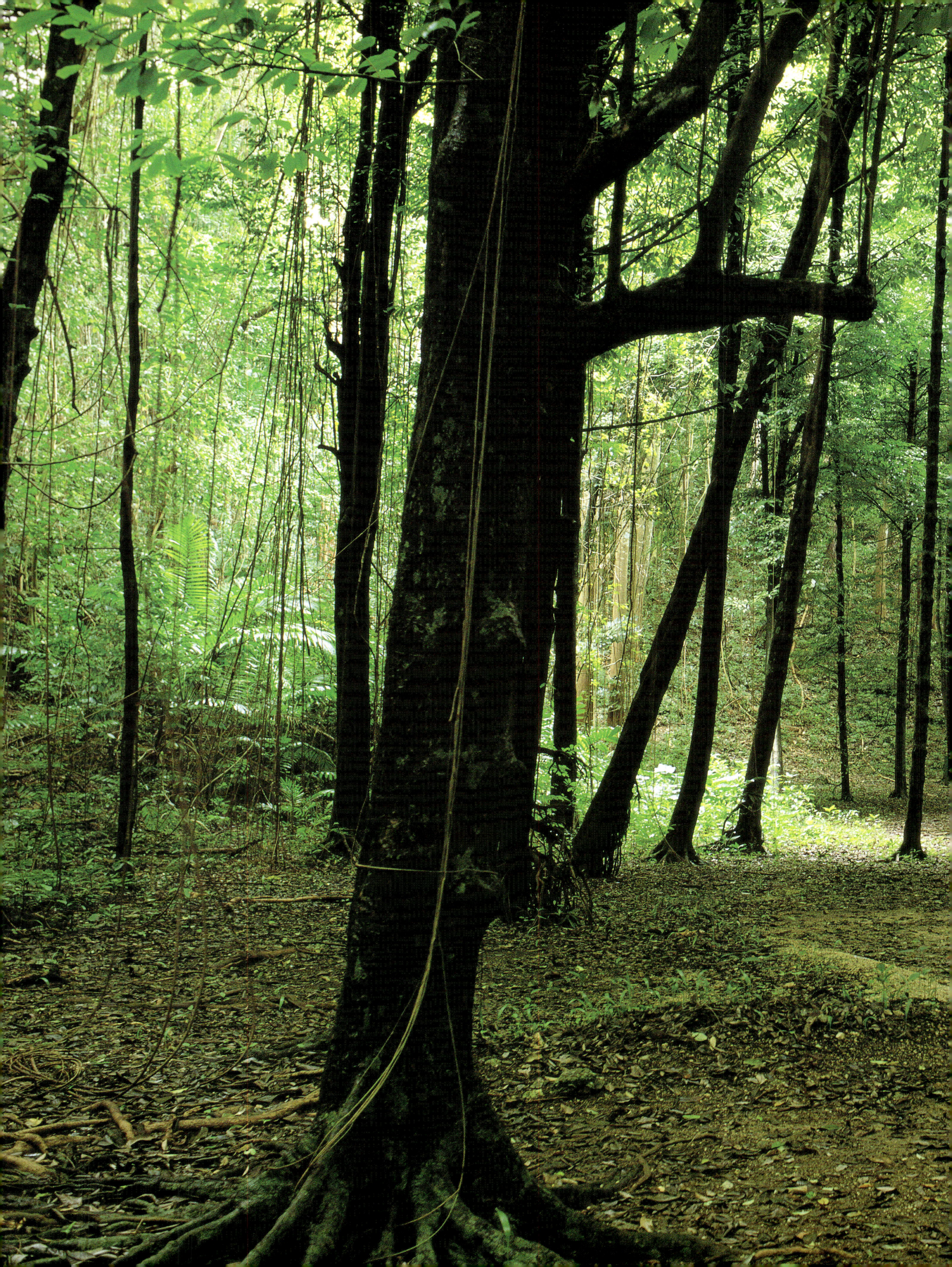

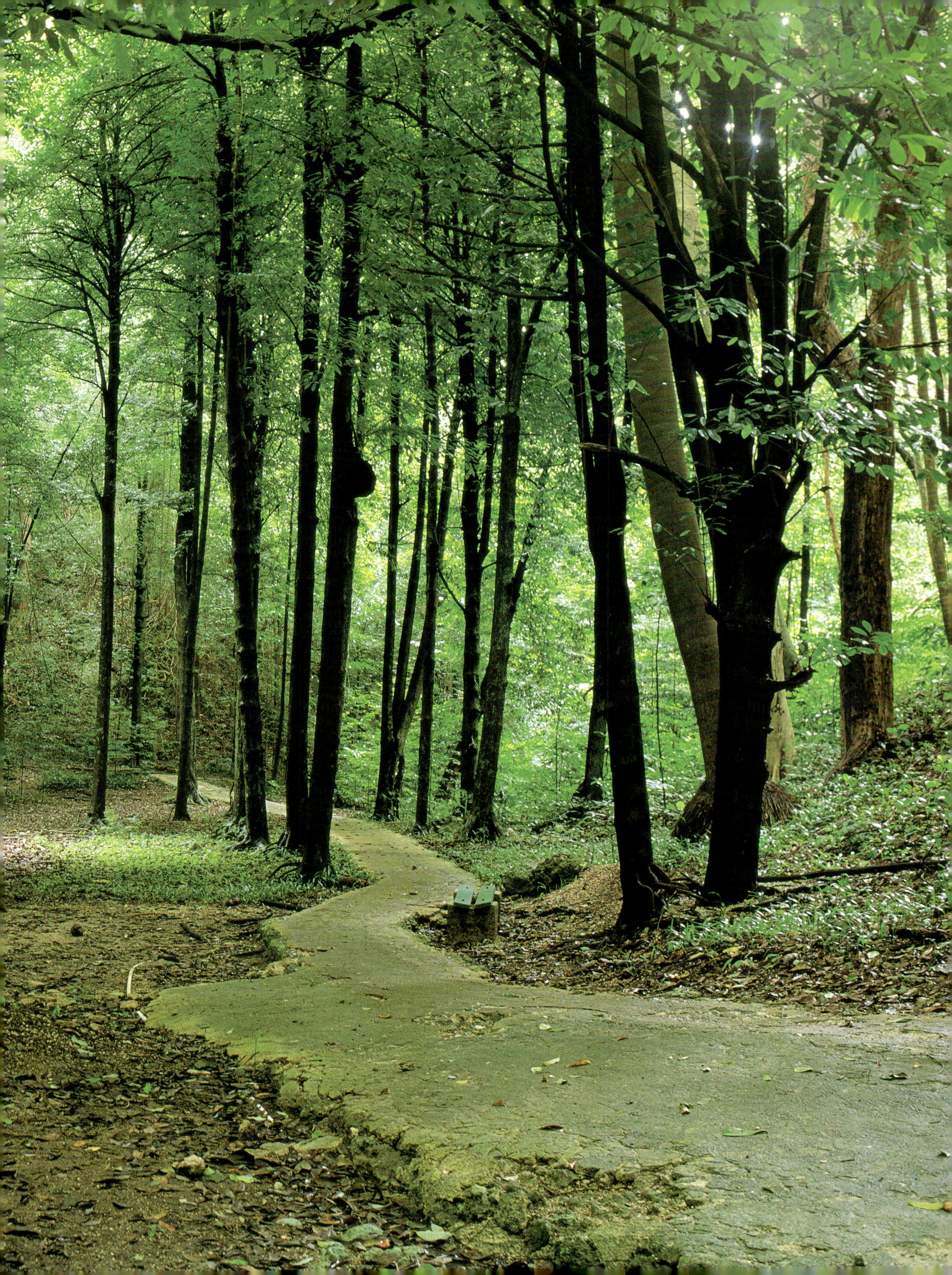

Welchman Hall Gully is part of the complex network of wooded gullies extending over 150km in length across Barbados. These gullies first developed as underground rivers, the roofs of these waterways finally collapsing as a result of water erosion of the coral limestone cap that covers much of the island. Some of the gullies are 60m (200ft) deep and exhibit a variety of plants, animals and geological formations that few people see as they go about their daily lives.

Historic Welchman Hall Gully was first described about 200 years ago as "a fine valley of fruits which offered the most grateful refreshment". The Gully is at an elevation of some 270m (880ft) above sea level, is about 1.25 km (3/4 mile) long and, in places, over 15m (50ft) deep.

The initial development of this orchard and grove of exotic trees is credited to General William Asygell Williams who was of Welsh descent, hence the name Welchman Hall. The Williams family vault can still be seen to this day on the adjoining Vault Road. The property further changed hands several times until it was bought in 1962 by the Barbados National Trust, who then enhanced the ornamental aspect of the gully and opened it to the public.

Welchman Hall Gully is a site blending the past, present and future uses of gullies in Barbados. It extols the beauty and tranquility of a natural gully, a moist sheltered environment where indigenous plants and animals can thrive. It shows how gullies were used as orchards for fruit and spice trees and as areas for the gathering of firewood and bush teas. Gullies were the natural boundaries between plantations and, in days of yore, plantation labourers would annually return soil that had washed down into the gullies back to the fields. Lastly, Welchman Hall Gully shows the future potential to put some gullies into cut flower production for the home and export markets.

Opening page: A magnificent stand of Bamboo. In the foreground, a young West Indian Royal Palm, *Roystonea oleracea*, stands amongst *Heliconia psittacorum* cv: 'St. Vincent Red' and *Costus speciosus* to the left. • **Previous pages**: A shady grove of Nutmeg Trees, *Myristica fragrans*, an uncommon plant in Barbados but a well-known feature of Welchman Hall Gully. The Nutmeg, a native of the Molucca islands, is a large evergreen tree with separate male and female trees. Both the spices, nutmeg and mace, are produced by the female tree; the nutmeg being the seed and the mace the red mantle clothing the seed. These are enclosed within an outer fleshy fruit. It should be noted that Nutmeg has mildly hallucinogenic properties and should only be consumed as a spice in small quantities • **Above**: Moss and lichen-covered prop roots of the Nutmeg, *Myristica fragrans*, scramble over a rocky outcropping. The high humidity in the gully, and greatly reduced sunlight, encourage the growth of moss and lichens on many surfaces. .Other seedlings visible on the gully floor around the roots include Nutmeg and Macaw Palms, *Aiphanes minima* • **Opposite**: The majestic avenue of Coconut Palms close to the entrance to the gully. Several other trees are also present behind the Coconut Palms and these include: on the left side going towards the centre – Red Sandlewood, *Adenanthera pavonina*, a native of Asia that produces small red seeds which are used in local handicraft and jewellery; a Rubber Tree, *Ficus elastica*, native of India and Malaysia; Blue Mahoe, *Hibiscus elatus*, a native of West Indies and source of wood for fine furniture; Lucky Seed Tree, *Thevetia peruviana*; on the right side going towards the centre – Guava tree, *Psidium guajava*, native of Central and South America, that produces an edible fruit which contains more than five times the Vitamin C content of an equivalent weight of oranges; Fiddle Wood Tree, *Citharexylum spinosum*, native of the Lesser Antilles and Northern South America, which has various medicinal properties and produces an excellent hardwood; Pomerac or Plumrose, *Syzgium malaccensis*, native of Malaysia, produces an edible rose-red or crimson coloured fruit. It is worthy to note that like the Breadfuit, the Pomerac was also introduced into the Caribbean by Captain Bligh.

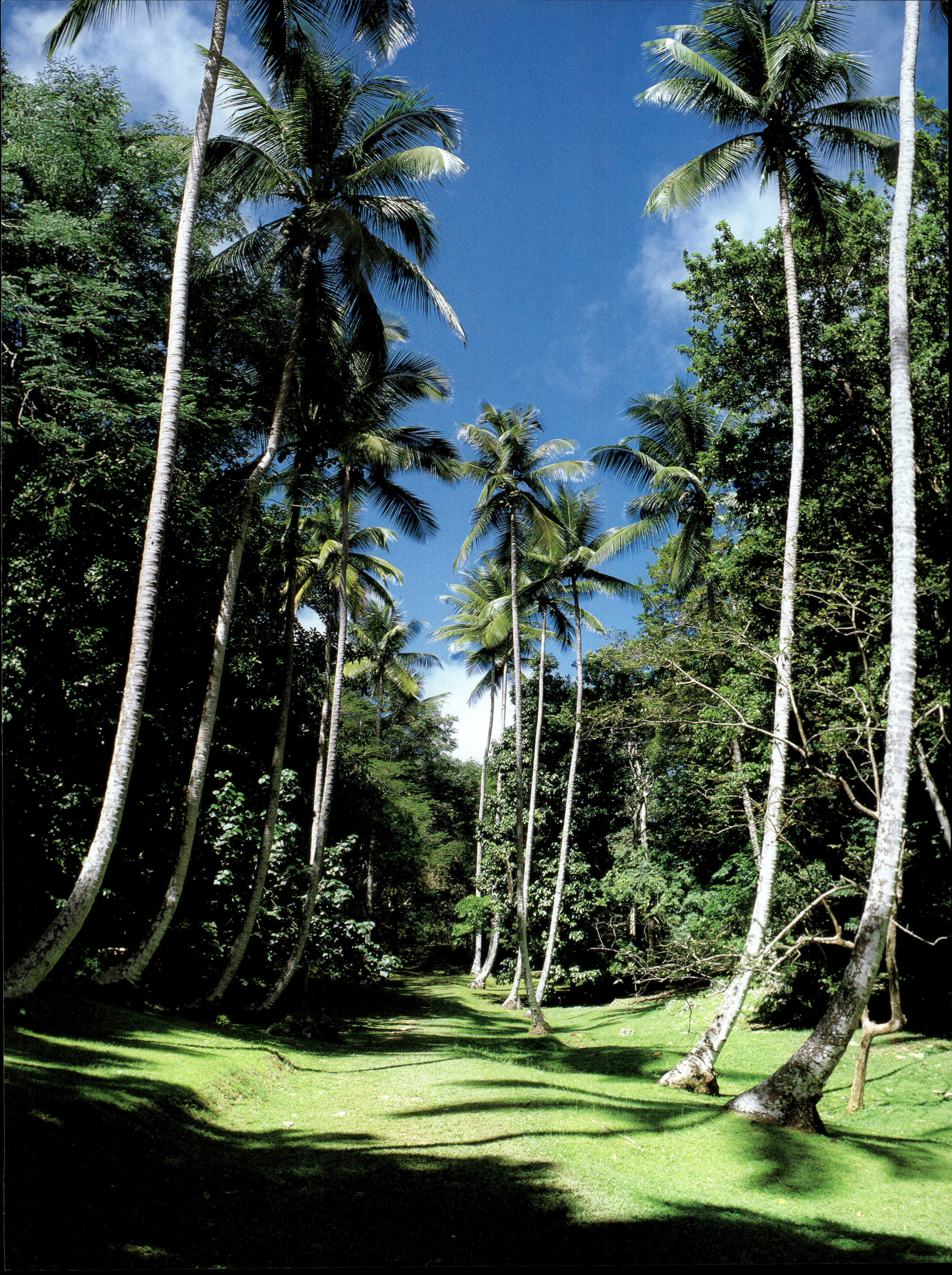

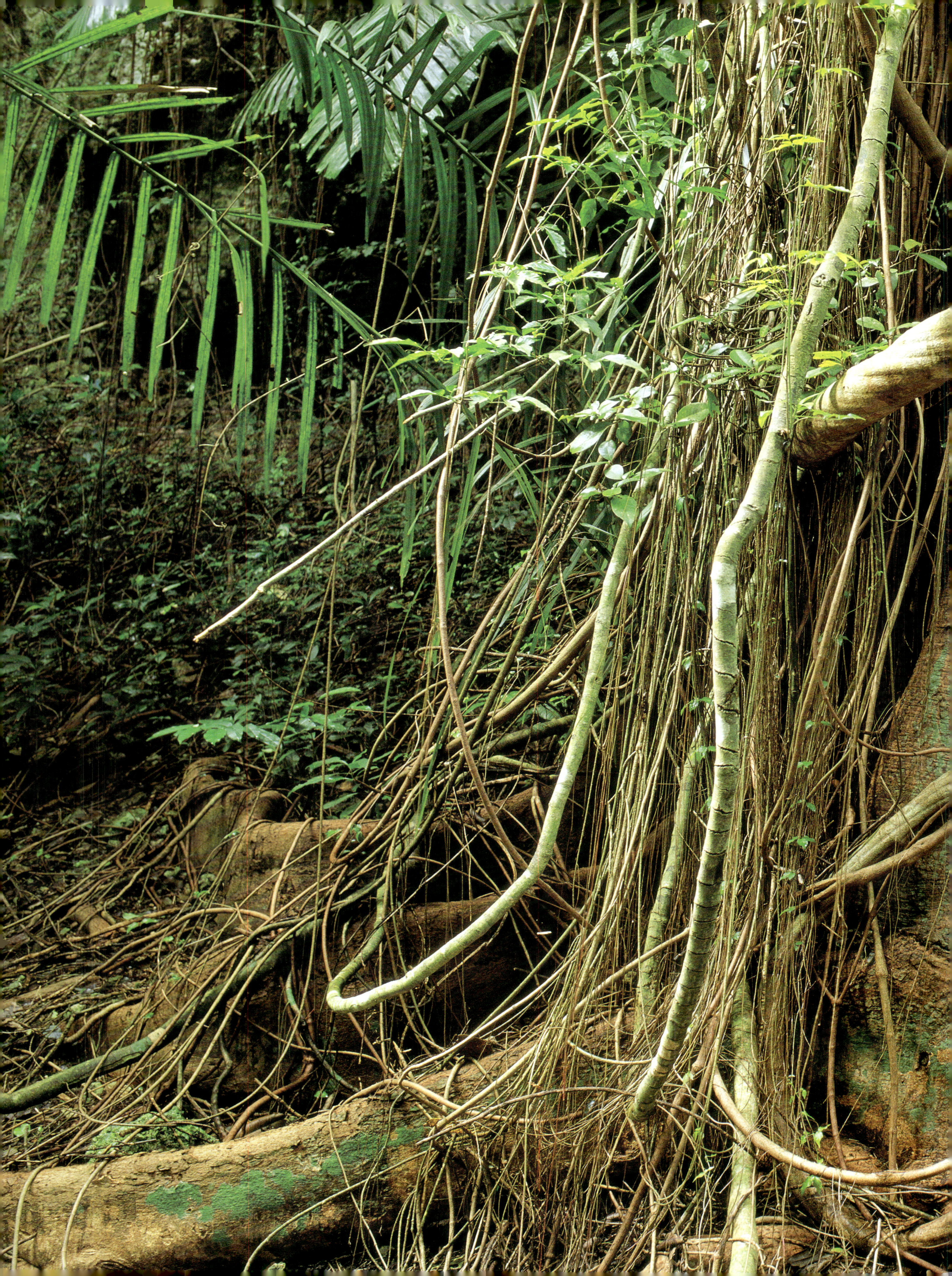

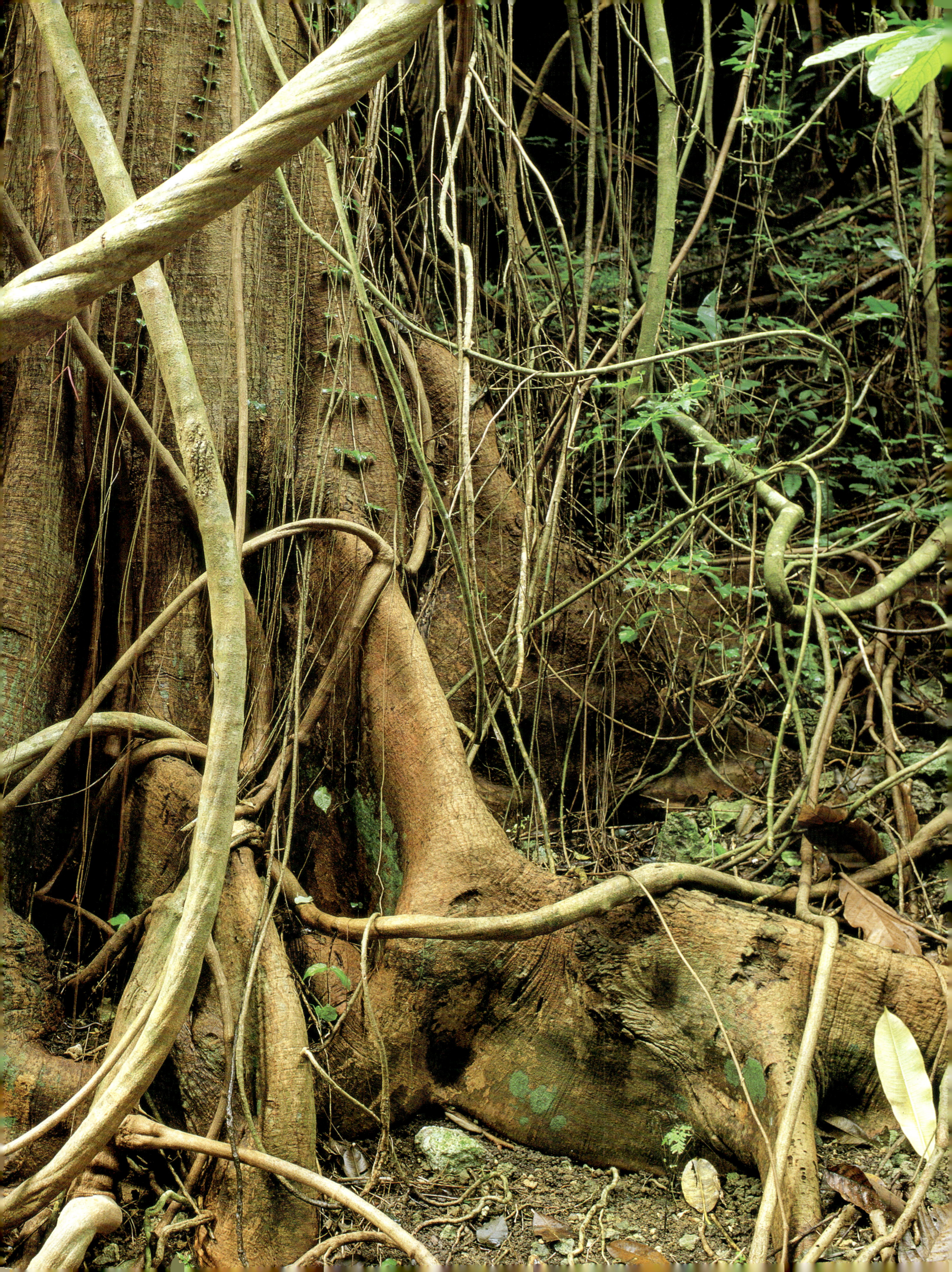

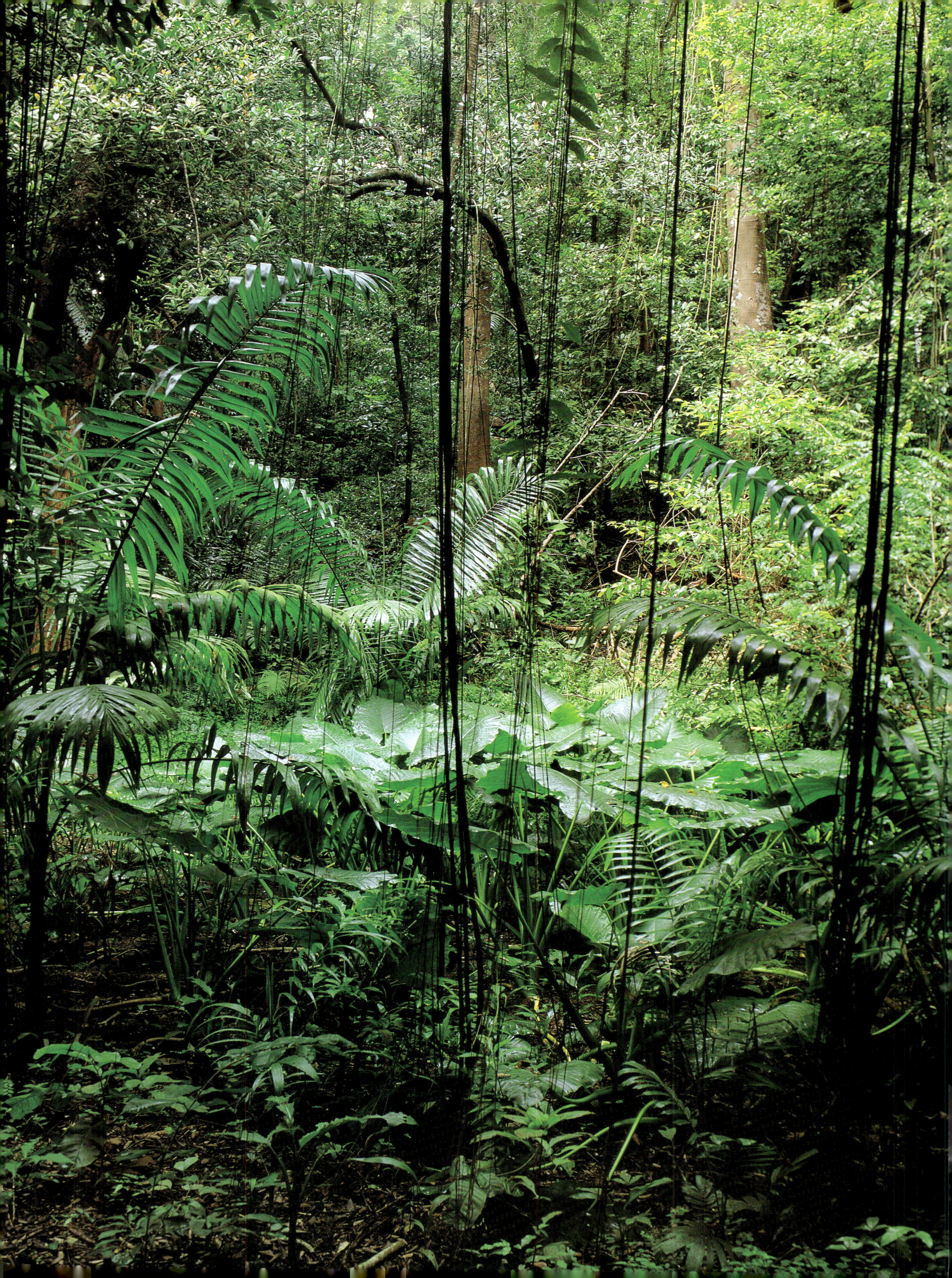

Previous Pages: An image of natural abstract expressionist artwork, made up of Lianes and buttressed roots. The roots are of the Poison Tree, *Sapium hippomane*, this individual being in excess of 100 feet in height. It gets its name from the fact that its caustic sap causes blisters and even temporary blindness. It is a common tree in the gullies of Barbados and is native to the island, Trinidad and South America. • **Facing Page**: The natural vegetation of Barbados as it would have been seen many centuries ago. This scene is typical of the gully. Lianas hang from overhead trees, while young West Indian Royal Palms, *Roystonea oleracea*, surround a clump of Giant Elephant Ear, *Alocasia macrorrhiza*, with a stand of young Nutmeg trees, *Myristica fragrans*, to their right. Seedlings of West Indian Royal Palms and Macaw Palms, *Aiphanes minima*, cover the forest floor. • **This Page:** A large boulder is covered with Creeping Club Moss, *Selaginella serpens*. This plant has its origin in the West Indies and its ancestors would have been prominent during the age of the dinosaurs. It is one of the few remaining members of this group of plants and is only found now in Barbados at Welchman Hall Gully. Other plants inhabiting the boulder include a variety of ferns, St John's Bush, *Psychotria nervosa*, a common gully plant that is native to the Greater Caribbean and whose leaves are used in a 'bush tea' concoction for the treatment of colds, fever and stomach ailments, and Rock Balsam, *Peperomia magnoliifolia*, another common gully plant that is native to Tropical America and one which also had medicinal properties in the treatment of colds and coughs.

Flower Forest

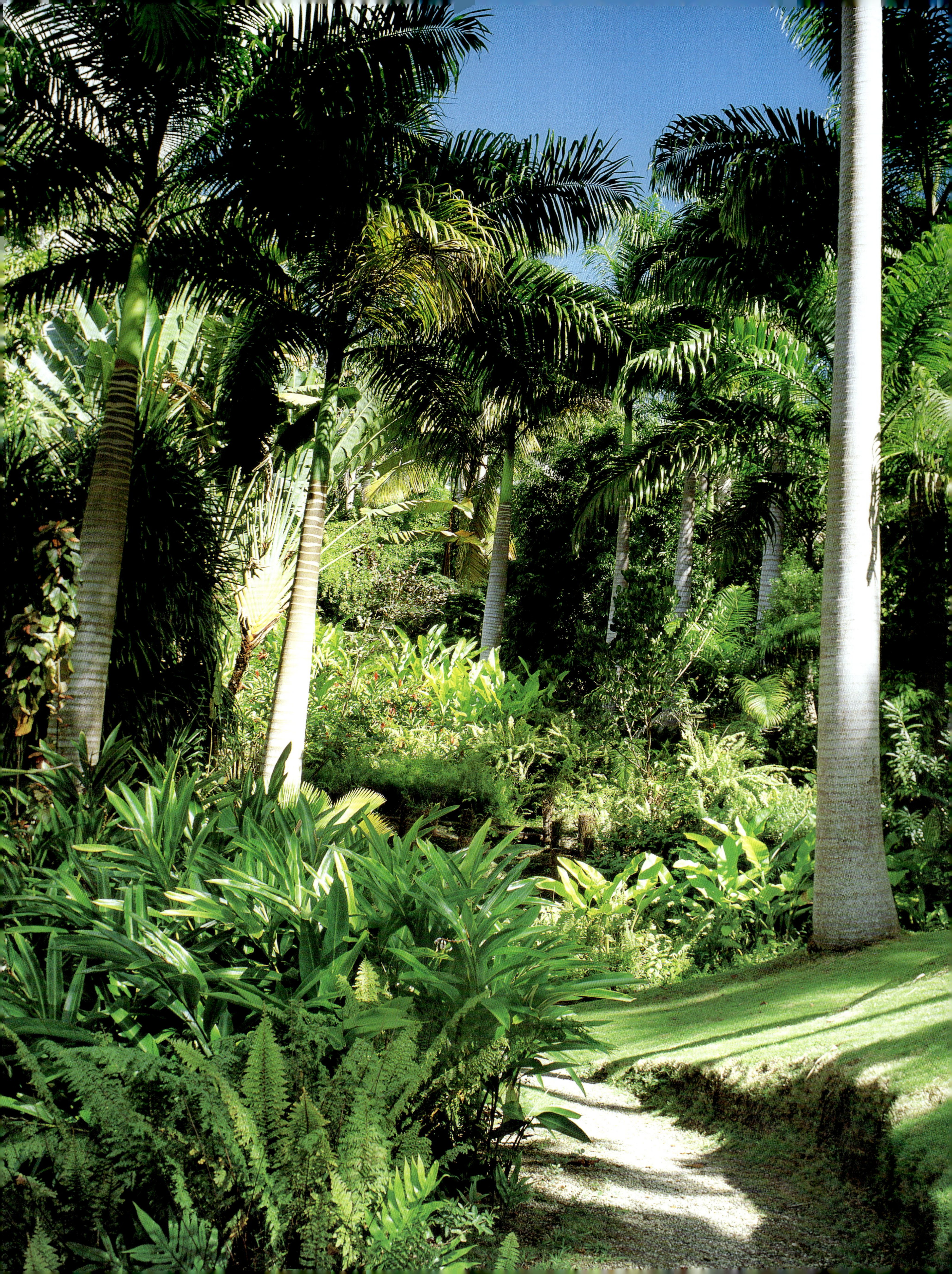

Opened in 1983 on the site of the former Richmond Sugar Plantation, the aptly named Flower Forest is neither a botanical garden nor a nature trail, but rather a peaceful blend of both, with swathes of colourful flowers, groups of majestic palms, rolling green lawns and an occasional glimpse of semi-jungle conditions.

Offering equal appeal for experts and amateurs alike, fifty acres of natural beauty have been enhanced by imaginative landscaping, using plants from throughout the West Indies and other parts of the world.

The original landscape consultant was Richard Coghlan, who studied at the Cambridge University Botanic Gardens and at the Royal Botanic Gardens at Kew. The Flower Forest is a reflection of his knowledge and expertise, as well as his love for plants and their development within a healthy environment.

Situated some 850 feet (260m) above sea level with spectacular panoramic views, the Flower Forest presents tremendous variation, depending on the time of year as well as the time of day, regardless of whether the sun is shining or rain is falling.

Opening page: Royal Palms, *Roystonea oleracea*, tower above Hill's Boston Fern, *Nephrolepis exaltata* cv: 'Hillii', and Shell Gingers, *Alpinia zerumbet*, in the left foreground, and Crape Gingers, *Costus speciosus*, and Red Gingers, *Alpinia purpurata*, in the centre of this view. A Gully Balsam, *Clusia plukenetii*, is seen just to the right of centre rising above the Red Gingers. The Gully Balsam is commonly found in the gullies of Barbados growing on the rocky cliff faces and occasionally as an epiphyte on other trees. It typically grows to a height of 30 feet and has long hanging roots. It has traditionally been an important plant in Barbados as the roots are used in basketry – an art which has been traced back to the pre-history of Barbados in the time of the Amerindians, the original inhabitants of Barbados. A group of Traveller's Palms, *Ravenala madagascariensis*, may be seen behind the pair of Royal Palms to the left of centre, partially obscured by a large clump of Pandanus. Pandanus is another plant that has been used in Barbados in basketry. The Traveller's Palm, native to Madagascar as indicated by its species name, is considered one of the most striking and unique plants in nature. However, it is not a palm but a member of the Bird-of-Paradise family, *Strelitziaceae*, and a relative of the bananas. Its name is derived from the fact that the leaf bases are hollow and collect and hold rain water which is then available to thirsty travellers. • **Above**: Shell Ginger, *Alpinia zerumbet* • **Opposite**: *Heliconia wagneriana*

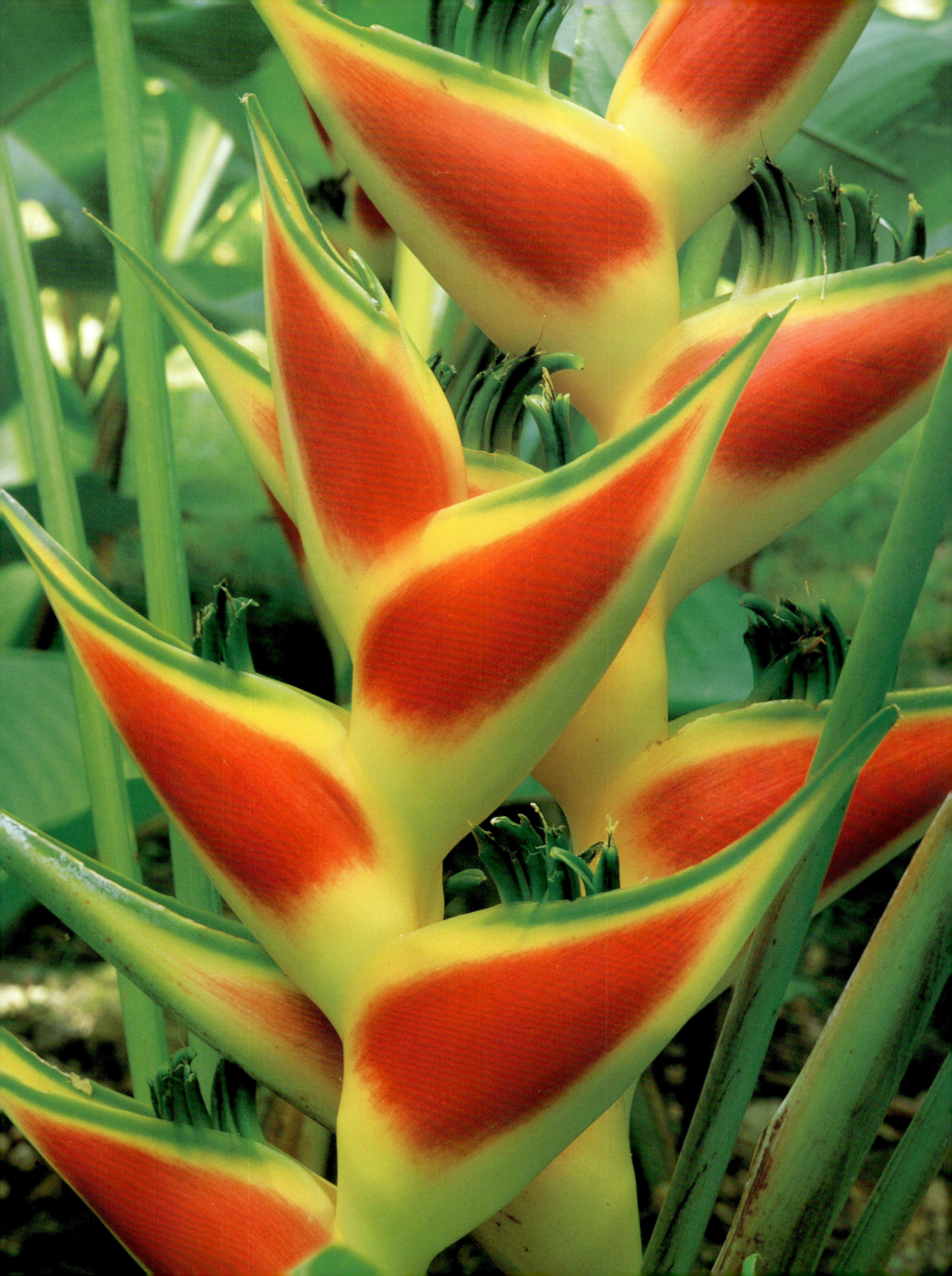

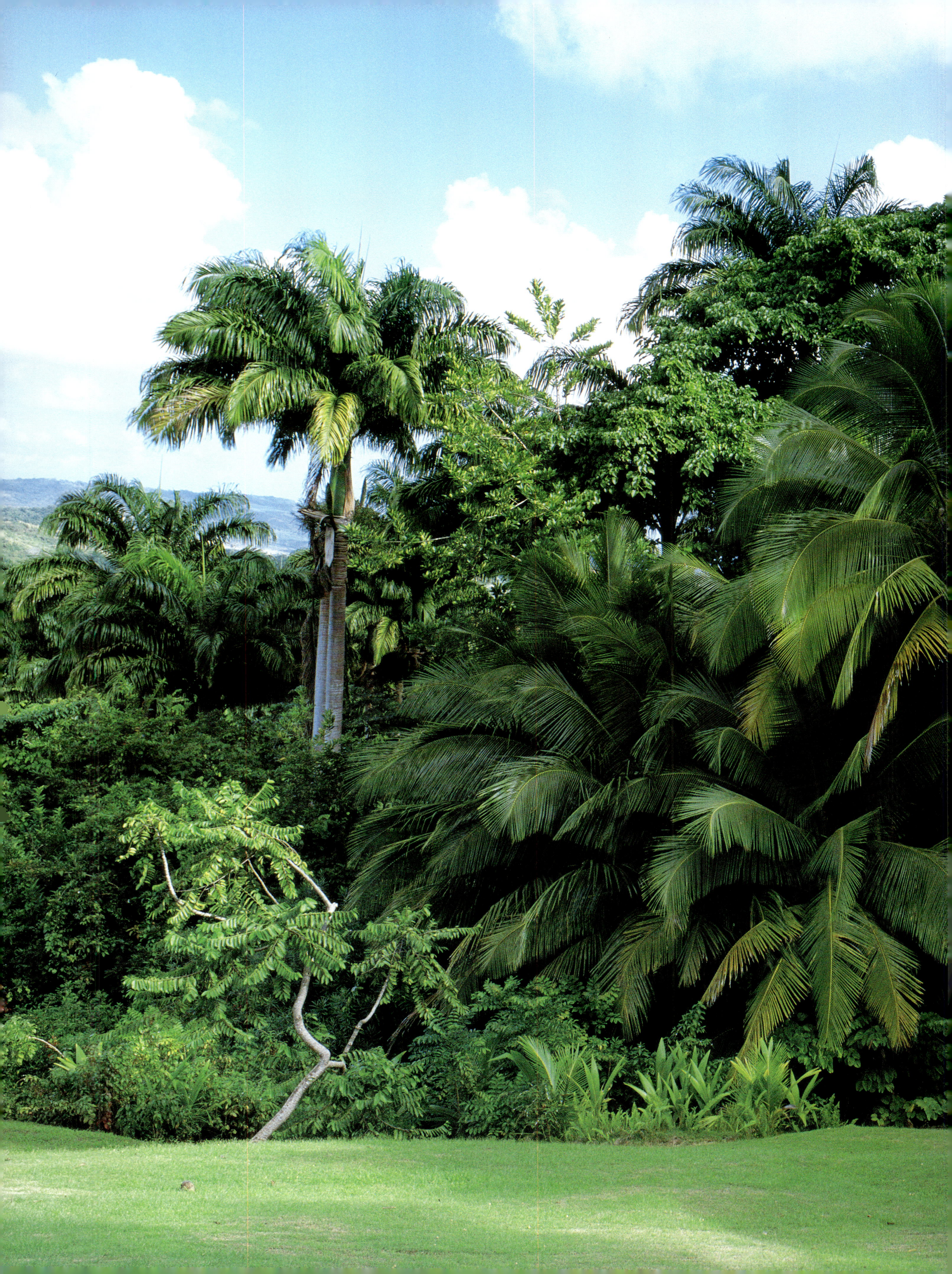

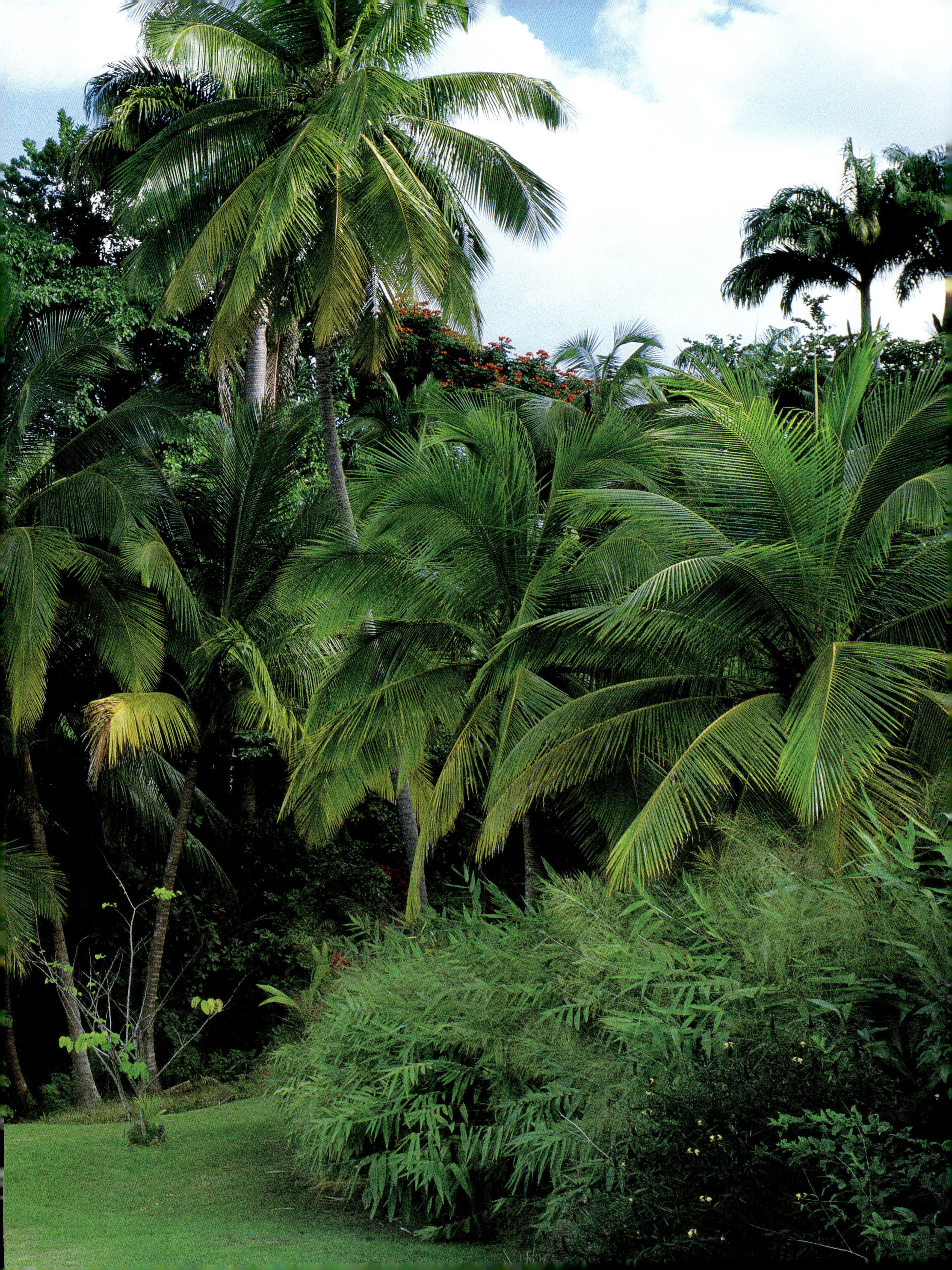

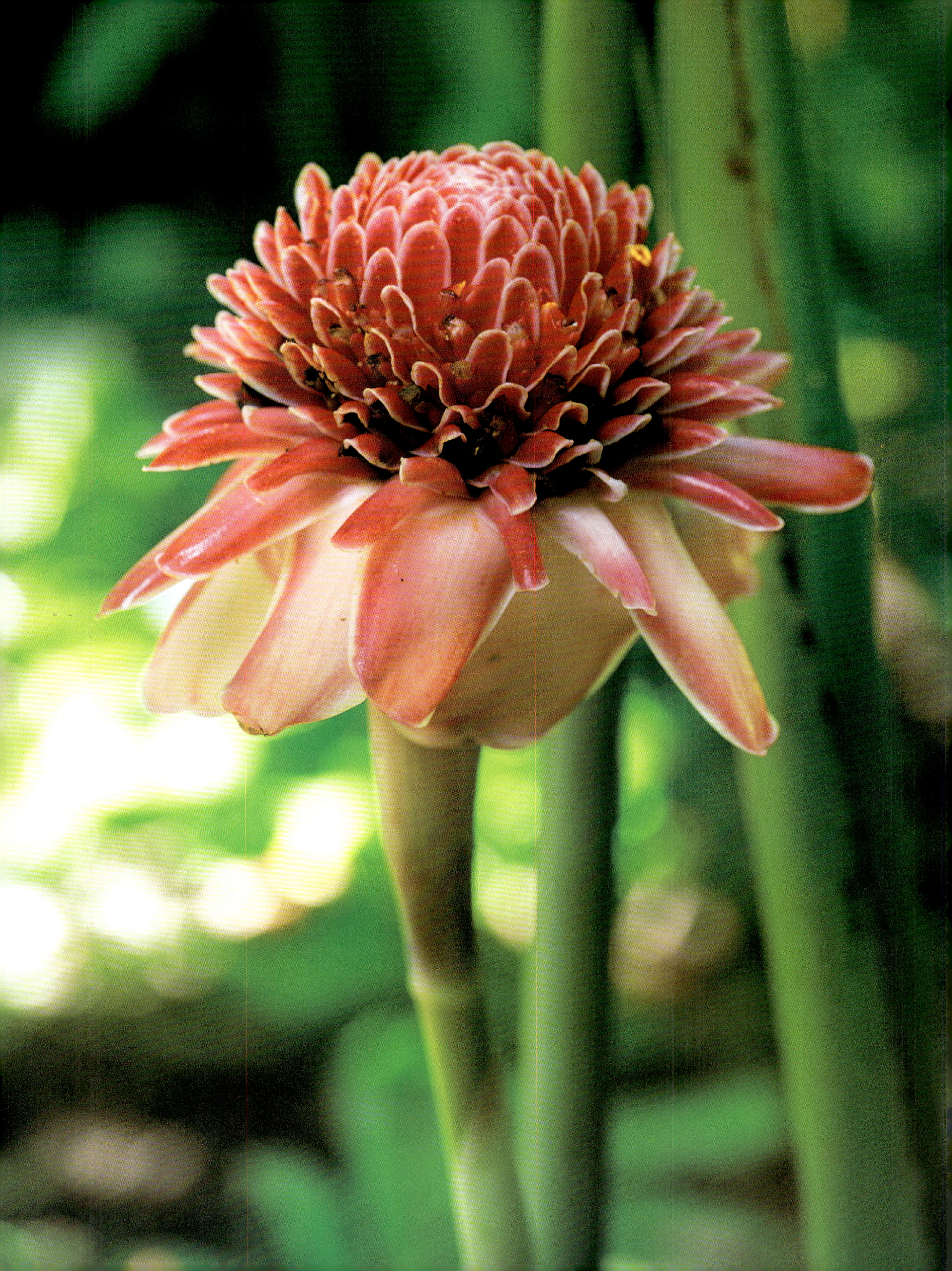

Previous pages: A grove of magnificent palms including Coconut Palms, *Cocos nucifera*, in the foreground and Royal Palms, *Roystonea*, in the background. The large tree behind the Coconut Palms in the center is a Sandbox tree, *Hura crepitans*. The Sandbox is a very large tree that can reach heights in excess of 100 feet and has great spreading branches. The trunk is armed with large conical spines. The seed pods produced are pumpkin-shaped and 3-4 inches across. As the seed pods mature and dry out they explode with a loud bang and disperse their seeds over a very wide area. The segments of the seed pod are often used in the creation of jewelery. A poisonous milky sap is secreted by the tree that is used by Amerindians to poison darts. Left foreground: A small Ylang-ylang tree, *Cananga odorata*, the flowers of which are very fragrant and are used in perfumery. Right foreground: A large clump of the ornamental grass *Panicum virgatum*, in flower • **Opposite**: Torch Ginger, *Etlingera elatior*, sometimes referred to as Porcelain Ginger • **Above**: Golden Trumpet, *Allamanda cathartica* cv; 'Hendersonii'.

Above: Yellow Iris, *Trimezia martinicensis* • **Opposite**: *Hibiscus rosa-sinensis*

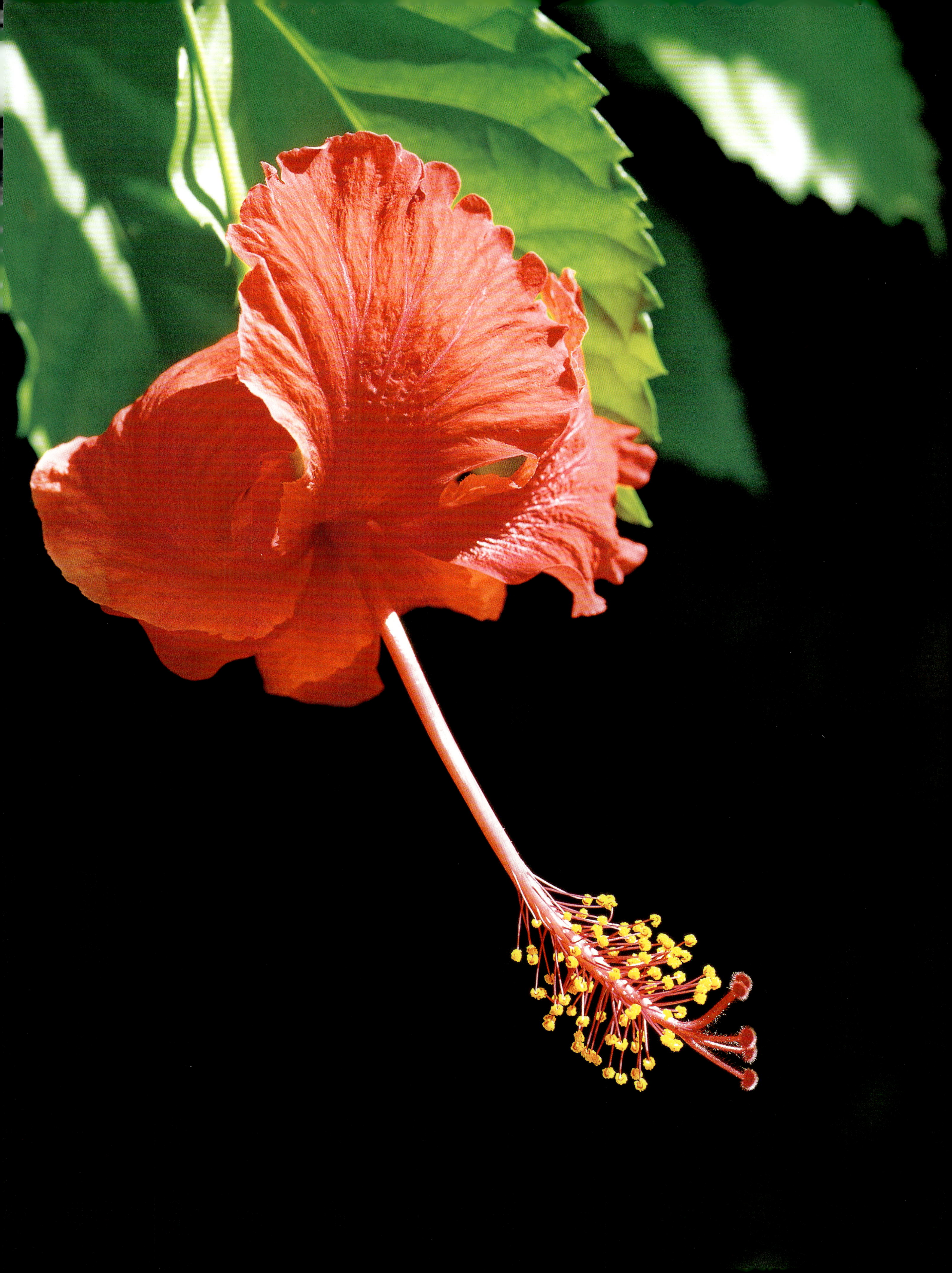

Orchid World

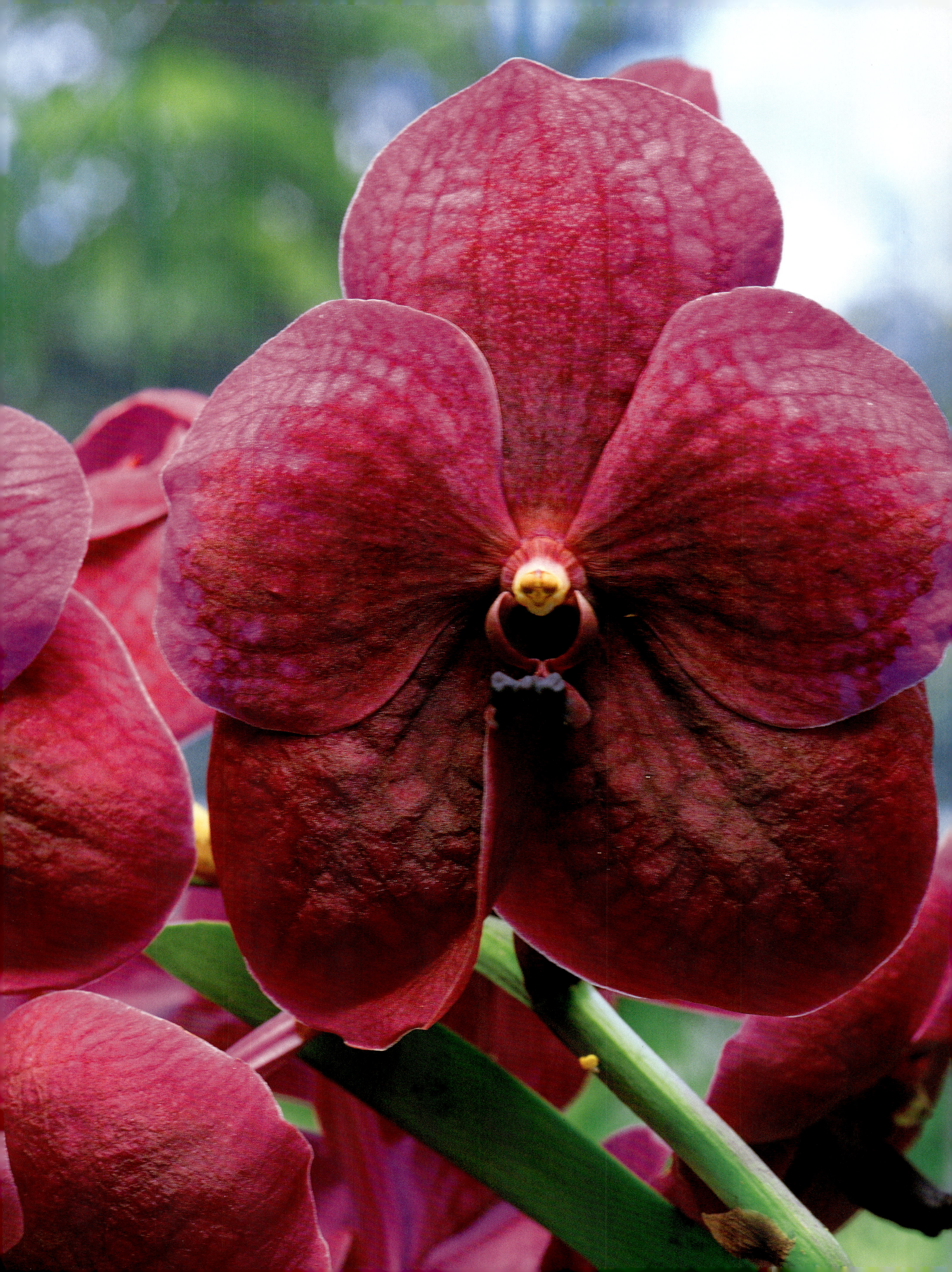

Orchid World, first opened in 1998, is one of the finest orchid gardens in the entire Caribbean. Thousands of orchid enthusiasts from all around the globe visit Orchid World each year, invariably complimenting the owners for the wonderful feat that they have achieved in creating such a beautiful natural environment.

Located in the rural parish of St. Thomas, and perched some 800 feet above sea level, Orchid World benefits from constant cooling breezes and a good average annual rainfall of approximately 80 inches; an essential element for a garden where most of the plants need to be irrigated as often as two to three times per day.

The vast array of orchids on display includes imported varieties, from places such as Thailand, Singapore, Hawaii and the USA, as well as Barbadian grown plants. Orchid World has been very fortunate to benefit from the acquisition of a number of outstanding locally amassed private orchid collections, as well as the donation of many individual plants.

Orchid World has made full use of its existing natural surroundings, as well as tastefully designed supporting structures, to re-create as closely as possible the natural growing conditions most enjoyed by orchids, both the terrestrial varieties and the epiphytes, which usually grow on other plants with no contact with the ground.

Above: Orchids growing outdoors at Orchid World. Dark pink flowers are Mokaras with quarter-terete vandas behind
Opposite: Ascocenda Tubtim Velvet x Vanda Kasem's Delight, a strap-leaf ascocenda hybrid

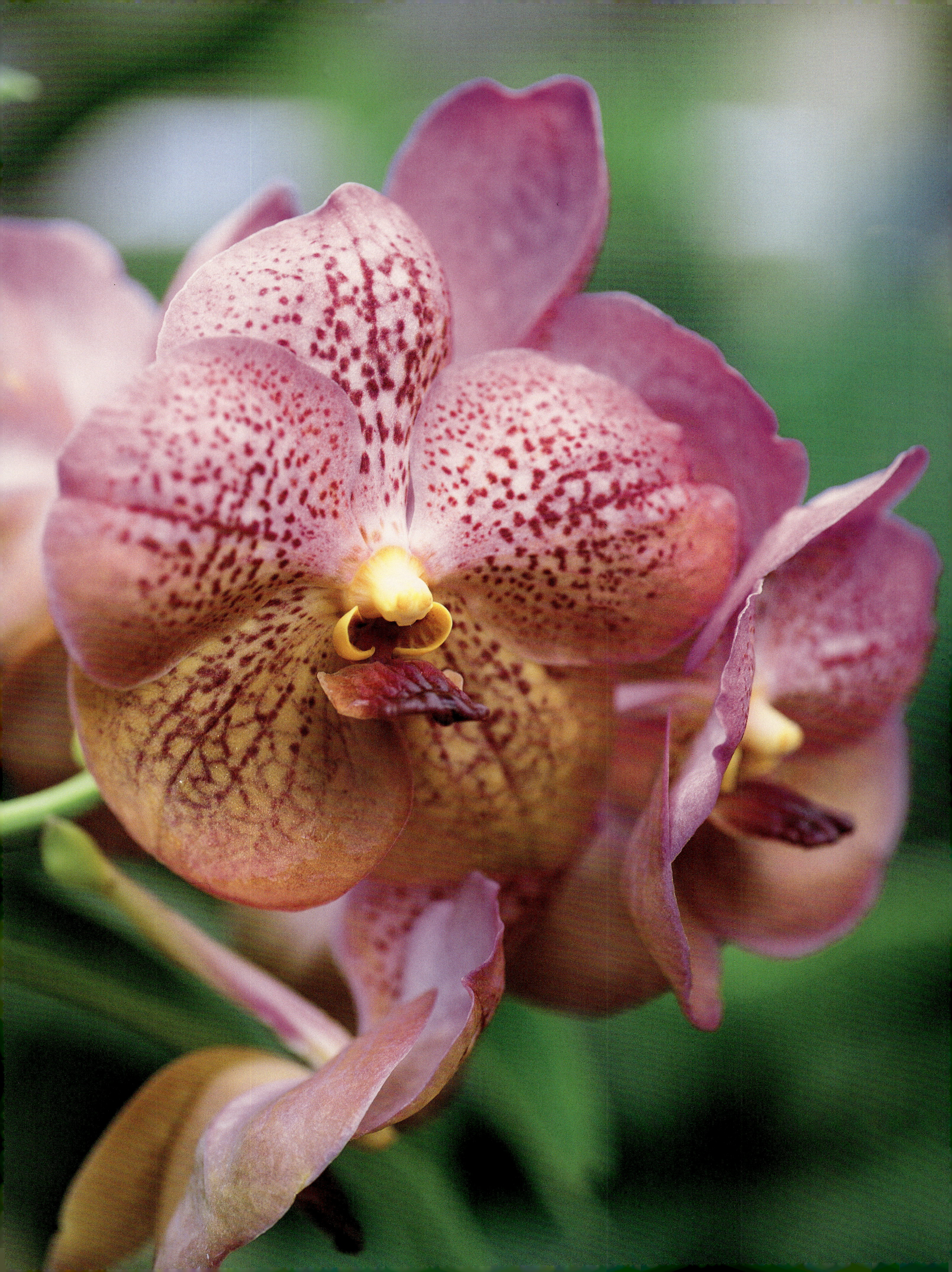

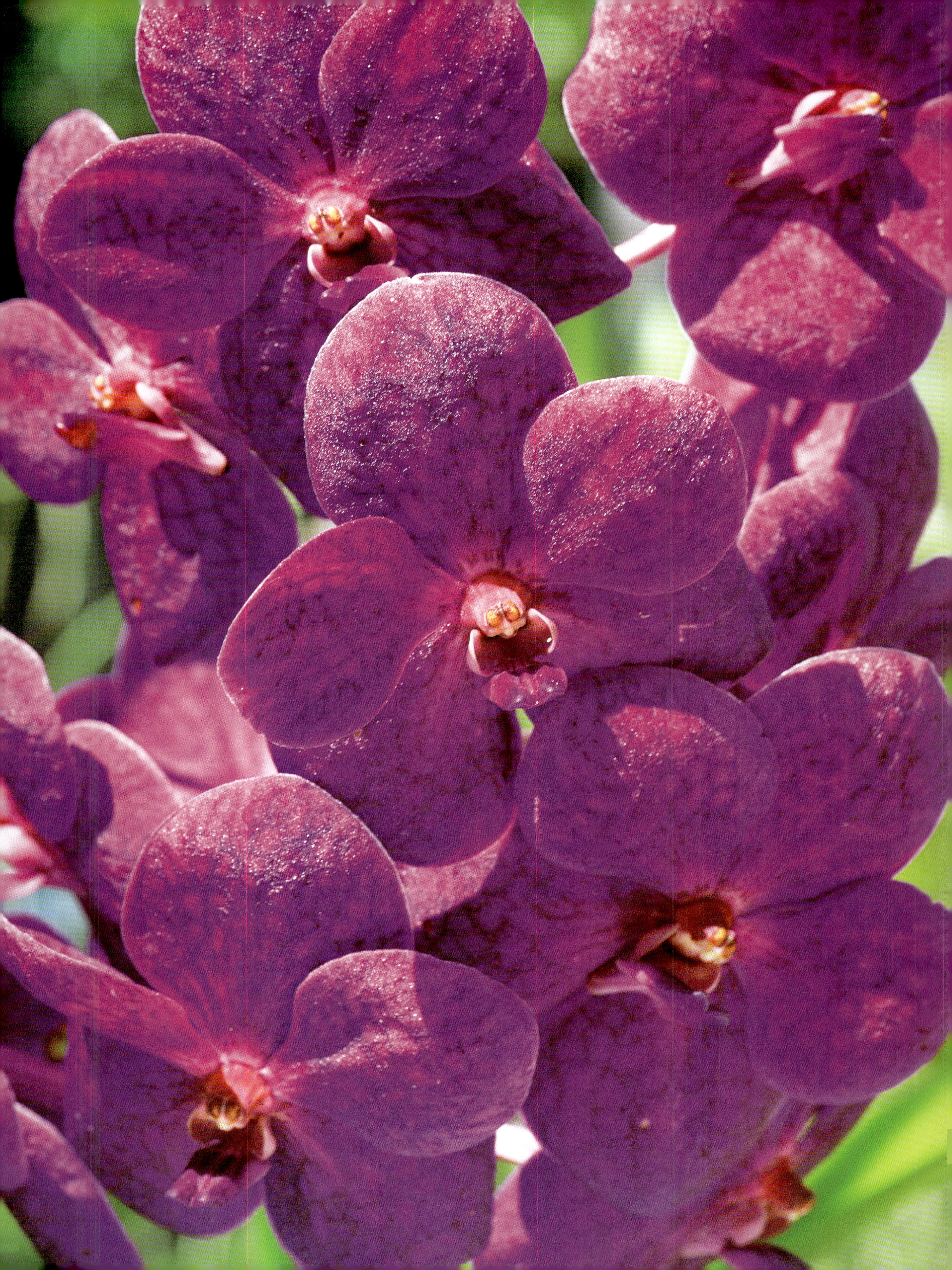

Opposite: Ascocenda Yip Sum Wah × Vanda coerulea, a strap-leaf ascocenda hybrid • **Above clockwise from top left**: Potinara Twenty-Four Carat 'Lea', A Potinara hybrid; Striped Phaleaenopsis hybrid; Standard white Phalaenopsis hybrid; Mokara Chark Kuan

Above: View inside Orchid World • **Opposite**: Mokara Madame Panni

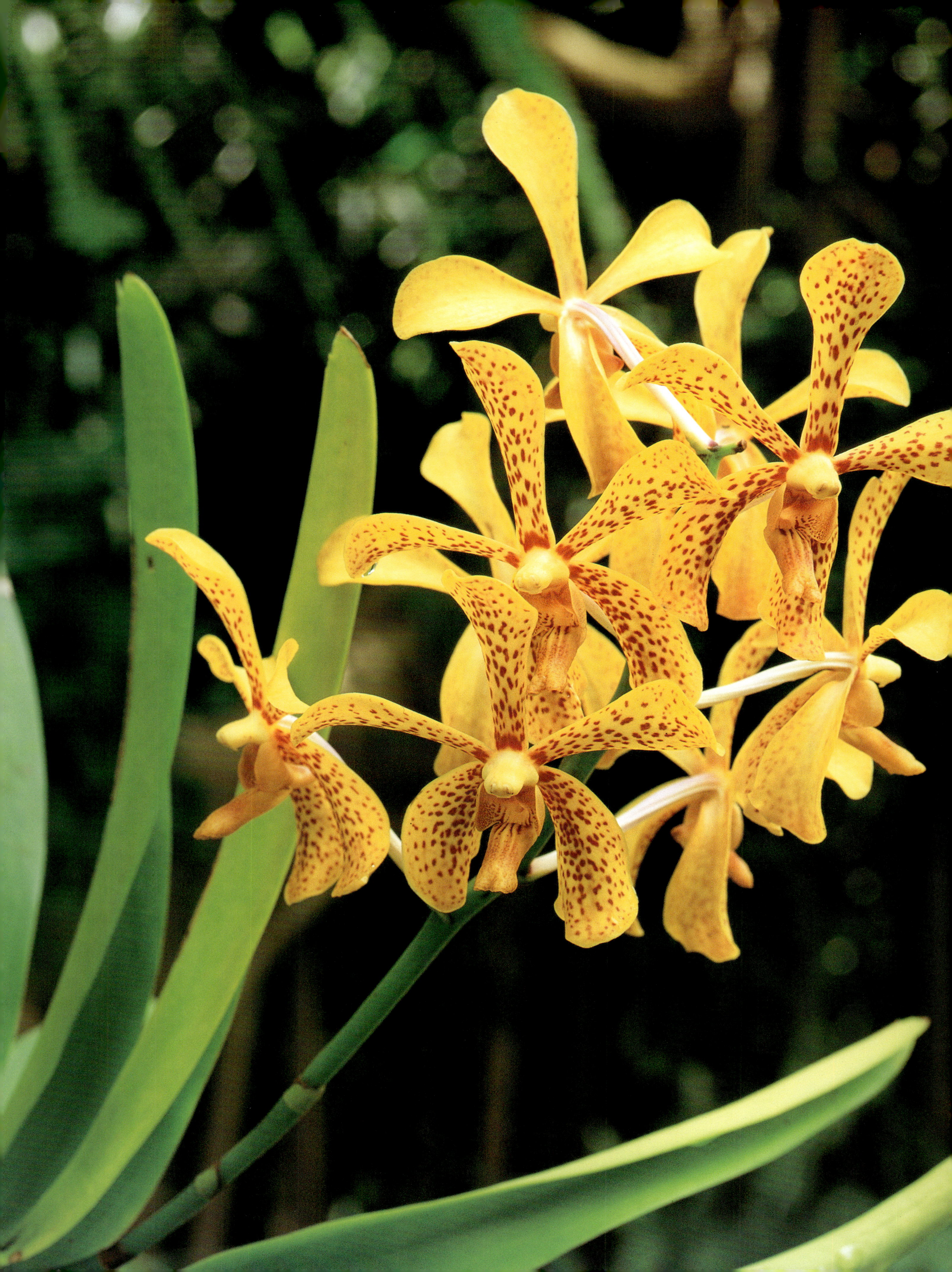

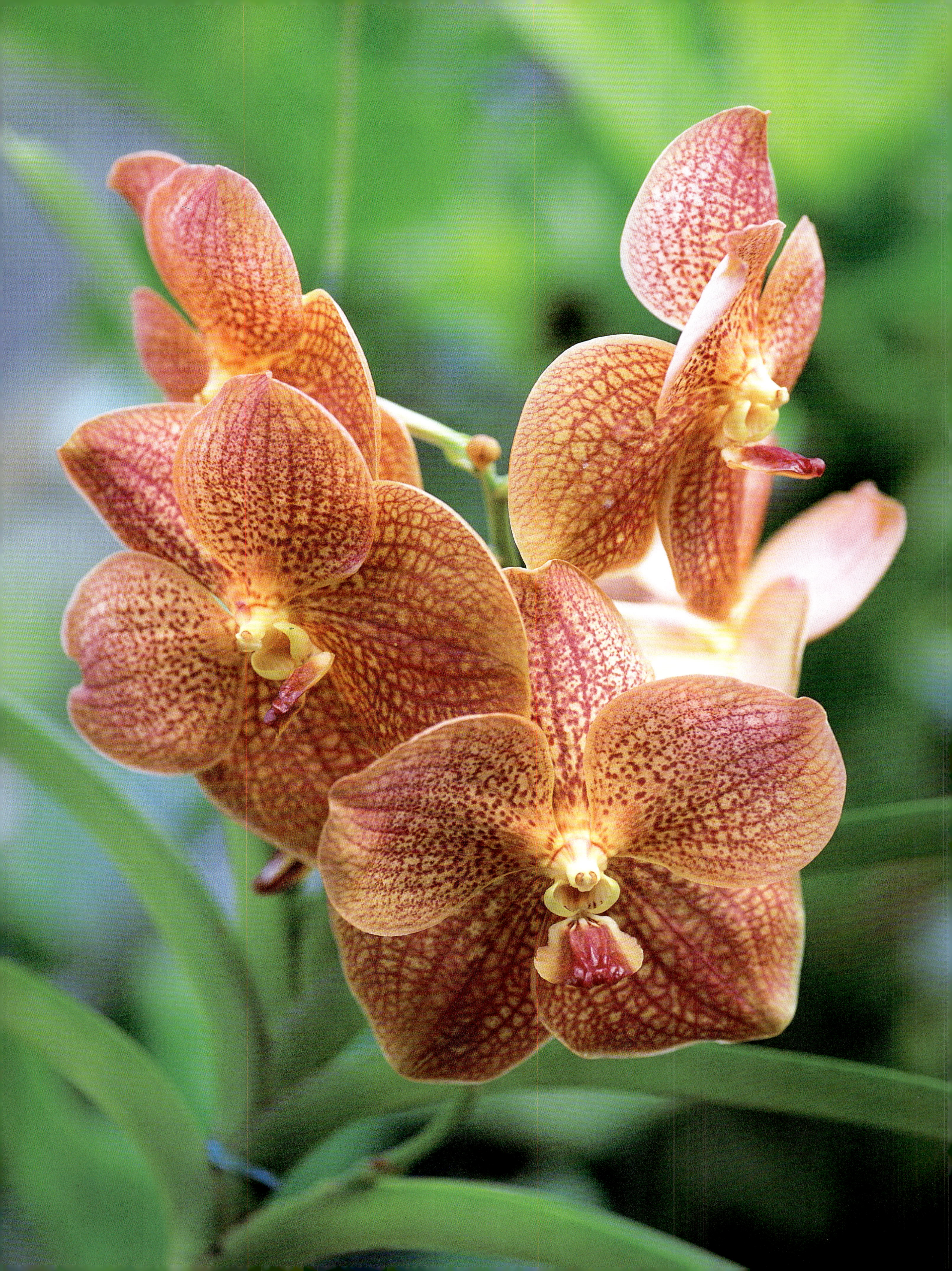

Opposite: Strap-leaf ascocenda hybrid • **Above**: Orchids growing outdoors at Orchid World. Mokara Madame Panni in the foreground with quarter-terete vanda hybrids in the background

ORCHIDS IN BARBADOS

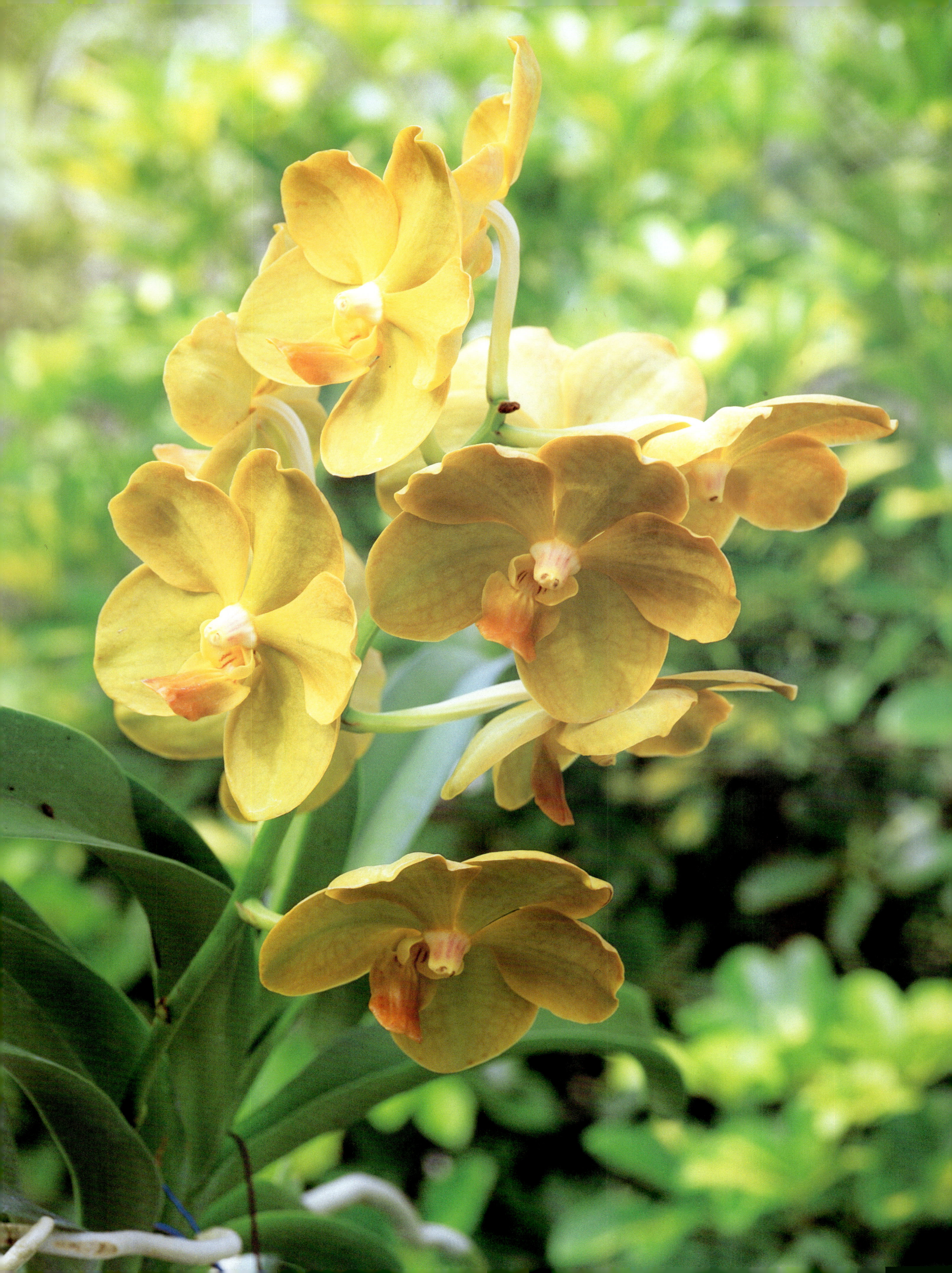

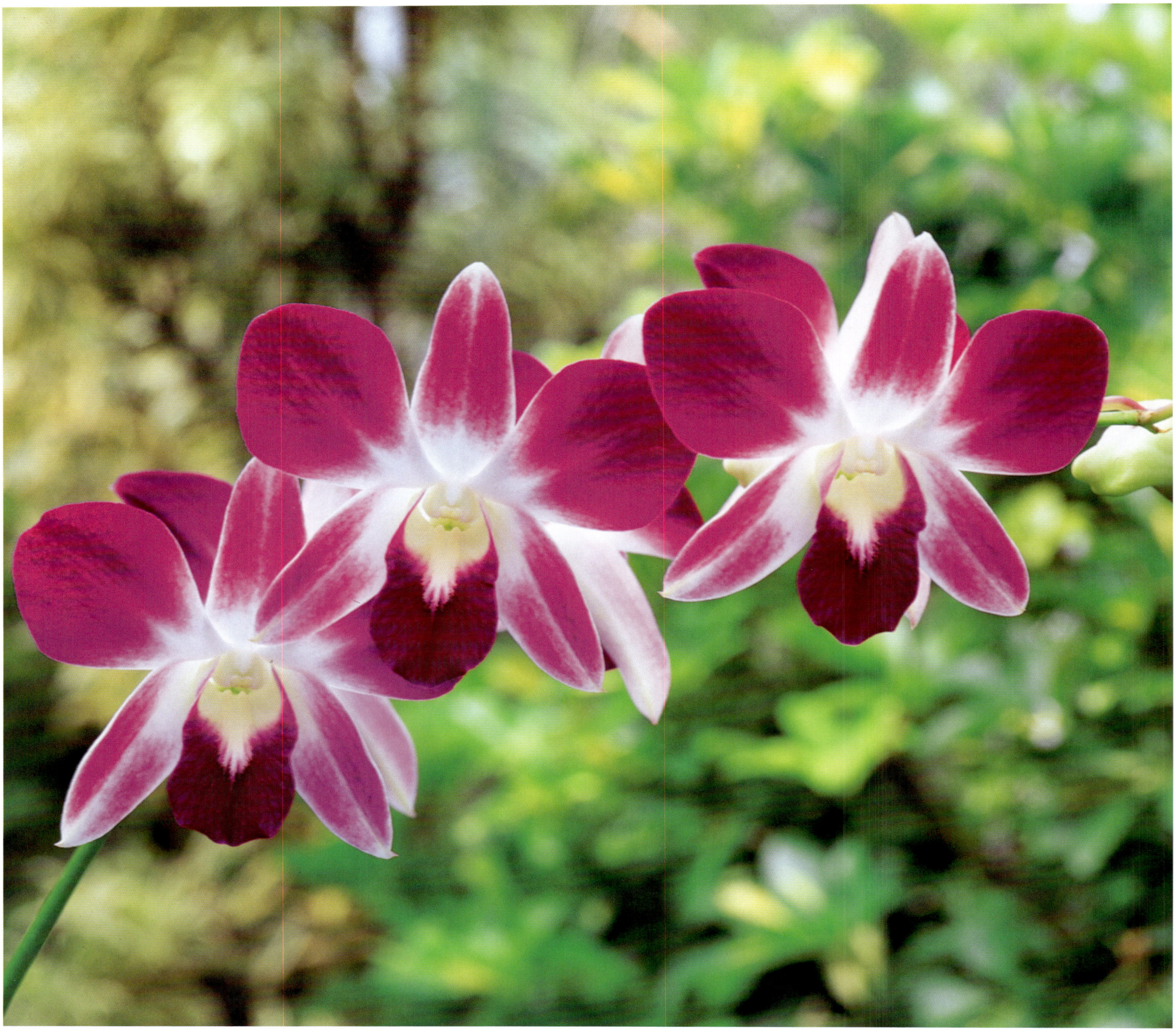

Opening page: Ascocenda Motes Tangelo • **Opposite:** Dendrobium Sonia, a well known cut-flower Dendrobium • **Above:** Vanda Gordon Dillon. A well known strap-leaf vanda hybrid developed in Thailand in the 1960's and named after the first secretary of the American Orchid Society

Above: Rhyncostylis gigantea • **Opposite**: Brassidium Gilded Urchin 'Ontario'. This hybrid is well known for its long spidery petals and sepals

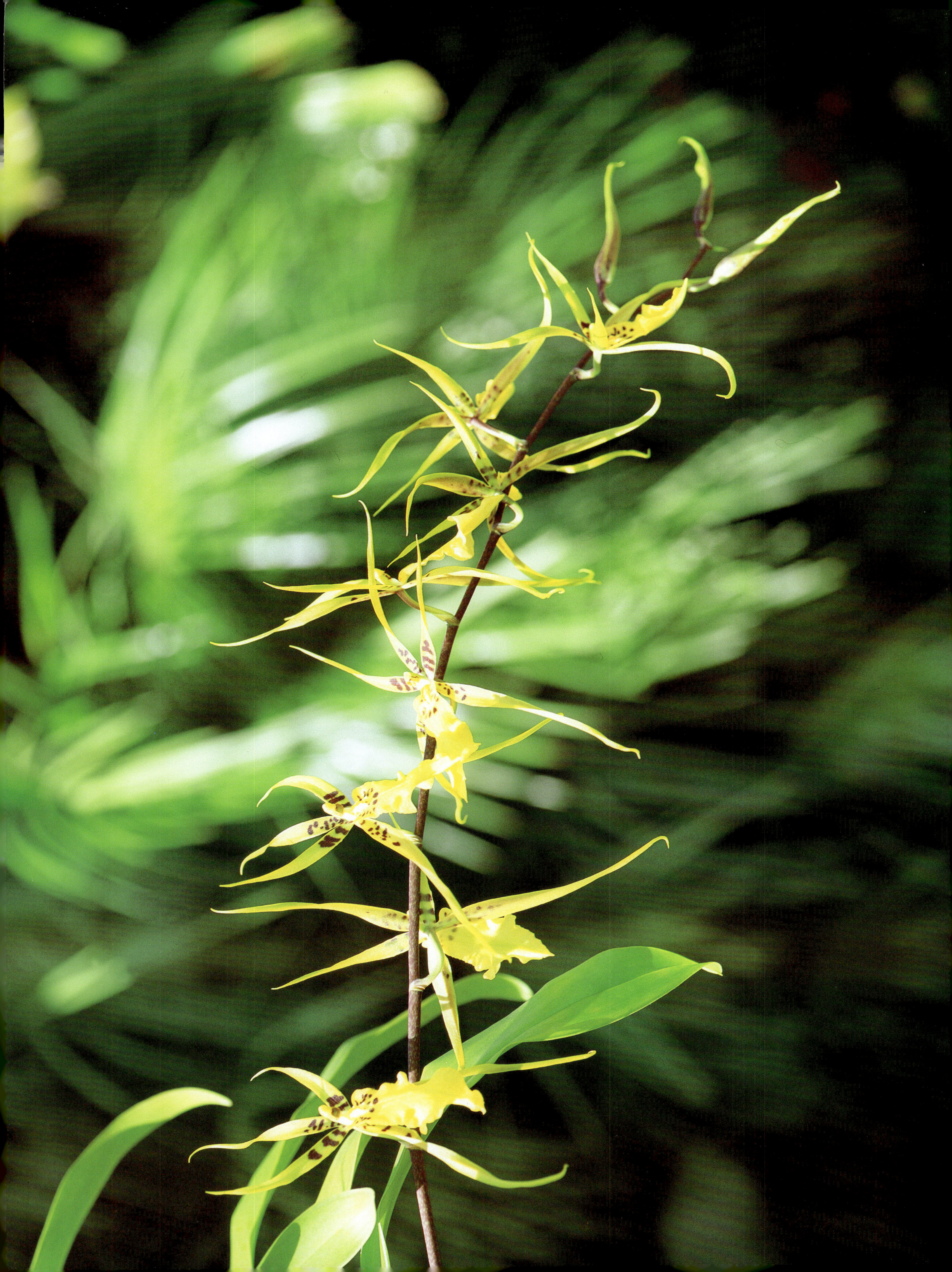

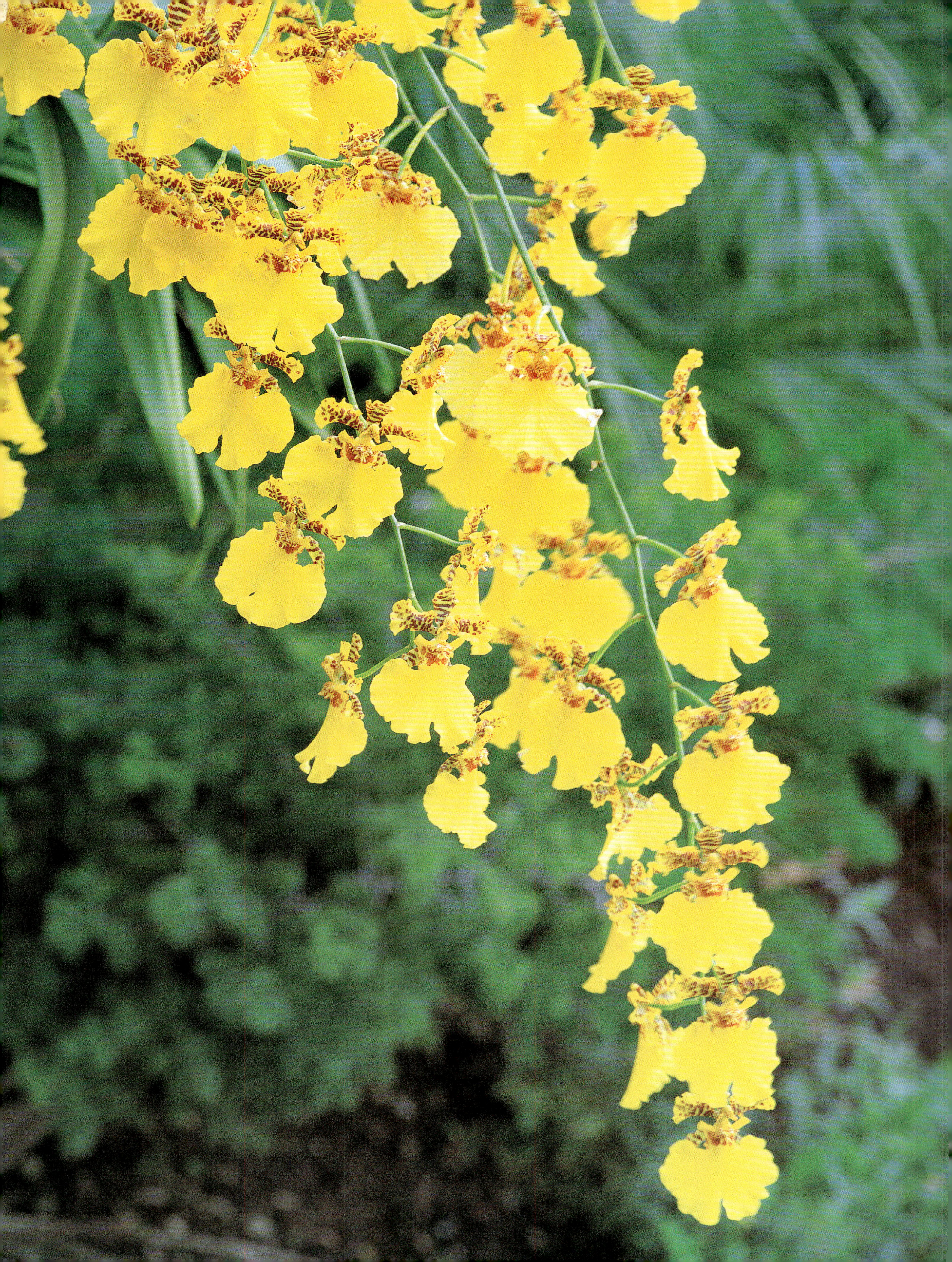

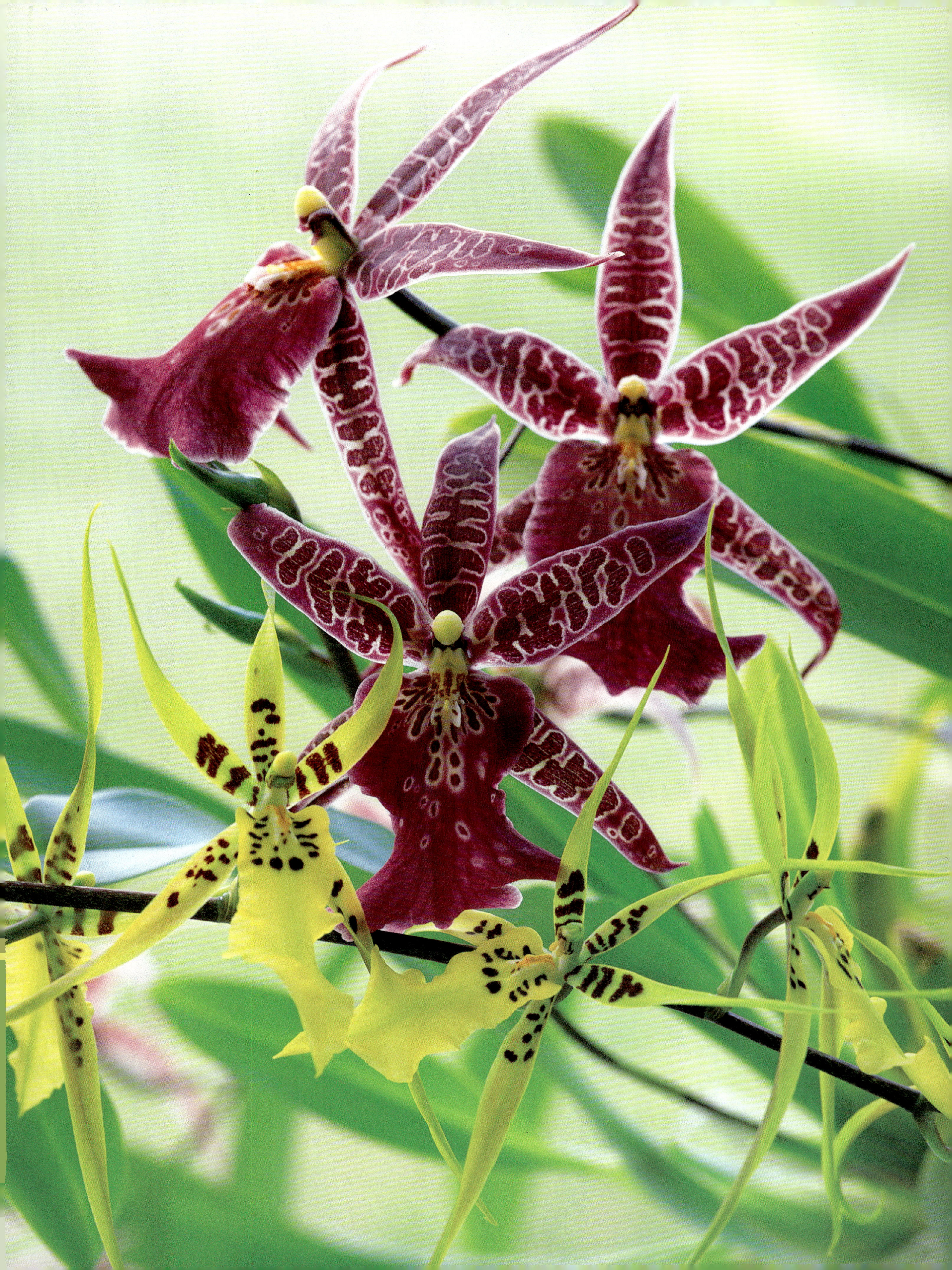

Previous page left: Oncidium Sweet Sugar • **Previous page right**: Miltassia Aztec 'Nalo' - background, Brassidium Gilded Urchin 'Ontario' - foreground • **Above**: Phalanenopsis Minho Princess. A novelty type of phaleanopsis gaining in popularity today • **Opposite**: Phalaenopsis hybrid

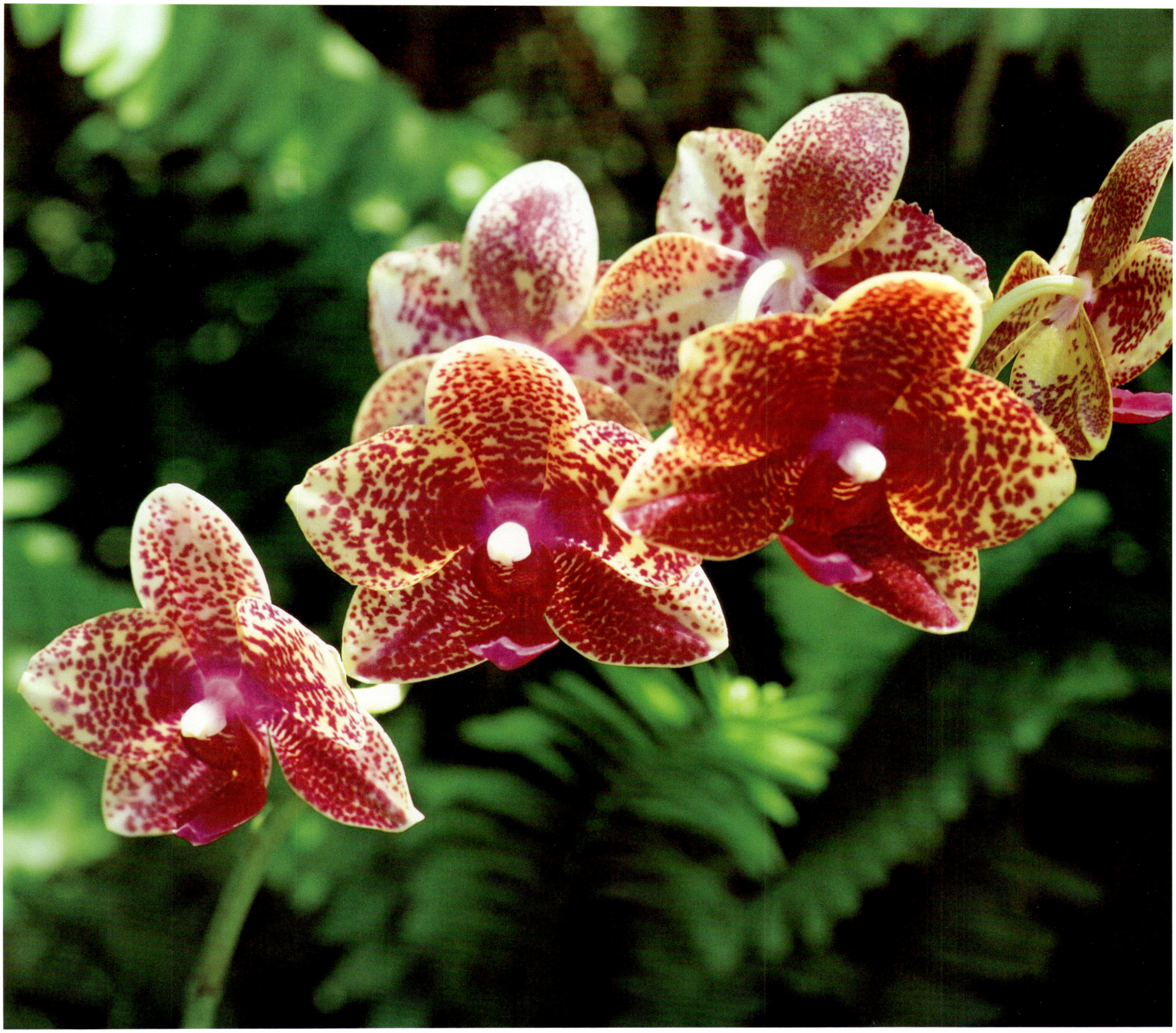

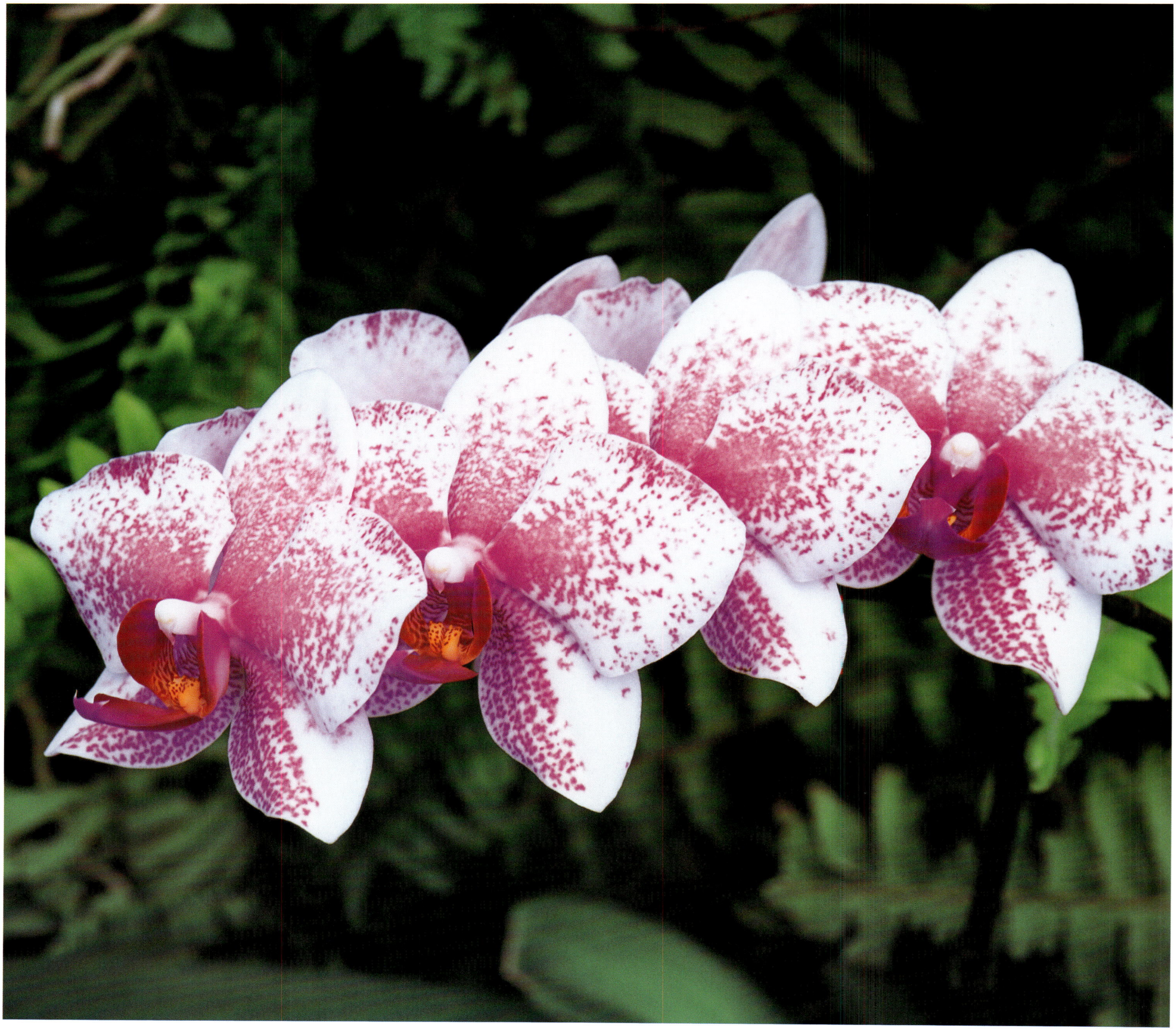

Opposite: Phalaenopsis hybrid • **Above**: Mokara Chark Kuan

PALMS IN BARBADOS

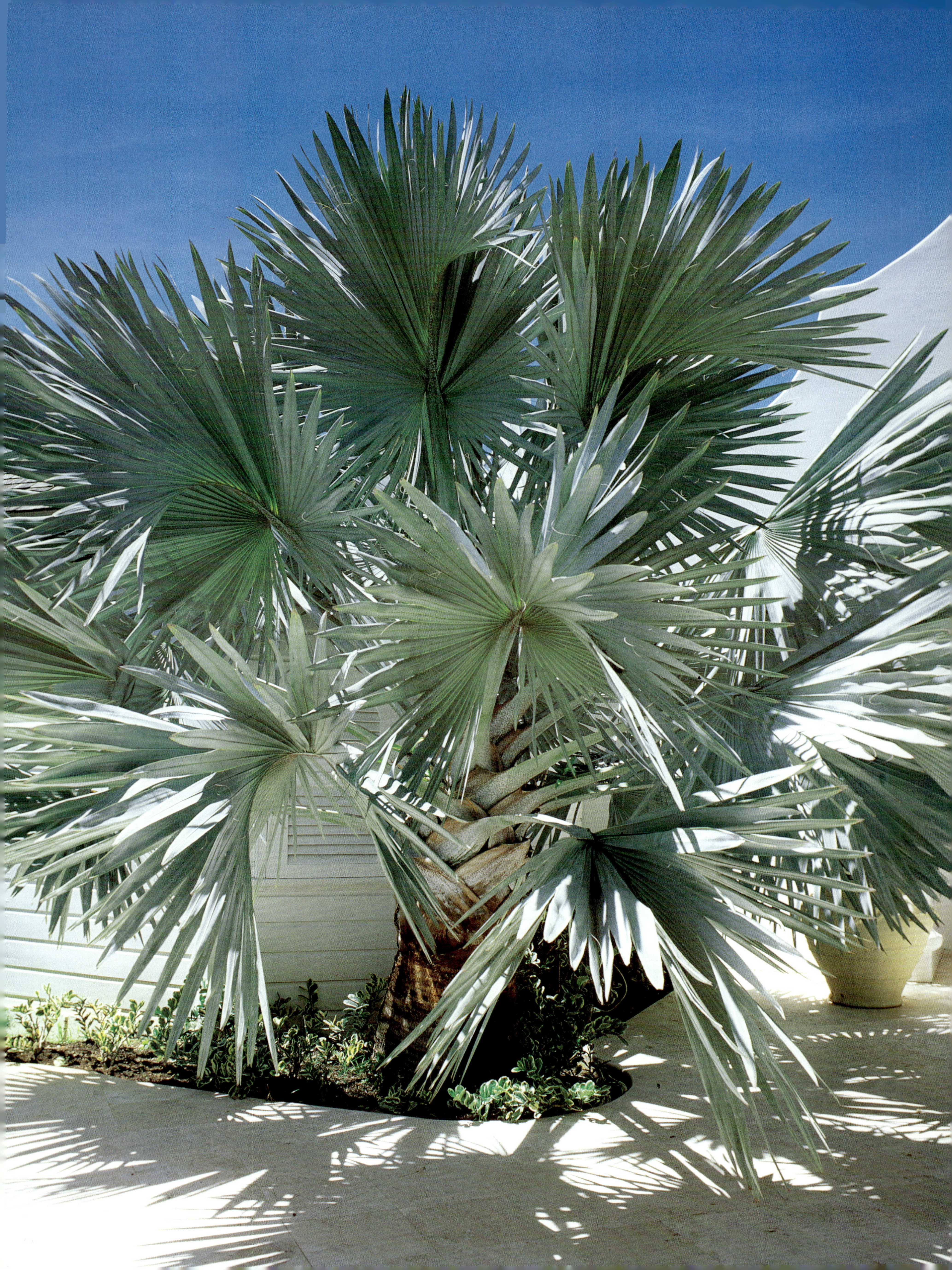

Until modern times there were only a few kinds of palms commonly found in gardens in Barbados, with the most evident being the indigenous varieties such as the West Indian Royal Palm (*Roystonea oleracea*), the Lesser Antilles Thatch Palm (*Coccothrinax barbadensis*), the Silver Thatch Palm (*Thrinax excelsa*) and, of course, the king of them all, The Coconut Palm (*Cocos nucifera*).

Several other varieties, including the Macaw Palm (*Aiphanes minima*) and the Gru Gru (*Acrocomia aculeate*), were generally found in gullies but not often used in landscaping due to the proliferation of thorns on their trunks and leaves.

However, as interest in gardening and landscaping grew in Barbados then so did the demand for a greater variety of palms, thus leading to the introduction of a much wider range of exotic varieties. This list of new arrivals featured many of today's more popular palms, most notably the Golden Palm (*Dypsis lutescens*), the Macarthur Palm (*Ptychosperma macarthurii*), the Solitary Palm (*Ptychosperma elegans*), the Clustering Fishtail (*Caryota mitis*) and the Queen Palm (*Syagrus romanzoffiana*).

Today, through the importation of palm seeds, the island has acquired over a hundred more different introduced varieties from around the world. Indeed, as palms are now being used more and more in landscape gardening, certain varieties are grown for specific purposes. Thus the local supply can now offer specimen palms, salt-tolerant palms, shade-tolerant palms; palms for hedges, ground cover or interior use; and palms of a variety of colours, shape and size for just about every use in any landscape.

Opening page: Bismarck Palm, *Bismarckia nobilis*. The Bismarck Palm, a native of Madagascar, is one of the more recent additions to the Landscape Designer's palette in Barbados. Provided they are located in a sunny area, given sufficient root room and water, they are large, fast growing, spectacular fan palms that are well worthy of a prominent position in any garden that can accommodate them. They are planted in locations where the designer wants to make a 'statement'. They do however require a lot of room for growth as the large blue-coloured leaves can expand to 10 feet across, and within 5 years the plant can attain a height of 25 feet and a similar width. The Bismark Palm is also available in a less attractive green form. • **Above**: Chinese Fan Palm, *Livistona chinensis*, in the centre, with a young Fiji Fan Palm, *Pritchardia pacifica*, to the right, and a grouping of Solitary Palms, *Ptychosperma elegans* to the left. Chinese Fan Palms are extremely adaptable palms, lending themselves for use as beautiful container plants in their early years and are suitable for both full sun and shaded landscapes. In this setting, where there is moderate to heavy shade, dependent on the time of the year, an extremely graceful growth habit has developed with long slender petioles of 8-10 feet in length and a deep green leaf colour. Contrast this growth habit with that of a Chinese Fan Palm later in this section that has been grown in full sun.

• **Opposite**: West Indian Royal Palms, *Roystonea oleracea*, creating a magnificently lined avenue for this driveway. They are underplanted with Yuccas or Spanish Bayonet, *Yucca aloifolia*, and numerous other plants, thereby creating a very tropical entrance to this property. The classic use of West Indian Royals in Barbados over the last 200 plus years, has been in the lining of driveways to many of the stately mansions and plantation great houses. West Indian Royals, which are indigenous to the Caribbean, are tall palms, achieving heights in excess of 100 feet, and as tall as 130 feet under ideal situations, with a trunk diameter of 2 feet. They therefore need to be carefully sited in the landscape.

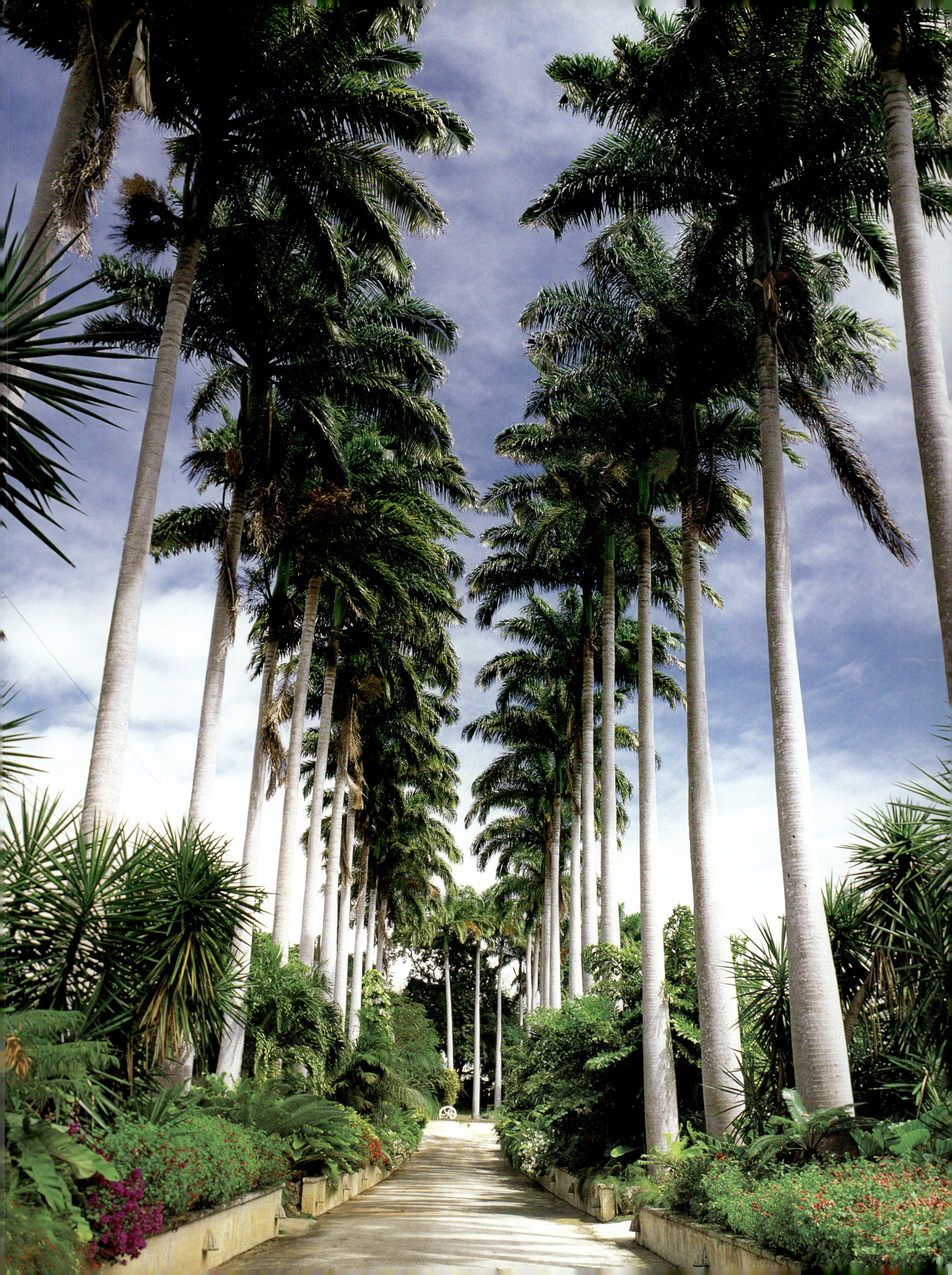

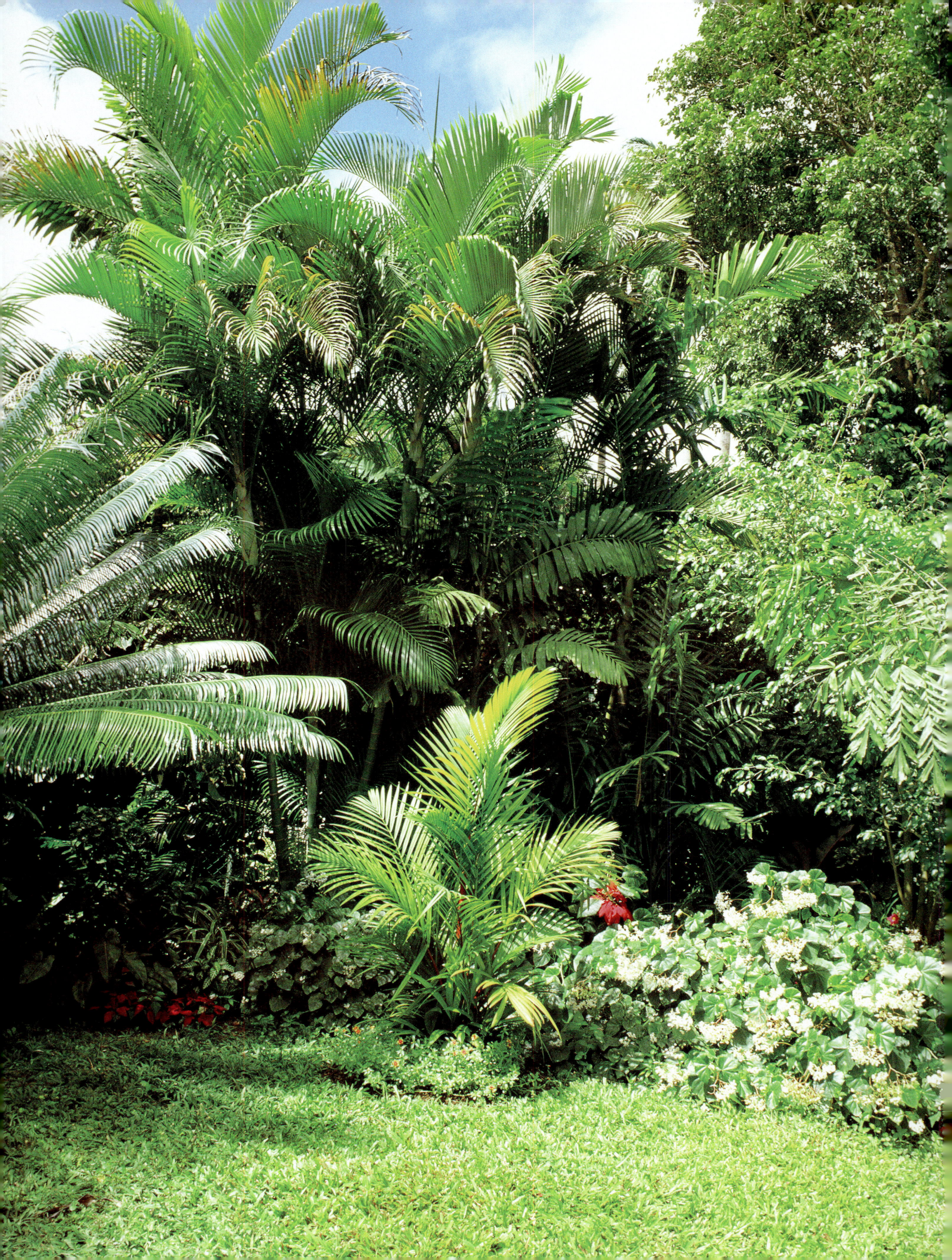

Opposite: A young Sealing Wax or Lipstick Palm, Cyrtostachys renda, enjoys a place of honour in front of a clump of Golden Palms, Dypsis lutescens, to the left and a clump of Macarthur Palms, Ptychosperma macarthurii, on the right. The leaves of a Sago Palm, Cycas circinalis overhang on the left while those of a Solitary Fishtail Palm, Caryota urens, overhang on the right. The Sealing Wax palm is a much sought-after palm on account of the incredible red colour of its petioles and leaf bases. Unfortunately, it is a very challenging palm to grow successfully in Barbados as a result of the high calcium content of our soils and the resulting high soil pH. Sealing Wax palms originated in the swampy coastal areas of Thailand and Malaysia. They therefore thrive under very wet acidic soil conditions, quite the opposite situation to that which prevails in Barbados. In order to grow the Sealing Wax successfully in Barbados an artificial environment must be created to mimic those conditions of its origin. The palm also requires regular treatment with chelated iron and other soil amendments to keep it looking in peak condition. An excellent specimen has been grown for years at Andromeda Gardens and is featured in that section of this book • **Above**: A spectacular view of a Talipot Palm, Corypha umbraculifera. Talipot Palms are GIGANTIC palms. The leaves attain a diameter of up to 20 feet and are borne on very stout petioles, 10-12 feet long which are armed with black teeth. Although slow growing, the trunks reach heights of 90 feet and a diameter of 3 feet, and support a crown of 40-50 feet in diameter. The Talipot are monocarpic palms that die once they have flowered, but they go out in style. When they flower they produce the largest inforescence in the plant kingdom, 20-25 feet tall and containing millions of flowers, right out of the crown of the palm, sticking straight up. It is truly a spectacle once seen, never forgotten. These are obviously not palms for the average garden, but rather for estates or parks with lots of room. This spectacular specimen exists at Andromeda Gardens.

Above clockwise from top left: Base of the crown of a Triangle Palm, *Dypsis decaryi*; Close up of a Skyduster Palm, *Washingtonia robusta*; Close up of the trunk of a Golden Palm, *Dypsis lutescens*; Close up of the underside of the Red Latan Palm, *Latania lontaroides* • **Opposite**: A cluster of immature West Indian Royal Palms, *Roystonea oleracea,* and Solitary Palms, *Ptychosperma elegans*. The Solitary Palm is truly an elegant palm, befitting of its Latin name, and is used extensively in landscaping in Barbados. It flowers regularly and the resulting large bunches of small red fruit add striking splashes of red to the landscape. The fruit are enjoyed by the wild Ramier pigeons, *Columba squamosa*

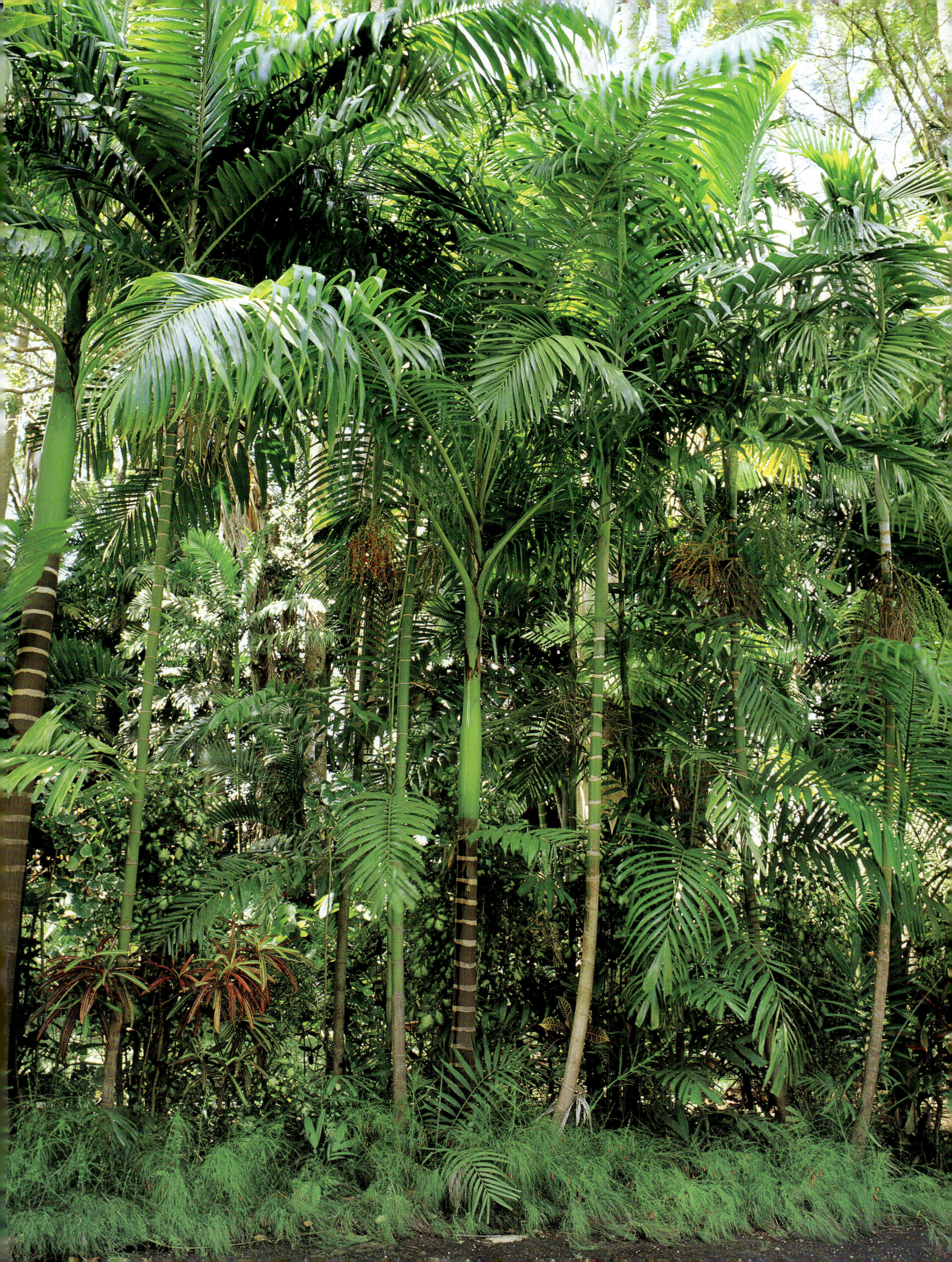

Above left: Senegal Date Palm, *Phoenix reclinata*, which traditionally grows along rivers and streams and in clearings in the rain forest in Tropical Africa, has been used in landscaping in Barbados for many years. Its use however has been limited since, like most *Phoenix species* it is very spiny, and as a clustering palm produces almost impenetrable thickets if left unpruned. However, in the right location and with periodic pruning, it becomes a very handsome palm, and one that can be used as an attractive, but impenetrable, hedge if plants are located close enough together. • **Above Right** - Barbados Fan Palm, or Thatch Palm, Cocothrinax barbadensis. An important plant to Barbados as it is indigenous and is one of very few plants that carry the name of Barbados – barbadensis. It is now considered a threatened species in the wild. In the 17th century, Ligon in his History of Barbados described it as the "Palmetto the Lesse" and considered it a common plant of the littoral forest. Limited numbers of the species exist in the gullies of Barbados. It was much prized for thatching. In St Lucia it is referred to as the "Latanye" and is the mainstay of local broom production and other craft manufacturing. At the current rate of harvesting (2000) the industry was not considered to be sustainable with the existing stock of trees. It is a very adaptable palm and makes an excellent container plant for use in the house or on the porch. In the landscape it is a very beautiful palm and will eventually reach heights of about 40 feet under ideal conditions.

Above left: Clustering Fishtail Palm, *Caryota mitis*, a native of the tropical rainforests of India, Indonesia and the Philippines, has long been a staple in landscape design in Barbados. It is fast growing, very easy to grow and since it clusters, the size of the clump of palms increases with age. However, like all *Caryota* species, the Clustering Fishtail palm is monocarpic, which means that once the stems have flowered and fruited, they die off. Flowering normally starts at the leaf node at the top of the plant and proceeds downwards to the node at the base of the plant. This process usually takes several years. In a multi-stemmed palm, such as this, the death of a stem is insignificant as the plant is always producing more stems to take its place. A word of caution about the seeds. The seeds of all *Caryota* species have high levels of oxalic acid crystals which are a severe irritant to the skin and mucous membranes, and can result in severe pain and discomfort if handled incorrectly. This should be borne in mind when placing these palms in the landscape, especially where children are involved. • **Above Right**: Fiji Fan Palm, *Pritchardia pacifica*, a native of the Tonga Islands and arguably one of the most beautiful fan palms available. The Fiji Fan Palm has been used as a landscape plant in Barbados for generations. It is very fast growing, requires little care, and is especially attractive when planted in odd-numbered groups of 3 or 5 palms. The sound of a breeze rushing over and around the leaves adds a special tonal quality to the landscape where these palms are used!

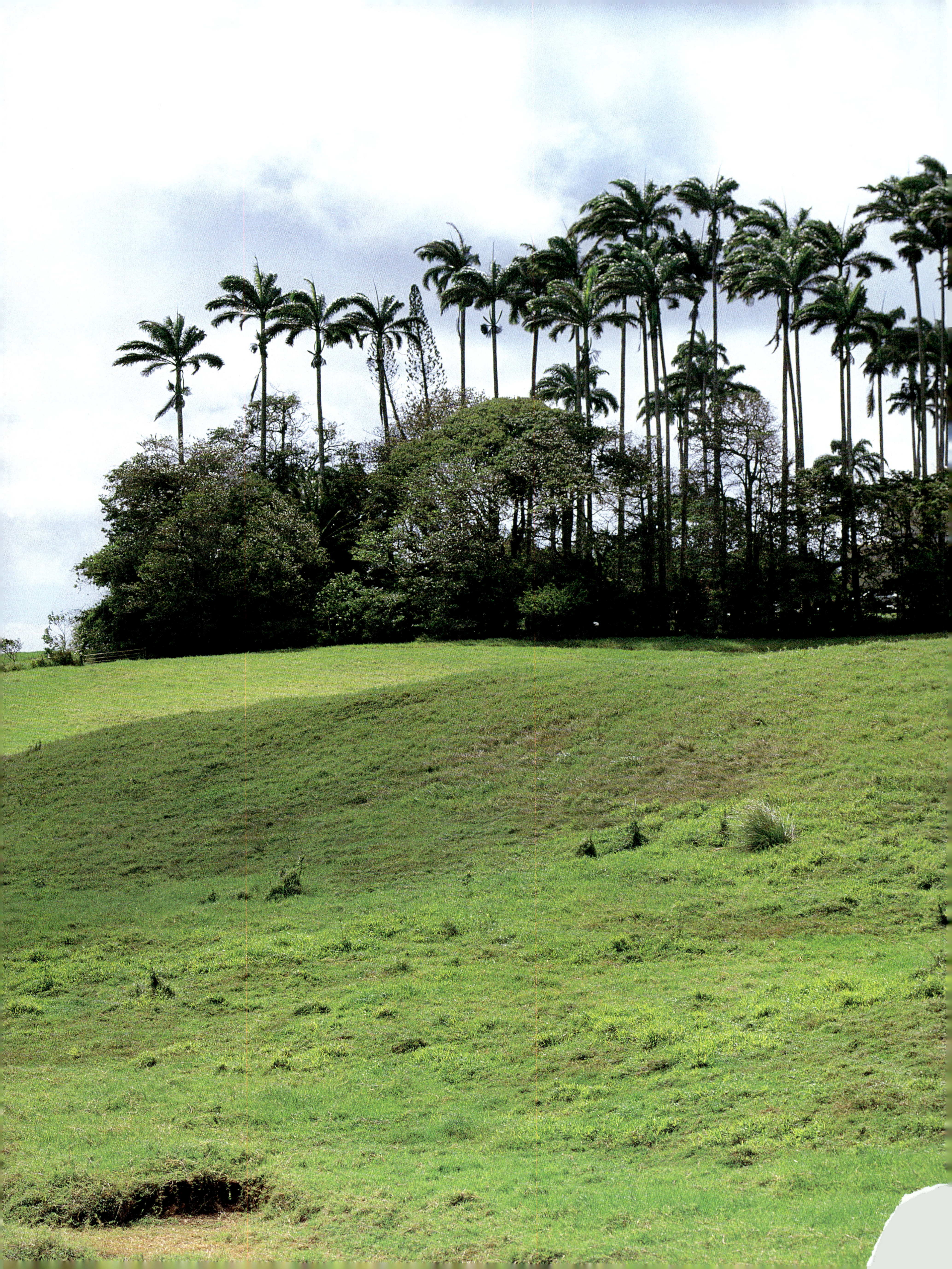

Opposite: West Indian Royal Palms, *Roystonea oleracea*, silhouetted against the skyline. • **Clockwise from Top left** - *Phoenix* hybrid - a local hybridization between the Date Palm, *Phoenix dactylifera*, and the Canary Islands Date Palm, *Phoenix canariensis*, has produced this very attractive plant. The resulting plant has retained much of the bluish colour of *P. dactylifera* but has lost the very stiff leaflets of that species. The leaflets of the hybrid have a much softer texture and gives the plant a slightly weeping appearance. There are 13 members in the genus *Phoenix*, all of which hybridise freely with each other. This results in considerable variability in size, texture, form and colour of the resulting hybrids, particularly in seeds collected from cultivated specimens, grown in environments with more than one species of *Phoenix*; **Top right** - Chinese Fan Palm, *Livistona chinensis* – this specimen has been grown in full sun and has produced a much tighter crown than the specimen in an earlier photo in this section which has grown in a shaded environment; **Bottom right** - A pair of Gru Gru Palms, *Acrocomia aculeate* – a very spiny but attractive palm that on account of its armament has seen limited use in landscaping projects. Most specimens are found in collectors' gardens and occasionally in some of the gullies of Barbados. It is however a very common palm in the natural landscape of many of the other islands of the Caribbean and is seeing an increased usage in landscaping projects in St Vincent. **Bottom left** - Queen Palm, *Syagrus romanzoffiana* – a very popular landscape palm in Barbados which is used primarily because of its long, very gracefully drooping, plumose leaves. Once mature it flowers and fruits profusely, producing large numbers of round one inch diameter fruit. Some persons consider this to be a nuisance requiring constant sweeping and cleaning, depending on where the palm has been located.

Index

Acalypha godseffiana - 15, 19, 34, 135
Acalypha wilkesiana - 15, 62, 125
Acrocomia aculeate - 197
Adenanthera pavonina - 148
Adenium obesum – 23, 52, 83, 118
Adiantum sp - 19
Adonidia merrillii - 91
African Tulip Tree, see *Spathodea campanulata* - 113
Agave horrida - 43
Aglaonemas - 70
Aiphanes minima – 140, 148
Allamanda - 23
Allamanda cathartica cv. 'Hendersonii' – 87, 161
Allamanda violacea – 48, 135
Alocasia macrorrhiza - 34, 51, 52, 135, 153
Alocasia macrorrhiza cv. 'Rubra' – 48, 70, 135
Allocasia macrorrhiza cv. 'Variegata' – 125, 135
Aloe species - 125
Alpinia purpurata – 87, 156
Alpinia zerumbet - 156
Alternanthera bettzickiana - 125
Alternanthera tenella - 9
Amaryllidaceae - 23
Amazon Lily, see *Eucharis amazonica* - 27
Ananas bracteatus cv. 'Variegata' - 24
Angel's Trumpet, see *Brugmansia versicolor* - 23
Annonaceae - 113
Anoxopus compressus - 48
Anthurium scherzerianum - 113
Apocynaceae – 23, 70
Araceae - 139
Araucaria hetrophylla - 9
Artocarpus atilis - 135
Ascocenda Motes Tangelo - 177
Ascocenda Tubtin x Vanda Kasem's Delight - 166
Ascocenda Yip Sum Wah x Vanda Coerulea - 169
Ashoka Trees, see *Polyalthia longifolia* cv. 'Pendula' - 113
Asparagus Fern, see *Asparagus densiflorus* cv. 'Sprengerii' – 48, 67
Asparagus densiflorus cv. 'Sprengerii' – 48, 67
Asparagus myriocladus - 84
Bamboo Palm, see *Chamaedorea seifrizii* – 52, 129, 148
Barbados Fan Palm, see *Cocothrinax barbadensis* - 194
Beaucarenea recurvata - 51
Beaumontia - 23
Beefsteak Acalypha, see *Acalypha wilkesiana* – 15, 62, 125
Begonia semperflorens – 92, 125
Begonia sempervirens - 126, 139
Bignoniaceae - 7
Billbergia species - 125
Bird-of-Paradise, see *Strelitzia reginae* – 125, 156
Bismarck Palm, see *Bismarckia nobilis* – 24, 48, 187
Bismarckia nobilis – 24, 48, 187
Black Pearl Tree, see *Harpullia zanguebarica* – 83, 87
Blue Butterfly Bush, see *Clerodendrum ugandense* - 24
Blue Latan Palm, see *Latania loddigessii* - 51
Blue Mahoe, see *Hibiscus elatus* - 148
Blue Salvia, see *Salvia farinacea* - 125
Boston Fern, see *Nephrolepis exaltata* – 83, 84
Boston Fern, see *Nephrolepis exaltata* cv. 'Bostoniensis' – 52, 135
Boston Fern, see *Nephrolepis exaltata* cv. 'Hillii' – 156
Bottle Palm, see *Hyophorbe lagenicaulis* – 27, 139
Bottlebrush Tree, see *Callistemon viminalis* - 52
Bougainvillea 'Nairobi Orange' - 125
Bougainvillea glabra – 24, 31
Bougainvillea spectablis – 7, 15, 31, 48, 70
Brassidium Gilded Urchin 'Ontario' – 178, 182
Breadfruit Tree, see *Artocarpus atilis* - 135
Breynia disticha - 27
Bridal Bouquet Plumeria, see *Plumeria pudica* – 61, 125
Bromeliad, see *Neoregelia carolinae* cv. 'Volkaert's Pride' – 19, 125, 139

Brugmansia versicolor - 23
Brunfelsia Americana - 117
Buddha Belly Plant, see *Jatropha podagrica* - 39
Busy Lizzy, see *Impatiens walleriana* – 9, 135
Caesalpinia pulcherrima - 100
Calanthe - 19
Calliandra haematocephala - 143
Calliandra surinamensis - 139, 143
Callistemon viminalis - 52
Cananga odorata - 161
Canariensis, see *Galphimia glauca* - 139
Canary Island Date Palm, see *Phoenix canariensis* – 113, 197
Cardboard Palm, see *Zamia furfuracea* – 23
Carissa - 23
Caryota mitis - 195
Caryota urens - 191
Casuarina equisetifolia - 9
Casuarina Tree, see *Casuarina equisetifolia* - 9
Cat's Whiskers, see *Orthosiphon stamineus* - 125
Cestrum nocturnum - 117
Chalice Flower, see *Solandra maxima* - 70
Chamaedorea seifrizii - 52, 129, 148
Chinaman's Hat plant, see *Holmskioldia sanguinea* - 51
Chinese Fan Palm, see *Livistona chinensis* – 187, 197
Christmas Palm, see *Adonidia morillii* - 91
Citharexylum spinosum - 148
Clerodendrum "Firework", see *Clerodendrum quadriloculare* - 113
Clerodendrum quadriloculare - 113
Clerodendrum ugandense - 24
Clusia plukenetii - 156
Cochineal Plant, see *Nopalea cochenillifera* - 92
Coconut Palm, see *Cocos nucifera* – 39, 40, 48, 75, 148, 161
Cocos nucifera – 39, 40, 48, 75, 148, 161
Cocothrinax barbadensis - 194
Codiaeum variegatum - 23, 27, 58, 70, 125, 126, 135
Coleus, see *Coleus blumei, Plectranthus scutellarioides* – 62, 135
Coral Plant, see *Jatropha multifida* - 48
Coral Plant, see *Russelia equisetiformis* – 34, 67
Coral Tree, see *Erythrina variegata* – 7, 91
Cordia sebestena - 83
Cordyline - 117, 125
Cordyline terminalis - 135
Cordyline terminalis cv. 'Firebrand' - 51
Corkscrew Ginger - 51
Corkwood Tree, see *Sesbania grandiflora* - 24
Corypha umbraculifera - 191
Costus speciosus - 156
Costus speciosus cv. 'Variegata' – 51, 148
Crape Gingers, see *Costus speciosus* - 156
Crassulaceae - 27
Creeping Club Moss, see *Selaginella serpens* - 153
Crinum Lily, see *Crinum asiaticum* cv. 'Variegata' – 23, 125
Crinum asiaticum cv. 'Variegata' - 23
Croton, see *Codiaeum variegatum* – 23, 27, 58, 70, 125, 126, 135
Crown of Thorns, see *Euphorbia milli* – 7, 43, 125
Cup and Saucer plant, see *Holmskioldia sanguinea* - 51
Cup of Gold, see *Solandra maxima* - 70
Curcuma - 117
Cycas circinalis - 57, 58, 70, 79, 92, 117, 125, 191
Cycas revolute - 58
Cyperus alternifolius – 34, 75, 84, 135
Cyperus papyrus – 52, 75
Cyrtostachys renda - 139, 191
Date Palm, see *Phoenix dactylifera* - 197
Delonix regia - 58
Dendrobium Sonia - 177
Desert Rose, see *Adenium obesum* – 23, 52, 83, 118
Diacrium bicornutum - 44
Dracaena godseffiana - 129

Dracaena marginata – 9, 34,
Dracaena marginata cv. 'Tricolour' – 9, 92
Dracaena reflexa – 125, 139
Duranta repens - 139
Dypsis decaryi – 117, 192
Dypsis lutescens – 15, 48, 83, 125, 139, 191, 192
Echinocactus grusonii - 43
Eichhornia azurea – 51, 52, 57, 113
Eichhornia crassipes - 57
Elephant Ear, see *Alocasia macrorrhiza* – 34, 51, 153
Epipremnum pinnatum cv. 'Aureum' - 70, 91
Eranthemum andromeda - 125
Erythrina variegata – 7, 91
Etlingera elatior - 161
Eucharist Lily, see *Eucharis amazonica* - 27
Eucharis amazonica - 27
Euphorbia lactea cv. 'Variegata' – 43, 113, 135
Euphorbia leucocephala - 39
Euphorbia milli – 7, 43, 125
Euphorbia pulcherrima - 135
Euphorbia pulcherrima cv. 'Plum Pudding' - 24
Euphorbiaceae – 39, 67
Feather Grass - 48
Fern – 117, 129, 135, 153
Ficus – 39, 67, 117
Ficus elastica - 148
Fiddle Wood Tree, see *Citharexylum spinosum* - 148
Fiji Fan Palm, see *Pritchardia pacifica* – 58, 75, 76, 91, 187, 195
Firecracker Plant, see *Russelia equisetiformis* – 34, 67
Fishtail Fern, see *Nephrolepis biserrata* cv. 'Furcans' - 83
Fishtail Palm, see *Caryota mitis* - 195
Fittonia verschaffeltii - 113
Flamboyant, see *Delonix regia* - 58
Foxtail Palm, see *Wodyetia bifurcata* – 57, 61
Frangipani, see *Plumeria, P. obtuse, P. pudica, P. rubra* – 40, 61, 70, 76, 91, 100, 125, 143
Furcraea foetida – 39, 43
Furcraea foetida cv. 'Medio Picta' - 39
Furcraea foetida cv. 'Striata' - 140
Galphimia glauca - 139
Gardenia, see *Tabernaemontana divaricata* - 91
Gardenia taitensis - 125
Geiger Tree, see *Cordia sebestena* - 83
Ghost Cactus, see *Euphorbia lactea* cv. 'Variegata' – 43, 113, 135
Gmelina hystrix - 9
Golden Barrel Cactus, see *Echinocactus grusonii* - 43
Golden Dewdrop, see *Duranta repens* - 139
Golden Palm, see *Dypsis lutescens* – 15, 48, 83, 125, 139, 191, 192
Golden Trumpet, see *Allamanda cathartica* cv. 'Hendersonii' – 87, 161
Gouty Foot Plant, see *Jatropha podagrica* - 39
Graptophyllum pictum - 125
Gru Gru Palms, see *Acrocomia aculeate* - 197
Guava Tree, see *Psidium guajava* - 148
Gully Balsam, see *Clusia plukenetii* - 156
Harpullia zanguebarica – 83, 87
Hawaiian Jasmine, see *Gardenia taitensis* - 125
Hawaiian Pineapple - 118
Heliconia psittacorum cv. 'St. Vincent Red' - 148
Heliconia wagneriana – 9, 156
Heliconia - 117
Hibiscus – 34, 176
Hibiscus elatus - 148
Hibiscus rosa-sinensis – 62, 162
Holmskioldia sanguinea - 51
Hura crepitans – 117, 161
Hyophorbe lagenicaulis – 27, 139
Hyophorbe verschaffeltii - 135
Impatiens walleriana – 9, 135
Ixora casei – 34, 104

Jasmine, see *Cestrum nocturnum* - 117
Jatropha integerrima - 67
Jatropha multifidia - 48
Jatropha podagrica - 39
Justicia betonica - 135
Justicia brandegeana - 135
Kalanchoe blossfeldiana – 39, 43, 125
Kalanchoe daigremontiana - 27
Lady of the Night, see *Brunfelsia Americana* - 117
Lady Palm, see *Rhapis excelsa* – 51, 70, 83, 84, 139
Lantana camara - 32
Lantana montevidensis – 57, 58
Latania loddigessii - 51
Latania lontaroides – 139, 192
Leguminosae - 143
Licuala grandis - 70
Lilac Sage, see *Lantana montevidensis* – 57, 58
Lipstick Palm, see *Cyrtostachys renda* – 139, 191
Livistona chinensis – 187, 197
Lotus Plant, see *Nelumbo* species - 113
Lucky Seed Tree, see *Thevetia peruviana* – 16, 148
Macarthur Palm, see *Ptycosperma macarthurii* – 83, 139, 191
Macaw Palm, see *Aiphanes minima* – 140, 148
Madagascar Palm, see *Pachypodium lamerei* - 70
Mahogany Tree, see *Swietenia mahogoni* – 61, 104, 125
Maiden Hair Fern, see *Adiantum sp* - 19
Mandevillea – 23, 100
Marigold, see *Tagates lucida* – 9, 23, 125
Mauritius Hemp, see *Furcraea foetida*, *F. foetida* cv: 'Medio Picta' – 39, 43
Mgambo Tree, see *Harpullia zanguebarica* – 83, 87
Mile Tree, see *Casuarina equisetifolia* - 9
Miltassia Aztec 'Nalo' - 182
Mokara - 166
Mokara Chark Kuan – 169, 185
Mokara Madame Panni – 170, 173
Mother-in-Law Tongue plant, see *Sansevieria trifasciata* cv: 'Laruentii' - 70
Mother-of-Thousands, see *Kalanchoe daigremontiana* - 27
Mussaenda erythrophylla cv: 'Rosea' - 34
Mussaenda philippica cv: 'Aurorae' - 139
Myristica fragrans – 148, 153
Nelumbo species - 113
Neoregelia carolinae cv: 'Volkaert's Pride' - 19
Nephrolepis biserrata cv: 'Furcans' - 83
Nephrolepis exaltata – 83, 84, 135
Nephrolepis exaltata cv: 'Bostoniensis' - 52
Nephrolepis exaltata cv: 'Hillii' - 156
Nerium - 23
New Guinea Creeper, see *Tecomanthe venusta* - 7
New Guinea Trumpet Vine, see *Tecomanthe venusta* - 7
Nopalea cochenillifera - 92
Norfolk Pine, see *Araucaria hetrophylla* - 9
Nun Orchids, see *Diacrium bicornutum* - 44
Nutmeg Tree, see *Myristica fragrans* – 148, 153
Nymphaea - 139
Nymphaea caerulea – 52, 97, 109, 139
Octopus Tree, see *Schefflera actinophylla* - 40
Oncidium Sweet Sugar - 182
Ophiopogon – 70, 126
Ornamental Grass, see *Panicum virgatum* - 62
Orthosiphon stamineus - 125
Pachypodium - 43
Pachypodium lamerei - 70
Pandanus baptistii cv: 'Aureus' – 83, 104
Pandanus sanderi - 135
Panicum virgatum - 62
Papyrus, see *Cyperus papyrus* – 52, 75
Pennisetum setaceum cv: 'Purpureum' – 7, 31, 62
Pentalinon luteum - 100
Pentas lanceolata - 9
Peperomia magnoliifolia - 153
Phalanenopsis hybrid – 182, 185
Phalanenopsis Minho Princess - 182
Philodendron melinonii - 92
Philodendron xanadu - 51
Phoenix canariensis – 113, 197
Phoenix dactylifera - 197
Phoenix hybrid - 197

Phoenix reclinata - 194
Phoenix roebelinii - 117
Pigmy Date Palm, see *Phoenix roebelinii* - 117
Pilea microphylla – 58, 125
Pink Powderpuff Tree, see *Calliandra surinamensis* – 139, 143
Pistia stratiotes - 48
Pittosporum tobira cv: 'Variegata' - 139
Plectranthus scutellarioides - 62
Pleomele reflexa cv: 'Variegata' - 125
Plum Pudding Poinsettia, see *Euphorbia pulcherrima* cv: 'Plum Pudding' - 24
Plumbago auriculata – 19, 76, 125
Plumeria obtuse - 100
Plumeria pudica – 61, 125
Plumeria rubra – 40, 70, 76, 91, 143
Plumrose, see *Syzgium malaccensis* - 148
Poinsettia, see *Euphorbia pulcherrima*, *E. pulcherrima* cv: 'Plum Pudding' - 24
Poison Tree, see *Sapium hippomane* - 153
Polyalthia longifolia cv: 'Pendula' - 113
Polypodium aureum - 113
Polyscias filicifolia - 125
Pomerac, see *Syzgium malaccensis* - 148
Ponytail Plant, see *Beaucarenea recurvata* - 51
Porcelain Ginger, see *Etlingera elatior* - 161
Portlandia - 125
Portulaca grandiflora - 43
Portulacca grandiflora cv: 'Florepleno' - 48
Pothos, see *Epipremnum pinnatum* cv: 'Aureum' – 70, 91
Potinara Twenty-Four Carat Lea - 169
Pride of Barbados, see *Caesalpinia pulcherrima* - 100
Pritchardia pacifica – 58, 75, 76, 91, 187, 195
Pseuderanthemum carruthersii - 91
Psidium guajava - 148
Psychotria nervosa - 153
Ptychosperma elegans – 187, 192
Ptychosperma macarthurii – 83, 139, 191
Puerto Rican Frangipani, see *Plumeria pudica* – 61, 125
Purple Allamanda, see *Allamanda violacea* – 48, 135
Purple Bougainvillea, see *Bougainvillea spectabilis* – 7, 15, 31, 48, 70
Purple Fountain Grass, see *Pennisetum setaceum* cv: 'Purpureum' – 7, 31, 62
Purple Portulaca, see *Portulaca grandiflora* - 43
Quarter Terete Vandas – 166, 173
Queen Palm, see *Syagrus romanzoffiana* – 34, 197
Quisqualis indica - 15
Rangoon Creeper, see *Quisqualis indica* - 15
Ravenala madagascariensis – 75, 76, 156
Red Cordia Tree, see *Cordia sebestena* - 83
Red Dracena, see *Cordyline terminalis* cv: 'Firebrand' - 51
Red Ginger, see *Alpinia purpurata* – 87, 156
Red Latan Palm, see *Latania lontaroides* – 139, 192
Red Powder Puff, see *Calliandra haematocephala* - 143
Red Salvia, see *Salvia spendens* - 125
Red Sandlewood, see *Adenanthera pavonina* - 148
Red Shrimp Plant, see *Justicia brandegeana* - 135
Rhapis excelsa – 51, 70, 83, 84, 139
Rhyncostylis Gigantea - 178
Rock Balsam, see *Peperomia magnoliifolia* - 153
Royal Palm, see *Roystonea oleracea* – 9, 31, 104, 148, 153, 156, 161, 187, 192, 197
Roystonea oleracea – 9, 31, 104, 148, 153, 156, 161, 187, 192, 197
Rubber Tree, see *Ficus elastica* - 148
Russelia equisetiformis – 34, 67
Sage, see *Lantana camara* – 32, 57
Sago Palm, see *Cycas circinalis* – 57, 58, 70, 79, 92, 117, 125, 191
Salvia farinacea - 125
Salvia spendens - 125
Sandbox Tree, see *Hura crepitans* – 117, 161
Sansevieria – 125, 129
Sansevieria trifasciata cv: 'Laruentii' - 70
Sapium hippomane - 153
Savannah Grass, see *Anoxopus compressus* - 48
Schefflera actinophylla - 40
Screw Pine, see *Pandanus baptistii* cv: 'Aureus' – 83, 104
Sea Grape Bush, see *Cocoluba uvifera* - 48
Sealing Wax Palm, see *Cyrtostachys renda* – 139, 191
Selaginella serpens - 153

Senegal Date Palm, see *Phoenix reclinata* - 194
Sesbania grandiflora - 24
Setcreasea purpurea - 104
Shell Ginger, see *Alpinia zerumbet* - 156
Skyduster Palm, see *Washingtonia robusta* - 192
Snow Bush, see *Breynia disticha* - 27
Snow-on-the-Mountain, see *Euphorbia leucocephala* - 39
Solanaceae - 23
Solandra maxima - 70
Solitary Fishtail Palm, see *Caryota urens* - 191
Solitary Palm, see *Ptychosperma elegans* – 187, 192
Song of India, see *Dracaena reflexa* – 125, 139
Spanish Bayonet, see *Yucca aloifolia* – 135, 187
Spathiphyllum - 106
Spathodea campanulata - 113
Spider Lily, see *Crinum asiaticum* cv: 'Variegata' - 23
Spindle Palm, see *Hyophorbe verschaffeltii* - 135
Standard White Phalanenopsis hybrid - 169
Striped Phalanenopsis hybrid - 169
St. John's Bush, see *Psychotria nervosa* - 153
Stemmadenia galeottiana - 104
Strap Leaf Ascocenda hybrid - 173
Strelitziaceae - 156
Strelitzia reginae – 125, 156
Swietenia mahogoni – 61, 104, 125
Syagrus romanzoffiana – 34, 197
Sygonium - 70
Syzgium malaccensis - 148
Tabernaemontana - 23
Tabernaemontana divaricata - 91
Tabeuia pallida - 51
Tagates lucida – 9, 23, 125
Talipot Palm, see *Corypha umbraculifera* - 191
Tamarind Tree, see *Tamarindus indica* - 15
Tamarindus indica - 15
Tea Plant, see *Alternanthera bettzickiana*, *A. tenella* – 9, 125
Tecomanthe venusta - 7
Thatch Palm, see *Cocothrinax barbadensis* - 194
Thevetia peruviana – 16, 148
Thunbergia fragrans - 97
Thunbergia grandifolia – 91, 92
Tillandsia cyanea - 113
Torch Ginger, see *Etlingera elatior* - 161
Traveller's Palm, see *Ravenala madagascariensis* – 75, 76, 156
Triangle Palm, see *Dypsis decaryi* – 117, 192
Trimezia martinicensis - 162
Typhonodorum lindleyanum – 48, 118, 139
Umbrella Grass, see *Cyperus alternifolius* – 34, 75, 84, 135
Umbrella Tree, see *Schefflera actinophylla* - 40
Vanda Gordon Dillon - 177
Vandaceous Orchids - 44
Variegated Corkscrew Ginger, see *Costus speciosus* cv: 'Variegata' – 51, 148
Variegated *Ophiopogon* – 125, 126
Variegated Snake plant, see *Sansevieria trifasciata* cv: 'Laruentii' - 70
Variegated Wild Pineapple, see *Ananas bracteatus* cv: 'Variegata' - 24
Virgin Orchids, see *Diacrium bicornutum* - 44
Washingtonia robusta - 192
Water Hyacinth, see *Eichhornia azurea*, *E. crassipes* – 51, 52, 57, 113
Water Lettuce, see *Pistia stratiotes* - 48
Water Lilly, see *Nymphaea caerulea* – 52, 97, 108, 139
West Indian Royal Palm, see *Roystonea oleracea* – 9, 31, 104, 148, 153, 156, 161, 187, 192, 197
White Mussaenda, see *Mussaenda philippica* cv: 'Aurorae' - 139
White Shrimp Plant, see *Justicia betonica* - 135
Whitewood Tree, see *Tabeuia pallida* - 51
Wild Cane, see *Pandanus sanderi* - 135
Wodyetia bifurcata – 57, 61
Yellow Iris, see *Trimezia martinicensis* - 162
Ylang-ylang Tree, see *Cananga odorata* - 161
Yucca aloifolia – 135, 187
Yucca gloriosa - 92
Zamia furfuracea - 23
Zebrina pendula - 108

ACKNOWLEDGEMENTS

It would have been impossible for us to publish Barbados in Bloom without the assistance and cooperation of a great number of people who helped us to choose the gardens to be featured in the book, to gain access into those gardens and to identify the many plants shown in the photos. We are very grateful to all of you for your support and we publicly thank you and acknowledge your invaluable input.

Individuals

All the Garden Owners
Ali Sandiford
Andre Kelshall
Arthur Atkinson
Audrey Thomas
Billy Gollop
Cathy Alkins
Curtis Gibbons
David Leach
Dawn St Romaine
Dr. John Webster
Fiona Johnson
Hetty Atkinson
Jean Robinson
Jenny Sisnett
Jeremy Sisnett
Jocelyn Parris
John Leach
Kathy Taylor
Matthias Servais
Michael Birkett
Mona Walker
Nancy Binks
Nigel Jones
Philip Edwards
Rae Milne
Rene Margies
Roger Chubb
Sally Miller
Dr. Stephen Collins
Stephen Thomas
Steve Barnett
Tony Stoute
Vicky Stuart

Companies and Institutions

A and A Flora
Tel: (246) 427-2096

Exotic Palms Inc.
Tel: (246) 429-0316

Growing Things
Tel: (246) 435-6413

Palm World
Tel: (246) 433-1814

Plants Plus
Tel: (246) 420-4712

Stephen Thomas Landscaping
Tel: (246) 435-6413

Talma Mill Studios Landscape Architects
Tel: (246) 420-5137

The Flower Shoppe
Tel: (246) 426-7559

VIP Orchids
Tel: (246) 437-4442

The Barbados Horticultural Society
Tel: (246) 428-5889

The Barbados National Trust
Tel: (246) 436-9033

The Ministry of Housing, Lands and the Environment
Tel: (246) 467-7800

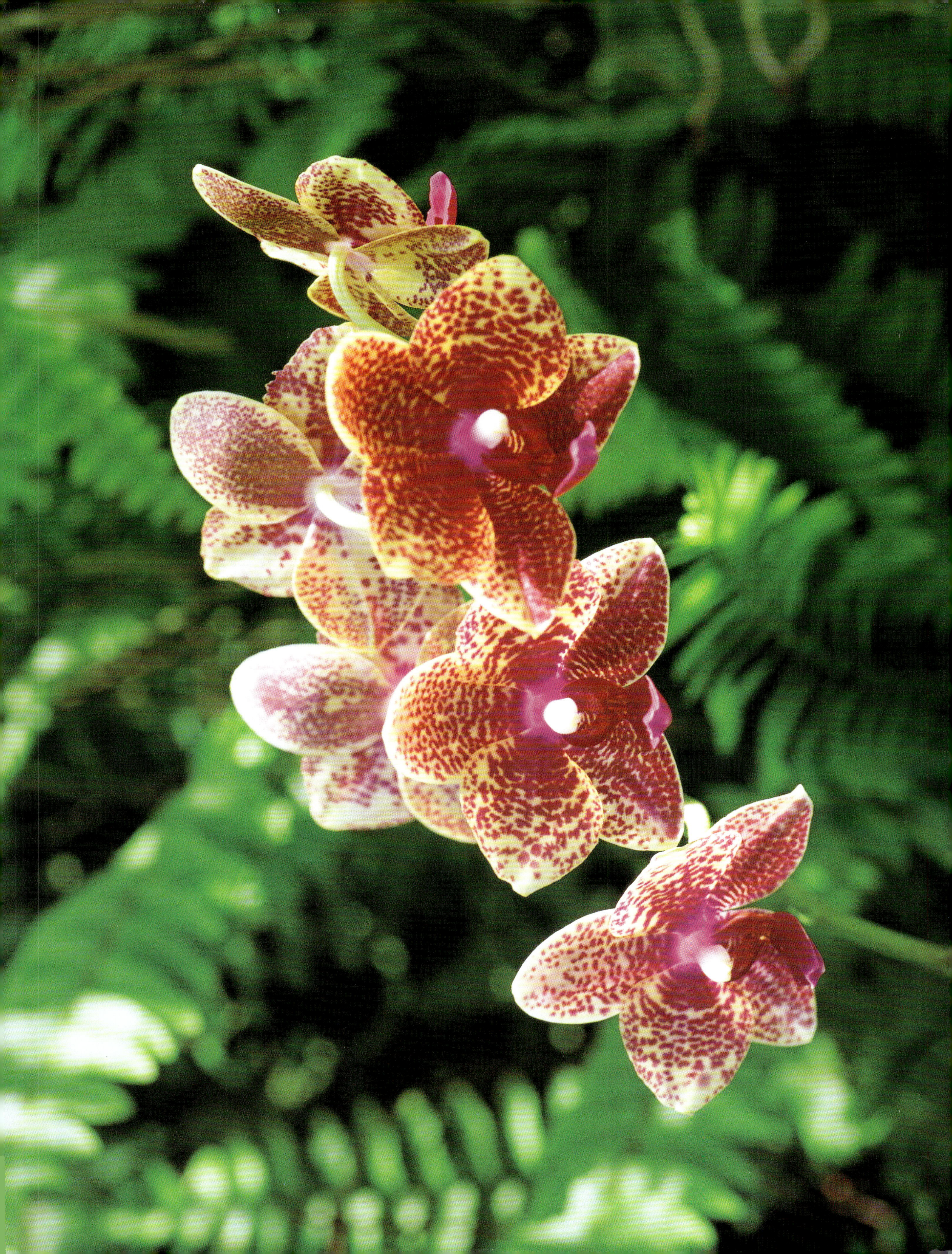

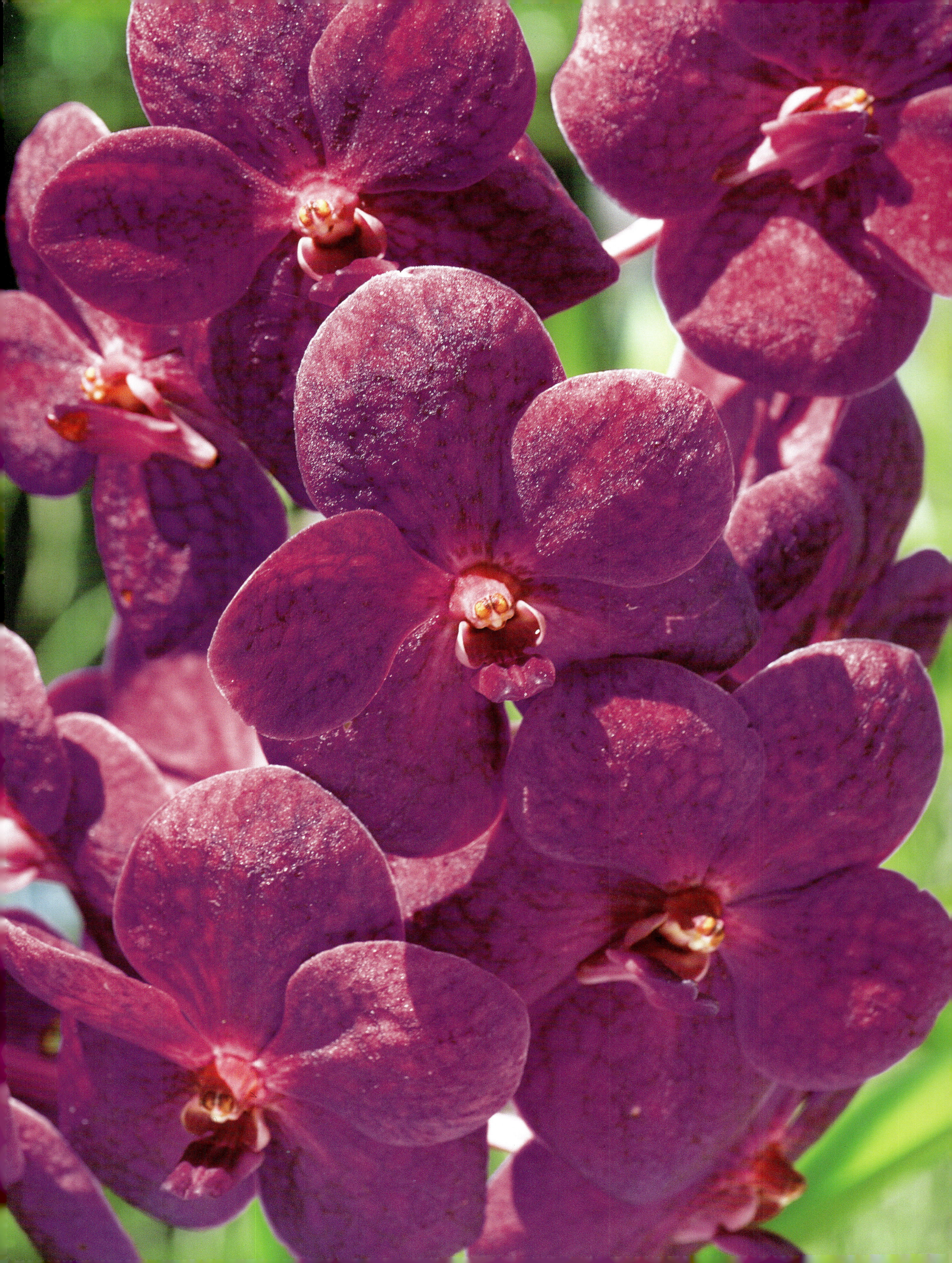

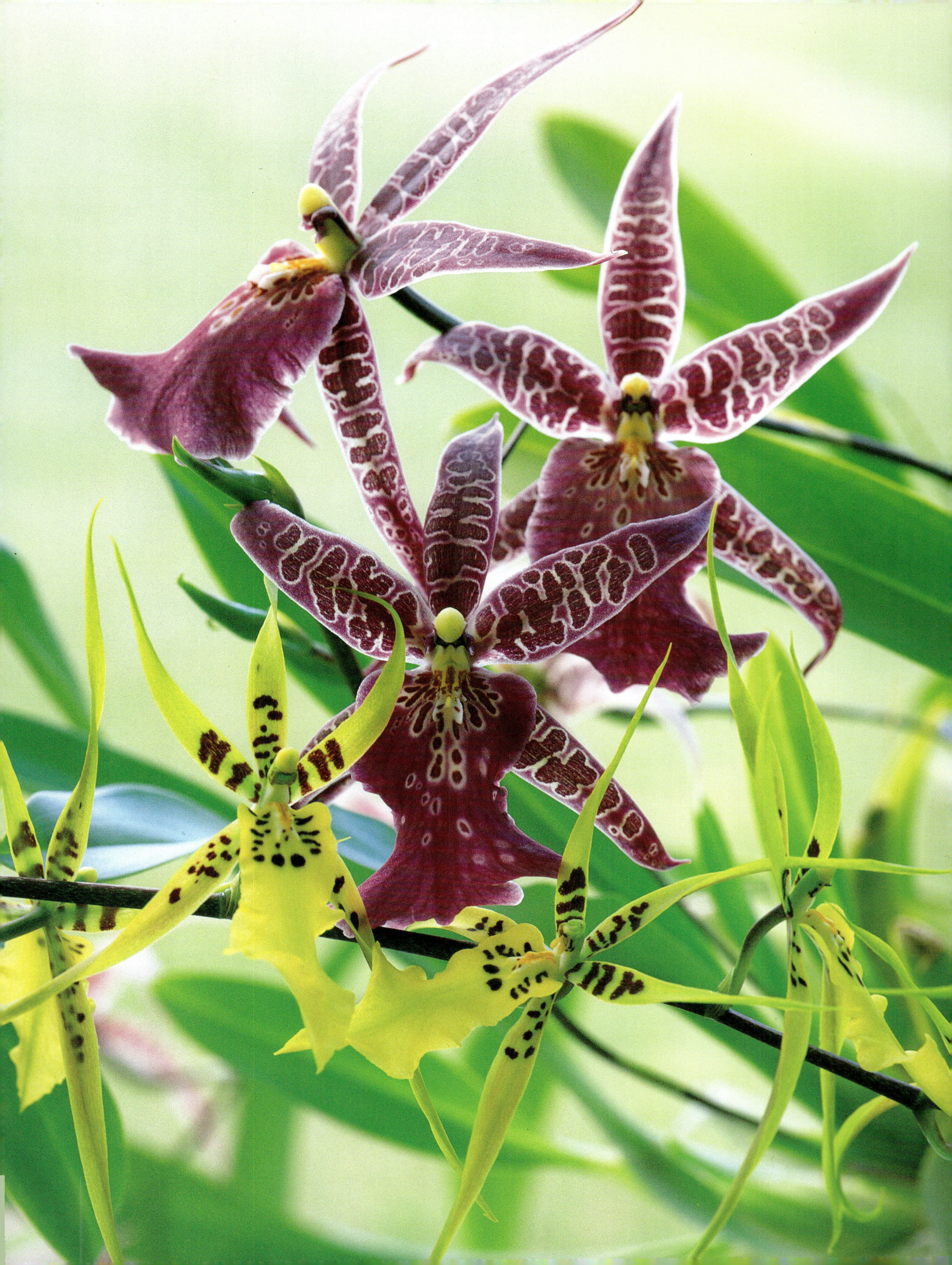